PRAISE FOR JACKSON BLISS

"Jackson Bliss paints with words. He is the Kendrick Lamar of the literary world."

—REGINA KING, Emmy-award-winning actress & director

"Take a life and fold it in half then fold that half into another half. Keep going until there is nothing left. Make it into something beautiful, dreamed, imagined; it can be any vision you want, that is, until it's time to take it apart, to examine just how such a self was constructed. You'll never be the same dreamer again. Jackson Bliss nonetheless exposes the creases, the wearing away of self and soul, the deterioration of appearances and the texture of the fragile nature of the idealized self against the reality into which we are constructed. Do you want to do this? he seems to ask, allowing us to spy or avert our eyes. If life is an adventure, what does it mean when you have to unfold, uncrease, unravel, destroy your life in order to live it? With candor and honesty, Bliss investigates how plans go awry, how following the pattern never leads to the perfection we seek. It is only through undoing, revisiting, and shredding our scraps that lead one to oneself. *Dream Pop Origami* is a beautifully made star. See for yourself."

—JENNY BOULLY, author of *Betwixt & Between: Essays on the Writing Life*

"By turns sly, sorrowful, pensive, and forthright, *Dream Pop Origami* makes us rethink the possibilities of nonfiction writing, and of how we name and shape our identities."

—BETH (BICH MINH) NGUYEN, author of *Stealing Buddha's Dinner*

"Empty of permanence and interlinked with infinite beings in a net of belonging, Jackson Bliss imagines the world of in-between places. In *Dream Pop Origami*, ceaseless migrations and reincarnations actualize playful transformation tales just like the samadhi of freedom folds across any and all barriers. A memoir of renga-like linked verse, a song of becoming and love."

—DUNCAN RYUKEN WILLIAMS, author of *American Sutra* and *Hapa Japa*n

"At the risk of sounding trite, this book is just so much fun! But, like, for real—fun is just a diversion tactic for Dream Pop Origami's honest profundity and Jackson Bliss's expert storytelling. Each adventure is delivered in its most perfect form, ready for your interactive pleasure: To feel the complicated pleasure of nostalgia, go to chapter 22. To feel the adolescent pleasure of a game, go to chapter 28. To feel the naughty pleasure of reading Jackson Bliss's prose, go to chapter 35. To fulfill satisfaction, read this book."

—LILY HOANG, author of *A Bestiary*

夢ポップ折り紙

Dream Pop Origami

A PERMUTATIONAL MEMOIR ABOUT HAPA IDENTITY

by

JACKSON BLISS

SHOUT OUTS

The following pieces appeared originally in the following journals, newspapers, and anthologies in various forms:

The New York Times

Guernica

Boston Review

Longreads

The Good Men Project

Kartika Review & 2012-2013 Anthology of American Pacific Island American Literature

News (Australia)

Discover Nikkei

The Beiging of America Anthology: Personal Narratives about Being Mixed Race in the Twenty-First Century

South Loop Review

Huffington Post UK

Twitter

Pology Magazine

Para LB, sos

Mi sol diario alimentando el aire con rayadas tuyas,

Mi oración matutina, mi sueño de vitral,

Mi cabaña en la tierra salvaje, y mi botecito en el Diluvio,

Te dedico este libro a vos, mi amor.

Te amo para siempre, desde ahora

Hasta el fin de los tiempos.

Pick a number between 1-74. Any number. Got it? Now turn the page and find the chapter that corresponds to that number.

夢ポップ折り紙
DREAM POP ORIGAMI

夢**(Dream)**: Pieces about the imagination, make believe, daydreams, reading, & travel

ポップ (Pop): Pieces about the Midwest, childhood, music, family, & food

折り紙 (Origami): Pieces about metamorphosis, love, writing, &
nostalgia

夢ポップ折り紙

Dream Pop Origami

1. Stumbling on Infinity

One day my teenage body turned into koi paper, so I folded myself into makeshift objects of enchantment. I creased the patterned kami of my flattened limbs. I reinvented new morphologies in every pleat, cultivating a love affair with the changing shapes of my crinkled identity. I learned that origami was kinetic sorcery: part dream sequence, part zoomancy, and part totem. I learned that my teenage paper heart could be a pixilation of desire. I learned that love could transform me into musical slurs. I learned that origami could be the erotics of my metamorphosis, and so I did what any literature student, linguaphile, and emerging writer would do, I studied the language of creation, vowing to become a metaphor of the metaphor in every movement my body made until my flesh and my spirit occupied the same oath. I learned that folding paper was an act of divination, so I prayed to the kami, I asked for paper cranes to intercede and rescue me from isolation, not knowing that one day I would wash my face in Baskerville font and memorize all the creation myths about my changing form, not knowing that one day I would devote myself to the storytelling of the crane and the ontology of the crease. I learned through origami that this life wasn't mine until the first fold. Since koi paper was sometimes gold-speckled or reinforced with silver foil and sometimes torn and ripped apart, origami became a book of magic spells about self-creation and reinvention that I recited after every Robert-Smith-black eye, after every clipped migration to the sun, and after every disintegrating kiss in the fickle shade. Origami was my salve of crushed myrtle and lavender oil to heal the inflammation of loneliness and sabotage the shovel digging of grief. Origami became an artform of profound longing straight boys were not supposed to feel because we did not fall in love, we must never fall in love, we must never be defined by our vulnerability to others, and our tears must only be the flares of Jericho, the poison-tipped bolts of outrage, never confessions of a fat ugly heart, never confessions of devotion and self-overcoming and infatuation and solicitude. In time, origami became my garbage can shield to protect myself from the ricochet of fire arrows shot in the cold brutality of the night. Origami became the graphic design of my own survival, my first and only solution to the disruption of the staggering flame and the enlightenment of the scar-tissue soul.

My life is a ledger of paper cuts and ripped origami squares: in 8th grade, my mom moved into a motel with a complete stranger. In 9th grade, she trekked 2,400 miles across the country from Northern Michigan to Southern California to inhale the ocean brine in the air and graze in the sparkly dander of sunlight on her pale hapa skin. And so, I learned that origami was not just a functional metaphor of my bony adolescence, but also a torn-and-taped road atlas for my itinerant hapa family, shapeshifters of the plane and mixed-race drivers of the mid-city, all of us. When my mom disappeared from our timeline, we abandoned Northern Michigan one by one like a decimated confederacy, all of us migrating to Portland, Seattle, LA, Denver, Chicago, Indianapolis, South Bend, Buenos Aires, the Gambia, and Burkina Faso where we stumbled into abandoned dreamworlds colonized by other dreamers as if our heliotropic existence had been blotted out by the fallout of our nuclear imaginations. I was no different. I was no outlier. During every crisis and migration, I refolded old koi paper, I rewrote apocryphal psalms of the self at the bottom of every dark cellar I fell down. I turned myself into a fairytale of palette knives and bleeding narratologies. I became a Shinto fever-dream of the Nisei body, making new creatures come alive in my hands like a St. Francis cartoon. I ignited phoenixes with the sparks of my brokenness. I drifted to new cities that sold different colors of koi paper and offered different rules of personal transformation. I joined cooperatives of loss everywhere I went. I joined search and rescue teams to measure the depth of my own voids. I practiced folding and pleating new destinies from warped astrology charts and wrinkled kami. This is how the West Coast, with its historical amnesia, three-hour-time-zone-distortion, and culture of self-creation became my workshop of dream language, the Japanese studio of my origami training, and the birthplace of my defiant obsession with love, which is the music of our bodies.

One Christmas day at San Elijo beach, the sun was a soft and lyrical whisper on my pores. Surfers bobbed in the ocean far away at the smudged horizon line, their black wetsuits flapping with every Japanese woodblock wave. Families hurled fluorescent frisbees down the beach. Old dudes with beach-ball stomachs and Santa beards sprawled out in frayed lawn chairs. Incestuous teenagers sunbathed on clashing bright towels. A golden retriever darted through the mechanical claws of the ocean to retrieve a blue rubber ball as I wandered through the counterpoint of shadow play like a detective searching for clues of happiness underneath octopoid vines of kelp and splintered chunks of calcified driftwood as the frothing waves dragged civilization back into the great blue void, nudged my ankles like lonely Tabbies, and glided over the sand like a shimmering verb. I squatted over tiny underwater volcanoes and miniature rock pools at the elevated tide pools that had been hollowed out, rendered osteoporotic by time and tedium. I witnessed a whole subdivision of miniature canyons and thumb-poked craters, most of them tucked inside sheets of porous rock, filled with lukewarm salt-water, misplaced algae, kidnapped stones, and dismembered starfish. The tide pool was a pelagic junkyard of predictable mystery, a chapel of protective devotion, and a sanctuary city under the tissue-paper sea where I tempted fate, jabbing my finger into one of the tiny submerged volcanoes as a sea anemone puckered up, releasing a cloud of sand and stone fragments as waves unrolled up the shoreline, crashing against the elevated tide pool and spraying my thin legs. The design of my koi body changed with every wave as the sun stalled in neutral on the shoreline, lingering in the procession of aquarelle waves and Vaseline sunlight, dragging the cultural flotsam of blond surfers, white families, Latino barbecues, and teenage lovers back into its vast canyon of restless gold linework while origami cranes (tacked to the skyline like a middle school art project) dangled their graceful beaks over the beach. This place of idle worship, where strangers transformed themselves into experimental fables of the self, where my hands could conjure paper dragons with a few seconds of distracted prayer, where no one knew the basic difference between craft, accident, and birthright, had wiped our memory clean for the day.

As we walked to my mom's car, the horizon like a gradient blue mosaic encrusted in the simple syrup of the punctured sun, I put my arm around my mom and kissed her face that had aged from the spectral hunger of the desert, the dotted signature lines of smoke breaks, and the replicating vows of happy hour. As we talked, we squinted. Our pilgrimage to the West Coast had brought us to a small surfing town in Southern California where cactuses bloomed on crowded roads and orphaned bulbs of kelp and algae popped underneath our heels on the shore. My mom's rebellion against the world meant divorcing my dad but also tearing up our family, which in its structural violence, accidentally gave all of us permission to leave the Midwest. This is how I recoded myself in the strange and complicated colors of koi paper again and again. While Northern Michigan was once a space I'd known intimately, a space I'd demonized and later longed for when I'd floated to the Pacific Northwest, Northern Michigan was still the site of trauma where my mixed-race identity had been torn apart, refolded, and stapled back together much like this memoir, where my life was always throbbing, half unzipped for the shoegaze daydream that only happens out west, where my mom had dragged me in this tipsy parabola of desperation, heartache, and amnesia against my will, where I somehow learned to crease myself into a tiny paper crane on this beach in high school after I'd lost my virginity to a girl in my English class who used to argue with me about *The Sound & The Fury*. This state of reimagining, this cradle of azure myopia, this love song of lethal shard and gold sparkle, this place as idea and invention was where I learned to fold myself into a paper frog, a hanging star, and three-bit dinosaur in grad school, where I smothered my garish colors and wrinkled edges and paper tears in obsessive Scotch tape after every mistake, where eight-bit castles floated in the sky, where every tossed daydream dangled from the rafters of heaven with sky blue string, and where backwards lyrics were pinned to cork boards and dropped from window sills in celebration. It was here that my flaws became my premises of discovery. It was here that I time-traveled thorough the intersecting maze of imagination, reality blur, and self-creation in California. My smooth and unblemished fingers stumbled into infinity here, where they learned to create schools of thin and wobbly starlings with my papercut, artist-soft hands, both absolved by clumsiness and forgiven by longing. I learned to fold, unfold, and refold reincarnation into new creatures of fragmentation here. I reimagined every life decision as a choice here. I crafted my own hapa voice from the grocery lists of my mistakes, communities, and racial illegibilities here. I learned to fight for my own metaphoricity as an imagined creature of the besotten universe and redefine origami as a spiritual exercise of my own impossible transformation here. I learned that only I could write the story of my paper metamorphosis here, only I could give bone marrow to this memoir here, only I could nourish this feral garden with my silk-soft hands here, because without the book you're reading right now, the ravenous joy and the mutable heartache of this world would be just tremors in my life, just tiny, burning tremors in the blown-out veins of the earth that I was once too shy to run away from and once too afraid to abandon. But with this memoir, I'm in love until the end.

次に/Next:

1. To see Jackson turn thirty, go to page 63.
2. I'm flying to Osaka and here's the plan/I'm gonna finally meet all the Japanese fam/we'll take the train to Nara and walk the staircase to the sky/we'll kick it at my aunt's, drink some tea, say goodbye (on page 224).
3. To read about Jackson searching for Jim Morrison's grave in Paris, go to page 94.
4. Or just turn the page.

2. Things that Saved My Ass as a Kid

1. Choose-your-own-adventure novels, where I used bookmarks religiously to keep track of my reading destinies

2. Hershey bars (with almonds) inside obāchan's fridge

3. Going on vacation to México with my fam, where I could reimagine my life in another universe

4. Having a nuclear-powered imagination, which included, among other things:

Believing I had a robotic guardian angel, was part of a secret ninja society for kids, was born in Bordeaux, had superhuman speed, could build an ice palace out of snow, was a veteran of the Great Snow Wars, had a modeling contract with Supermodels Inc., owned stock in generic pharmaceutical drug companies, was training for the Tour de France, was a misunderstood genius/musical prodigy, was the reincarnation of Mozart—or at least the reincarnation of Tom Hulce's performance of Mozart in *Amadeus,* got a perfect score on the SAT by accident, was the son of a famous designer, was an Uruguayo expat, attended an East Coast prep school, would soon be recruited by J. Crew scouts on the streets of Chicago, ~~who would offer me a modeling contract~~, was a French baron, pretending my life was an Atari video game, and wishing I was an exiled Russian revolutionary and émigré poet named Alyosha who wrote love letters to a homeland I'd never see again and a woman who would never love me

5. The tunnel vision of bony girls smiling at me in musty school hallways

6. Riding my bike at dusk

7. ~~Soccer~~. ~~Futból~~. *Fine*: Soccer on early Saturday mornings

8. Pretending I was an invisible ninja

9. Going sledding on snow days and then drinking hot chocolate, watching the snow fall through the window like celestial dandruff

10. Dancing to Duran Duran's *Rio* by myself with all the lights on in the house

11. Running through the rain and holding my boxers in my hand like a flag of the riffraff

12. Having fashion-forward parents

13. The respite of Christmas vacation

14. The day my brother became my confidant

15. Being something (part Japanese) the other kids could never take away from me

16. Knowing I had Japanese cousins in Tokyo living in a parallel world with different rules and different words for their parallel reality

17. The sound of rain on the back porch

18. Playing Schumann's *Traumerei* after school

19. Bougie Ramen because life was too short

20. Atari, text-based video games on our IBM PC Jr, and Shogi games on Christmas Eve

21. Transformers, Legos, and totally dope Japanese toys my parents brought back from Tokyo, some of which could shoot missiles across the room and blind a cat

22. Pretending I was a secret agent and/or spy (not to be confused with the trope of the permanent foreigner in Asian American literature)

23. Imagining I was a mixed-race MC in the mirror to impress a one-month girlfriend

24. Walking through the woods as the sun was setting in middle school

次に/Next:
1. To see Jackson learn how to swim underwater, go to page 82.
2. To learn how (not) to spot a hapa, go to page 296.
3. Jackson's fave Midwestern expressions of ALL TIME on page 223. ~~How rad is that shit?~~
4. To learn about Jackson's experiments with reality, go to page 230.
5. Or just, or just, or just, turn the page.

3. The Tiny Spoon (or How to Stay in Love after Trauma)

1. FIND YOUR TEENAGE COURAGE TO LOVE AGAIN: Love LB with everything you've got. Love her like you did seven years ago, back when you were the boldest version of yourself and you weren't afraid to be stabbed in the heart by the cholos of destiny, love her like you have nothing to lose except solitude, fear, and cynicism. The audacity you had then is the audacity you need now. Love is always audacious, the creation of a tiny endangered world for two. The cynics will always hate you for your noisy affection, shooting their slingshots at anything that moves.

2. DROP THE METRIC UNITS: When you lived in Argentina together, you taught English all over Buenos Aires like a traveling circus while she made empanadas, cleaned the tiny apartment, and did laundry. Later on, the two of you translated screenplays together for extra pesos under the table. Now you make all the dinners, walk the dogs, take out the recycling, clean the house, and water the plants while she works downtown as a pediatric nurse (the best kind). Part of your strength as a couple is your flexibility, your ability to negotiate and warp gender roles effortlessly. Because your love and your identities are dynamic, evolutionary, and fluid, both of you continuously evolve, a million tiny universes created inside one another, growing inside you both every instant.

3. STOP IDEALIZING EACH OTHER: In the beginning, your love is pure, unpackaged, and elemental like a lead singer of a death metal band shouting lyrics you can't make out but can feel in your chest. Your earliest moments are a whisper, based partially on deficient knowledge: you barely know each other, you don't know each other's middle names or your

favorite colors yet, you haven't discovered each other's quirks, your idiosyncrasies, your secret kinks, and repressed insanities, you don't even know if she's a dog person or a cat person yet (dog), but over time, you learn all about her life and celebrate it. Slowly, you realize you love LB for her flaws too. You love her hang-ups and her idiosyncrasies. You love her because of these things, not despite them. Because, because, because. What wounds you sometimes is that the things she hates about herself are the things you love about her. You prefer flawed heroes.

4. BURN THE FUCKING MAP: At first, your fledgling love is a wisp of snowflakes. Eventually your love becomes a buoyant riff inside your head, an emotional catechism inside your pocket, a cosmology of longing in your hands. Thirteen years later, you're still crazy in love years after the first rush. Your love is deep and unfathomable. You could get lost in each other. And sometimes you do.

5. ASSASSINATE RATIONALISM: You don't list the reasons why you love her when talking to strangers because those are the reasons you *like* her, the things you tell people when they ask. You love her because it's impossible not to, because nothing you have ever done has ever cured you of this brain fever when she looks at you with the world reflected in her eyes, because you're helpless when she smiles at you like you're the only motherfucker in the whole high school dance. The point is, your love isn't rational. Most of the time, you can't even explain how or why it works. You don't know why it's different with her. You don't know why her sadness inflicts you. You don't know why her joy infects you. You don't know why everything got better after she took you to a Peruvian restaurant in Wicker Park and told you to dip your bread in a mysterious green sauce that burned a hole in your mouth. You don't know why both of you are so childish one moment and then so responsible the next, why you buy LB Hello Kitty geishas, which she openly loves, why she pretends to comb out the tangles in your shaved head, the only thing you know is when she kisses your cheek or tells you she loves you, the whole world disintegrates into soft light. The joy you feel is a perfectly strummed chord.

6. LOVE THE TINY SPOON: Sometimes, you bust out laughing when you notice how small her shoes are, small enough to be kids' shoes. Sometimes, she points it out herself because she's secretly proud of how tiny but strong she is. Sometimes, when she looks at you with glowing tenderness, it breaks you down. Sometimes, when you talk about her to close friends, you start to cry like an asshole. Sometimes, when you watch her through the window walking to work, it fucking obliterates you. It's not that you're weak when she's gone either. It's just that you're stronger when she holds your hand, something you would never admit to anyone except your readers, something you didn't even realize until you wrote it down. Sometimes, when you're not looking, she tackles you on to the bed and shouts *touchdown*! She dances as you play *Mass Effect 2* and *NCAA Football 14*, makes you watch baby elephant videos, and sticks monopoly money in your wallet, and the truth is, you love every spoonful because it's her, it's her, it's always her.

7. SLOW THE FUCK DOWN: Sometimes, you watch her sleep as the morning sunlight sneaks through the blackout curtains and cast oblong shadows on her face, you smell her coconut-scented skin and kiss her balmy cheeks, when you rub her hair, bouquets deconstruct and her snoring slurs into a sigh. Sometimes, you spoon with her under the covers even though it hurts your back, which makes her clasp your hand in her sleep as Zoe and Gogo! (your two little dogs) protect her on either side like tiny sentinels. Even asleep, you love each other. This fact is incontrovertible. Sometimes, her eyelids flutter as she sleeps. Sometimes, you kiss the shadows on her face before sneaking into your office to write. Sometimes, after you do some yoga, meditate, and work on your novel about racial spies and mixed-race ninjas, she stutters into the office with her face smushed from sleep. She sits on your lap and hugs you, her skin still warm from the soft voltage in her dreams.

8. GO OUT ON DATES: Even when you were losing your shit during field exams, you still dropped grad school twice a week for a few hours to

conjugate your existence and share the gift of food with her. Even when you were chained to the couch, reading abstruse books about gender theory and racial melancholia for your dissertation, you still went out to cafés with her to watch the sunlight crashing into the Venice shoreline. Even when you were busy AF writing the next great Asian American/hapa novel or fiddling with a Garage Band track or breaking your thumbs on your PS4, the one thing you didn't compromise were your dates with LB. She's the only person in your life you can probably take for granted because she loves you as passionately as you love her and she's the only person you will never take for granted because it's her and because it's you and there is nothing between except the sun.

9. OPEN YOUR MOUTH: According to Hindu tradition, words have vibrations. The word *love* is an act of affection, confession, and healing. *I love you. Te amo. Je t'aime.* 愛してる。 Ich liebe dich. Я люблю тебя. Seni seviyorum. Mwen renmen ou. T'estimo. אני אוהב אותך (ani ohev otakh). You tell her these things all the time because you want to capture that moment of emotional identification before it croaks in the sunlight, before you forget the sound, before your phone rings and the world burns up from the inside out. Sometimes, telling her feels monomaniacal, crazy even. Sometimes, you're not in the mood, but when she asks you to, and often when she doesn't, you say the words with the elements, the buddhas, and the kami as your witnesses. You say, I love you, because it soothes her, calms her down, because it tells her where she is and who you are. You don't want her to forget she's loved, you don't want her to live one day not knowing how much you love her, how fleeting the syllables are, how quickly memory erodes into oblivion. You know it's supposed to get old. You know it's vulgar AF, redundant, obviously tacky to tell her you love her as much as you do, but declaring love is a complete action. It's a piecemeal mantra. Your love for her is a gospel that you preach whenever she loses faith in the world, which is so easy to do. Telling her you love her is the way you save yourself from the plague of old age and the termites of regret, the one perfect thing you can do every day of your life that will always matter even if you crush everything else in your hand like a felonious brute.

10. CREATE A NEW LANGUAGE: Every day of your life, you try to find a different language to express what you feel for her, telling her with and without the words: you tell LB every time you make love in the afternoon, every time you hijack her Facebook account to announce a new bowel movement and stick garlic cloves in her lunch bag, every time the two of you walk around the streets of Japan in the winter and take your shoes off in Millennium Park and play with the dogs on the bed, every time you take a picnic together on a beach in Edgewater, every time you ride the El holding hands, every time you construct primitive narrative love notes with emoji during her night shifts and hug her when she laughs, every time you spend hours thinking about how to make her birthday stranger, more unorthodox, and more mawkish, every time you watch *The Wire*, K-drama, *Terrace House, Insecure, Friday Night Lights, Empire,* and *Breaking Bad* together until you're hungover, every time you write her a ballad on the piano and text her when she feels lonely, every time you make green tea after dinner and dance with her in your underwear, you're telling her everything you've ever felt for her in a single instant, everything she's wanted you to say since the beginning.

次に/Next:

1. To read Jackson's pro/con list about living in Buenos Aires, go to page doscientos ochenta y ocho, compadre.
2. To see Jackson and his brother eating Chinese food for Christmas Eve, go to page 86.
3. "I don't wanna cry," except on page 243.
4. To learn about Jackson's favorite cities in the whole damn world, go to page 217.
5. Or just turn the blimey page.

4. Secrets of a Secret Ninja (or Stories I Told Myself as a Hapa Boy)

1. After meeting a young Uruguayo boy and his gorgeous sister on a Carnival cruise, that I was their cousin and that I spoke Spanish like a cartoon

2. That I was a secret agent (with a briefcase full of state-of-the-art gadgets) whose job was to protect the world from terrorists and Soviet psychopaths. And that I could solve global crises with my pen telescope and code-breaking skills

3. That the light fixtures I'd stolen from the Christmas tree were shuriken, that I was a secret ninja, and that a ninja club of one was still a club, just very exclusive

4. That I had a limo waiting for me at all times, ready in an instant to rescue me from trouble (or bullies). All I had to do was mutter one word into my sleeve

5. That I was born in Bordeaux, France, which was why sometimes I used the wrong words in English because being trilingual was so confusing

6. That I had French cousins (Jean-Luc and Claudette) I was in regular contact with, who were always writing me long, incomprehensible letters to me in fancy French

7. That I lived in an imaginary town called Victoria located somewhere between Traverse City, Old Mission, and Interlochen

8. That the living room was a studio at night for Pet Shop Boys music videos starring yours truly

9. That I was transferring to Choate Rosemary Hall in the fall (every fall)

10. That I was a musical prodigy who could remember musical scores simply by skimming through them or hearing symphonies on the radio (which I blame a hundred percent on Amadeus)

11. That being a virgin wasn't shameful

12. That my chin-length brown/gold hair proved I was the reincarnation of Franz Liszt

13. That touching sidewalk cracks or falling leaves or invisible trap doors lead to instant death

14. That I had my own talk show (where I interviewed mushy apples, the ones I felt the most bad for)

15. That I was the youngest Tour de France winner in the history of the sport whenever I rode my bike up hills and listened to New Wave music on my dad's "borrowed" Walkman

16. That Doritos had healing power to close up the deep gash in my ankle I got from trying to do bike stunts off the curb

17. That I knew every Shakespearean sonnet by heart whenever I was crushing hard on a girl

18. That my telekinesis skills just needed more "practice"

19. That there were secret passages inside our house, some of which lead to alternative dimensions without bullies or absent parents or

malicious/racist classmates, or to parallel worlds without memory or heartbreak or divorce, or to a bunker inside Tokyo two thousand years in the future (à la Akira), or to a control room in Bordeaux, France (pourquoi pas?)

20. That I had crazy b-boy moves but was just "too shy" to flaunt my shit during recess and/or was a secret MC ready to spit kerosene for my life

21. That I could be Asian and White, and that people would accept me for who I was and never force me to pick sides or deny my racial identity based on how Asian I looked or how good my Japanese was(n't)

22. That I wasn't allowed to be Asian because you had to look Asian to be Asian, because you had to have an Asian-sounding name, because you had to know how to paint kanji with a shōdo brush and own yukata and master the ojigi, everyone knew that

次に/Next:
1. To watch shuriken hurling towards Jackson's heart, go to page 103.
2. To learn how Jackson and LB survived the most traumatic episode of their relationship, go to page 25.
3. To read about the little, hapa/mixed-race girl that Jackson never had, go to page 246.
4. To "pass the gourd," so to speak and sip some mate with Jackson, go to page 201, boludo.
5. Or just do nothing . . . until you turn the page.

5. Appetite for Dust

1.

After dragging my lifeless limbs back to the compound, I sat on the dirt and cried. My body was weak and trembled. My mind feasted violently on opulent memories of my old life in America. In my irrefutable sickness, I dreamt about things that didn't exist in Burkina Faso like pink lemonade and Italian soda, vegetarian taco salads with cold organic vegetables, thick slices of Jarlsberg cheese on Wheat Thins, crisp, cold filtered water that didn't need to be boiled or prepared with chlorine solution or Iodine tablets, chilled watermelon that didn't need to be soaked in bleach and rinsed with treated water, and hot showers that didn't give you cholera when you swallowed the water by accident. In my damaged brain, I began reminiscing about ex-girlfriends, the lilt of their voices swirling in my subtitled mind, the little mutters they made when they were dreaming, the way they sighed in their sleep as I crawled in bed with them, the pillows still warm and fragrant like freshly baked Naan, the way they walked around the apartment in impressionistic underwear, resurrecting dead plants with their morning warmth, their skin smelling of fabric softener, Tibetan incense, and almond foot-scrub. I was lost in my primitive nausea, the dirt stuck to my knees and palms, and the slight hint of rain and leftover tô hanging in the air like hummingbirds.

2.

My ex-girlfriends lead antithetical lives: comfortable, secure, and (probably) sure of every decision they made while I was sick, soiled, hungry, and lost in Bobo-Dioulasso. They were (probably) enamored with new men who'd graduated from elite Quaker colleges in exactly four years, men who were practical lovers and stable companions, their professional trajectories working like clockwork. They would (probably) be men without debt, artistic delusion, tats, or Japanese matriarchs. They were (probably) too smart to be writers, too stable to fall apart. I was on the other side of the world, hunched over and exhausted, shivering and parched. I became in Africa what you become after your cracks get cracked open and your brokenness gets broken again. I was at the stage after dejection and before self-loathing. I doubted every single decision I'd made in the past year. My stomach rejected reality while I starved in the patchy darkness. Lost in the conflict of my own flesh, I was nostalgic for a world I'd never wanted before and have never wanted since. I craved women I'd never loved and foods I'd never eaten. I craved old apartments I once felt stifled in. I craved cities I was once suffocated in. As old, wrinkled Burkinabé men congregated outside for the first Call to Prayer and miscued chickens screamed at the shy sun, its gold inlay still buried inside the Gulf of Aden like a terrible secret, my stomach became a telethon of contractions, purging itself of phantom food and reconstituted memories.

3.

Two days later, a bunch of volunteers and I decided to bike all the way to La Grand Marché to buy pagne fabric. With two or three pagne squares, neighborhood tailors could transform simple pieces of fabric—with their outlandish designs and dizzying patterns—into polo shirts, cello-shaped dresses, goofy MC Hammer pants, '70's pillowcases, and Gipsy towels for the Hot Season (la saison chaude). After I'd finished bartering with the commerçants, a gesture done only to protect my own dignity, I folded the gray-blue fabric with a red print of giant fisheyes into a tight little stack, placing it inside my daypack with my water bottle, my passport, and some old bread. We then biked up the main road, dirt clouds rising up from our wheels like djinni liberated from the soil, my pedal became a time machine, spinning me back into the early morning before the smell of dried fish, Maggi cubes, and rotting yams got stuck in my skin, before the shoppers at the market had voices or knew how to sink their hooks into my tender flesh like a Wiliamson Speed Jig. With each pedal rotation, my life went backwards inside my head, going past the afternoon and the early morning into the day before when I was sick and ostensibly Muslim and slightly

Yogic, but completely empty inside, returning in my mind to the day we stepped off the plane in Ouaga, overshooting into my college and high school years, into the moment I lost my virginity in high school, and then I went prelapsarian to my first real kiss in sixth grade, my first crush in 1st grade, and finally to my infancy, to the very instant I learned to crawl across my parent's linoleum kitchen floor in Northern Michigan, stuck and entranced by the spongey fortress of my pink flesh, by the soft bliss of my own suspended animation. My infancy almost mirrored my life as a 27-year-old English volunteer throwing up plantains in West Africa, purging his cellular memory of the universe, stalling at the threshold of grief and transformation.

4.

Our pedals cycled through history. I lost myself in the rhythm of our cyclicity, reinvigorated by passing waves of fresh air, consumed in the spinning bike chains as our mountain bikes swerved around potholes, overcrowded bush taxis, and dodged disheveled men pushing tapette carts. We stopped for cows stuck in ditches and goats that chewed on imaginary bread. We passed swarms of avocado green taxis, piggy-back moped riders, and troops of muscular women carrying bundles of firewood and water amphoras on the flat of their heads, their neck muscles bulging out like sacks of basmati rice as they talked and sang in Jula. We biked forever it seemed, right into dust storms that swooped down upon us like giant dog-catching nets past half-naked kids, their shocked faces covered in chalky powder and crumbs of dead food, we biked past old Burkinabé men praying on the side of the road as duct-taped radios played French pop music from makeshift boutiques. The air vibrated and sparkled with bituminous gold speckles that framed the sunset in a temporary act of pointillism before disappearing into the sway of dusk.

次に/Next:

1. To listen to Jackson's babbling as a newborn, go to page 271.
2. To see Jackson going through culture shock, go to page 75.

3.   To watch Jackson strolling past canals in Amsterdam~~, biking in circles, watching sex shows, smoking high grade weed, and then making love to a group of dolled up Russian entrepreneurs who read him Pushkin in half-assed Scottish accents and feed each other caviar and Lemon Heads in the nude)~~, go to 241!

4.   Or just, you know, andá a pasar la página si querés.

6. Things I Used to Believe Had Magical Powers Until I was a Teenager

1. Handmade blankets and heating vents as sacred artifacts to remove the winter chill from my bones

2. Ramen as a cure for sadness and hypothermia

3. Tap water from my bathroom sink as an antidote to feverish dreams

4. Spring sunshine as a cure for cabin fever, unlovability, and melancholy

5. My Gundam Shell in the winter (i.e., snowsuit and moonboots)

6. Doritos as magical stitches to close the deep gash in my ankle

7. My obāchan the art patron, toy supplier, sōmen noodle chef, shogi dealer, chocolate bar smuggler, cultural translator, and backyard baseball thrower

8. *Breakin'* as a multicultural fantasia from the mid-city, monoracial, WASPY world of Traverse City, Michigan, I'd longed to leave since the sixth grade

次に/Next:
1. To read about Jackson's most successful pranks, go to page 129.
2. To learn about Jackson's favorite songs in junior high, go to page 73.
3. THE MOSAIC AS A GIANT METAPHOR OF THE SELF, tonight at ten on Channel 260.
4. To watch Jackson daydreaming, go to page 190.
5. Or just turn the page (if you dare).

7. Flowchart Reincarnation (A Visual Essay of Migration)

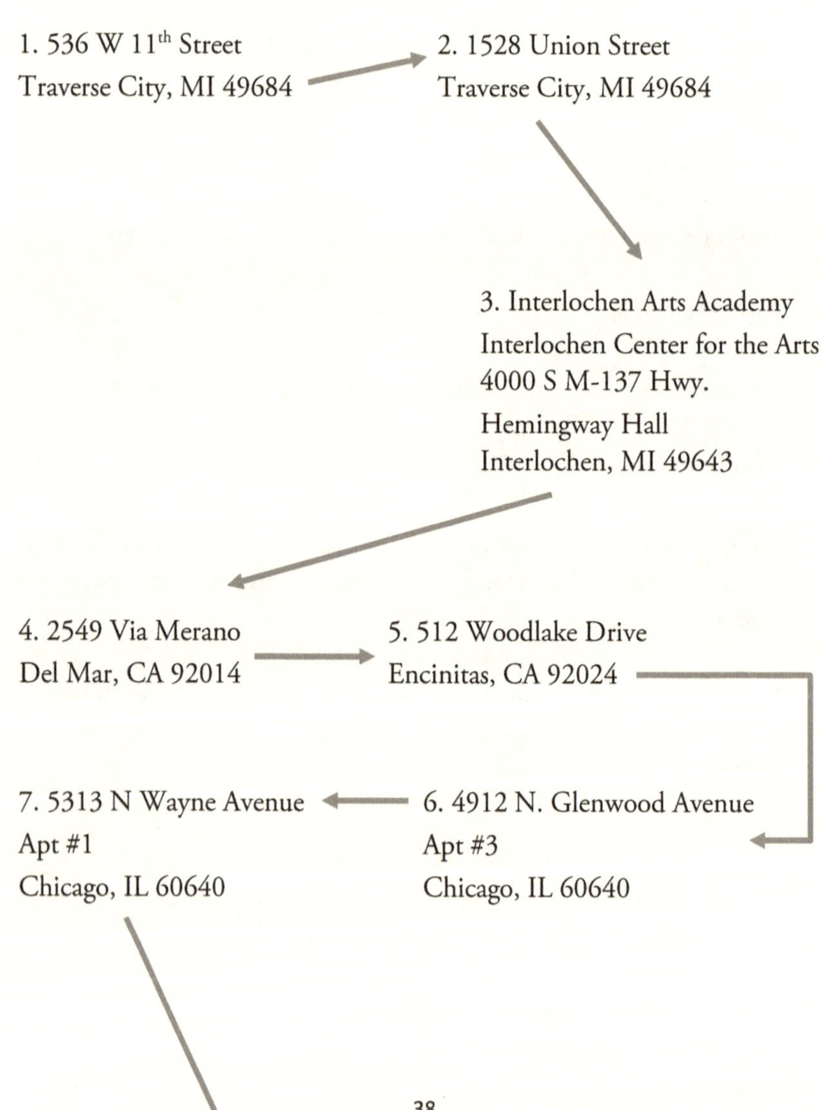

8. Oberlin College
Box #405
Oberlin, OH 44074

9. 164 Mansfield Street
New Haven, CT 06511

10. 4210 12th Avenue NE, Apt C
Seattle, WA 98105

11. 452 Pescado Place
Encinitas, CA 92024

12. C.E.G. de Djibasso, B.P #719
Djibasso, Burkina Faso
Province de la Kossi
L'Afrique de l'ouest/West Africa

13. 1335 NW 23rd Avenue
Apt #105
Portland, OR 97210

14. 1829 SW Cable Avenue
Apt #22
Portland, OR 97201

15. 3734 N Pinegrove Avenue
Apt #304
Chicago, IL 60613

16. 517 ½ W Wayne Street
South Bend, IN 46601

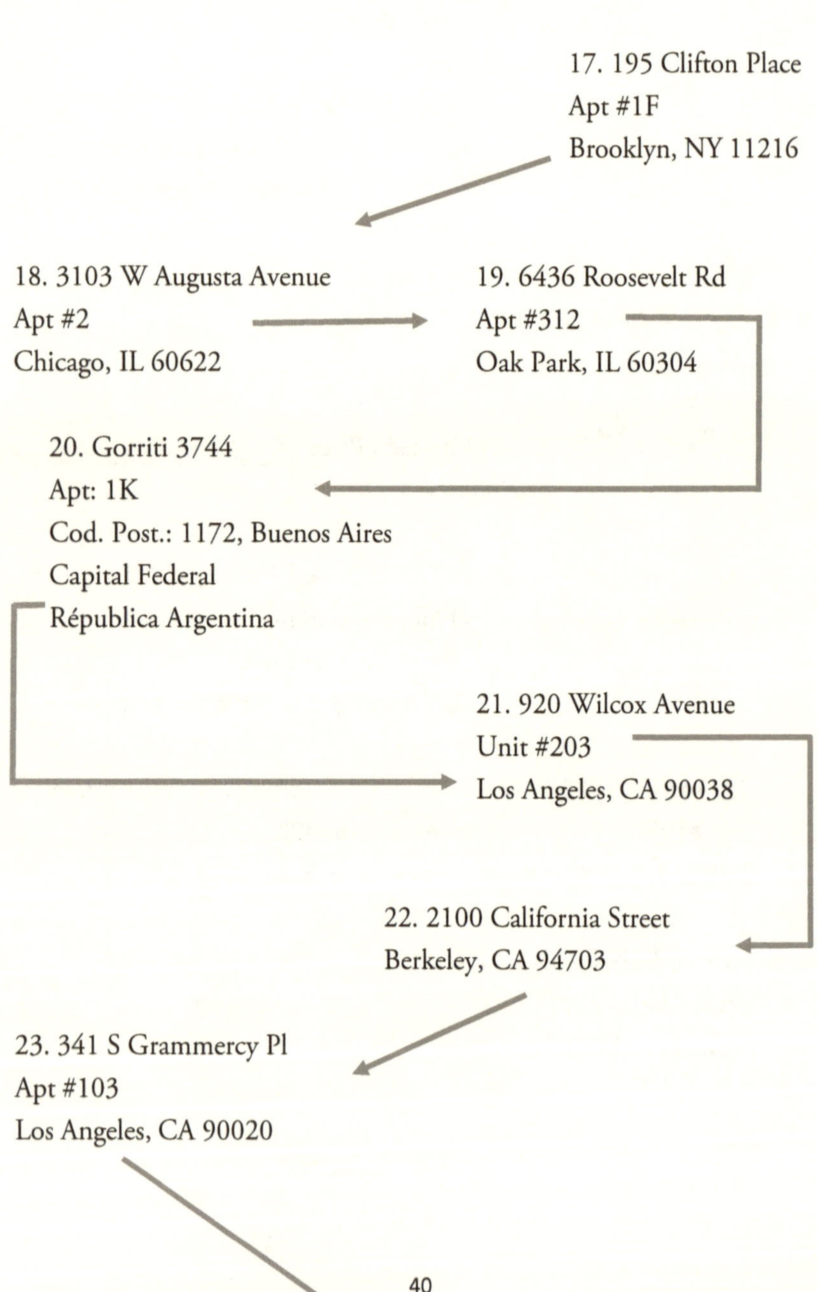

17. 195 Clifton Place
Apt #1F
Brooklyn, NY 11216

18. 3103 W Augusta Avenue
Apt #2
Chicago, IL 60622

19. 6436 Roosevelt Rd
Apt #312
Oak Park, IL 60304

20. Gorriti 3744
Apt: 1K
Cod. Post.: 1172, Buenos Aires
Capital Federal
República Argentina

21. 920 Wilcox Avenue
Unit #203
Los Angeles, CA 90038

22. 2100 California Street
Berkeley, CA 94703

23. 341 S Grammercy Pl
Apt #103
Los Angeles, CA 90020

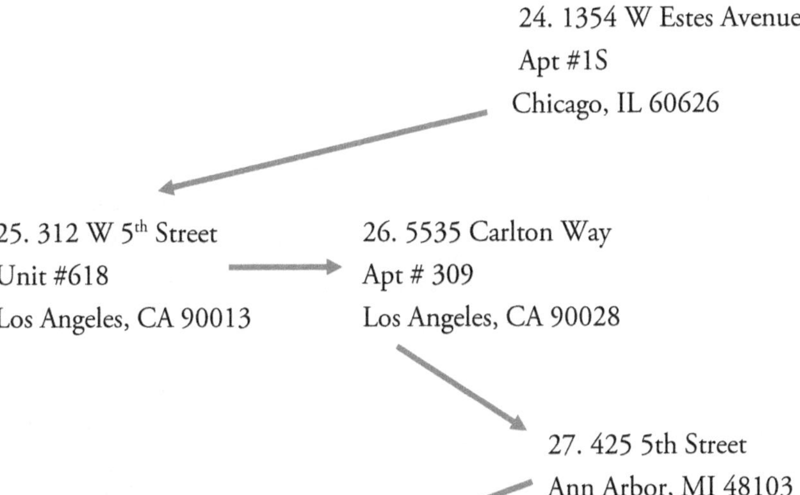

28. Back in LA, this time for LB. We thought about the sun. We came back to the sun.

次に/Next:

1. To see Jackson praying for rain in West Africa (and dude never prays, just to be clear), go to page 105.
2. Where the hapas at? Guess we should go to Bar 296 and find out!
3. To learn about the (surprisingly white, Eurocentrically male) books that changed Jackson's life in high school (because that's what the AP English curriculum used to look like), go to page 165.
4. Or just turn the page, ignoring the defensiveness in option #3 above.

8. The Bad Nisei Quiz

1. **Where was your mom born? Your maternal grandparent?**

-Yokohama and Iyo City. +4 points!

2. **日本語が話せますか。 Are you bilingual?**

-はい and no. 0 points!

3. **How often do you worry about group harmony?**

-Sometimes. +1 point!

4. **How often do you follow social or family hierarchy?**

-Almost never. -4 points!

5. **Can you use 箸 correctly?**

-Yes, my chopstick technique is legit. +2 points!

6. **Do you know at least 五百漢字 (500 kanji)?**

-I had to look up half the kanji on this quiz. -10 points!

7. **Do you own 浴衣 or 着物?**

-No, yukata and kimono are crazy expensive. -6 points!

8. **Have you read Confucius? Do you follow his teachings in the *Analects?***

-Yes, twice, and fuck no. -4 points and -2 for swearing! —What the fuck? -2 MORE points for swearing! -8 total!

9. **Do you speak indirectly in order to avoid confronting or shaming people?**

-Do you? -4 points!

10. **What マンガ are you reading?**

-I'm reading *Food Wars, Otomen,* and

Attack on Titan. +4 points! -That's it? -Now, +2 points!

11. Do you know how to make 卵焼き?

-I KNOW how to make it, but I keep burning the damn egg. -2 points!

12. Are you a Buddhist or a Shintoist?

-Buddhist. 0 points because Buddhists must overcome their attachments to point systems. (I'm showing you my teeth RIGHT NOW)

13. Do you love Yukio Mishima?

-No, I hate his hyper-nationalism and besides, this is a question of literary TASTE. -6 points!

14. Do you say "いただきます?" before every meal?

-Usually, but not always. -4 points!

15. Have you ever told your お母さん to "fuck off?"

-Yes, and I'm not proud of it. -10 points!

17. Do you like scorching hot お風呂?

-Hell no. -4 points and -2 points for swearing! -6 total!

18. Do you love お弁当 boxes and カラオケ?

-~~Fuck~~ yes! +4 points!

19. Do you love 相撲 and/or 野球?

-Not even a little . -10 points!

20. Do you have any tattoos (or other markers of organized crime)?

-Um, maybe. -20 points!

____

Final Score: -77 (Congratulations, you are a Terrible Nisei). ひどい!

次に/Next:

1. To see Jackson spending time with his mom on Christmas, go to page 17.
2. To watch Jackson playing piano for his obāchan (affectionate Japanese word for grandmother), go to page 100.
3. To learn about which words Jackson mispells the most (like *this* word), go to page 253.
4. Or just read this short essay about afternoon tea in Buenos Aires.

9. Por Lo Menos, Decile Chau!

Today was unextraordinary, even by expat standards, where every mundane detail of your life seemed to take on greater significance precisely because it wasn't yours to claim. I was taking my daily merienda at a café in San Telmo, studying for the GRE, and peoplewatching in the mid-afternoon. I'd just finished a second medialuna that was as good as it got in Buenos Aires: crispy on the outside but gooey and sweet on the inside, my cup of oversteeped black tea now a tiny stripe. As I took a break from my Vocabulary Hit List, gazing through the window as porteños walked down Avenida de Mayo smoking and laughing in groups (always groups) of twos and threes, suddenly, a boy dressed up like a little man ambled to my table like we were friends and plopped himself in the chair next to me. He stared at me and smiled, his teeth covered in half-melted chocolate and pastry flour. There was a cookie (or some type of disintegrating pastry) in his mouth like one of those soggy rawhide bones you see dogs chewing, both adorable and completely revolting. The boy chewed like a coca leaf addict, staring at me with huge brown eyes that resembled bloated coffee beans. Once I realized he wasn't going anywhere, I asked him his name in castellano. I asked him what he was eating. I asked him why he had granos de café for eyes and a dog bone for a treat. He smiled but didn't say anything. His mom observed us from a nearby table and shook her head as if to say, *he's at it again*, while her son gnawed on his soggy infinite pastry and then picked up my cellphone, examined it, and rubbed the camera lens with his thumb. I cringed, reminding myself to disinfect it when I got back home in Palermo Viejo.

—Alejandro, his mom said, no es tuyo! He ignored her. She tried again: —Che, no es *tuyo*.

The boy looked like he was about to surge into middle age: cardigan, button-down shirt, miniature shorts, and itsy-bitsy socks. He was pathologically cute in a way that said everything about his mom and very little about him. He pushed the buttons on my phone and looked disappointed when nothing happened. Then, he looked down at the unknown names in my contact list and pushed the illuminated buttons with furious randomness. My hand was on standby, ready to reach out, grab my phone, and end a call abruptly if necessary, the tension building in my arm as the soggy infinite pastry squished in his mouth, hanging by invisible string. As I listened to him suck on his snack, I began to feel nauseated. I began to get annoyed with how good Argentine children were at weaponizing their cuteness. I began to fantasize about prying that dirty thing out of his mouth with a fork and depositing it in a hazmat bin. I wanted to bat it to the floor with a butter knife, bicycle kick it into the trash, and shout *gooooooooool!* while the whole café cheered for me.

Che, no es *tuyo*, his mom repeated. —Dejalo Alejandro. Por favor, dejalo.

Ale micdropped my cellphone on the table and walked to the other side of the café with his spongy pastry still attached to his lips like a pacifier.

—Por lo menos, decile chau, she said with embarrassment, looking at me apologetically. You could at least say goodbye.

次に/Next:
1. Okonomiyaki is Kansai fare at its best. Explore all the best places in Ōsaka here on Channel 224.
2. Nostradamus didn't have SHIT on Jackson's miso soup prophecy on page 126.
3. To see Jackson spending time with his mom on Christmas, go to page 17.
4. Or just turn the goddamn page, will ya?

10. Things I Wanted to Be Growing Up (Many of them Astoundingly Unoriginal)

1. A baller (soccer or bball, I wasn't picky)

2. A concert pianist rock star with screaming rabid fans, long venue lines, popular tour t-shirts, and stylish groupies who wanted to give me hand-written love notes, Japanese markers, blowjobs in the elevator, and make out on transcontinental flights to nowhere

3. A marathon runner with his own soundtrack when he broke world records in ticker tape storms

4. A brilliant composer with frizzy hair and a serious weed addiction, who wrote symphonies inside his head incorporating everyday sounds into musical themes

5. A ripped b-boy with major top rock and famous legit freezes

6. A multilingual lawyer specializing in international law and cross-cultural romances

7. A blasé UN translator and/or lawyer specializing in international law who spent half the year living in Geneva and the other half in Chicago/Tokyo

8. A superhero that could read people's minds, stop time, predict the future, and also leap a thousand feet in the air with a jet propulsion backpack

9. The first American writer to win the Pulitzer Prize, the National Book Award, the Man Booker Prize, and the Nobel Prize in Literature (Dear Committees, I'm available and ready for nomination!)

10. A wide receiver for the Chicago Bears (superoriginal, I know)

11. A graphic novelist like Marjane Satrapi, Yoshihiro Tatsumi, or Adrian Tomine

12. A French philosopher who made his greatest discoveries while walking through the Latin Quarters, Oberkampf, and Saint-Germain-des-Prés

13. A professional (and by professional, I mean secret but totally richass) 忍び

14. A heart-broken samurai in the Tokugawa Shogunate who destroyed his enemies (and every friend, relative, and acquaintance of his enemy) to avenge his slain girlfriend, who was the love of his life

15. Another incomprehensible professor of comparative literature at Yale who casually spoke in seven languages and never translated shit for his students

16. The new lead singer of New Order called New New Order

17. A human reincarnation of a summer storm

18. A millionaire/philanthropist/playboy who rediscovered the meaning of life by helping those living in poverty and battling systemic racism and global injustice

19. The honorary mixed-race MC in Digable Planets

20. (Much much) more legibly Asian

21. The next Pelé

22. A socially conscious influencer who divided his life between Tokyo, Paris, Seoul, Stockholm, Vienna, Barcelona, Buenos Aires, Bali, & LA because I'm classic, bougie, ratchet like that

次に/Next:
1. To see Jackson going through culture shock, go to page 75.
2. When the Tower Records in the East Village was Church, and the coffee table books were the hymn books of pop culture on page 254.
3. To take a break, dream a little, and make some origami, go to page 57.
4. To read about the first time an Argentine boy stole Jackson's cell phone, go to page 45.
5. Or just turn the page gently and with understanding.

11. The Mesosphere in the Bedroom

Whenever Dad and Mary went out to eat at one of Chicago's jaunty restaurants, my brother and I became liberated subjects for a couple hours. Not because we were invited to their baby soirées, but because of the asylum of our Andersonville apartment that only existed in their absence. Sometimes, I felt like my brother and I were peacekeepers protecting a tenuous truce between warring factions. Other times, I felt like the apartment was flushed of its clunky ghosts, becoming a temporary safe haven from the half-life of our silent divorce from each other, from the painless forfeiture of our strained togetherness, and from the permanent exile of our old life in Northern Michigan that haunted us in the North Side, the personal brokenness trailing after you like an enamored sibling.

As a self-conscious act of escapism and social defiance, Wick and I turned the apartment into a weed smoker's paradise—the stuff that smudgy college memoirs should all be about but never are. We smoked weed together for euphoric immediacy, but also to free and rewrite ourselves from the structural erasure related to divorce and the emotional compartmentalization of two different timelines with two different families. Smoking weed helped us re-center ourselves in Chicago where we'd become nameless extras in the background of our parents' dramatic split, including our mom's wanderlust to Florida and our father's born-again biopic in Chicago. It was one thing to become invisible in your own family blackout. It was another to be forgotten in its rewiring. Smoking weed made us important again. It made our laughter mandatory. There were worse ways to reclaim your life.

One evening, Mary and Pops marched through the hallway like contradance amateurs, clicking their heels on the hardwood floor. Wick and I exchanged looks that said, *what the fuck is going on?* Dad and Mary stopped at the front door.

—Behave, you two, he said, pointing his index finger at us.

—Bye guys, she said, we'll see you around ten.

We nodded, shrugged, and turned to each other. When the front door closed shut, my brother and I put on R.E.M. on the stereo and cranked it as loud as it could go without pissing off our landlord who lived on the second floor, had grown tired of me blasting classical music overtures, hip-hop cultural criticism, and alternative music power chords at all hours of the night. He'd started fighting back one day by stomping his feet and shouting through his floorboards. Wick pulled out a Ziplock and sighed.

—Aw, man, he said.

—What? I asked.

—There's nothing but twigs and seeds left, he said.

Suddenly, our rebellion lost its teeth. It was exciting (possibly, even important) to violate our dad's hypocritical pot stance. After all, his half-blind, Reagan-loving best friend in Chicago, Bud—of all names—smoked the chronic like a reggae singer, but this night of rebellion got hamstrung so quickly.

As a last resort, we scraped the resin from an old pipe hidden in the bottom drawer of my hand-me-down armoire and then stuck the paste over a few Marlboro reds, my literature major smoke of choice in college. Ten minutes later, there was a thick, pungent cloud of cheap pot smoke in our bedroom that lingered in the corners like an industrial smog. It was a fucking terrible miscalculation considering we could have just as easily opened up our window and closed the bedroom door and then I wouldn't have to write the rest of this essay, but of course, that's not what happened.

—Wick, I said, my head full of clouds.

—What? he asked.

—There's a fucking *mesosphere* in our room. The only reason I knew this word despite my pathological fear of the hard sciences was because I was a policy debate nerd in high school and the first half of college, and one of the earlier debate resolutions involved space exploration beyond the earth's mesosphere.

—What?

—Mesosphere. In our bedroom.

—Okay.

I knew he was either too high or too proud to ask me what a mesosphere was. I didn't actually care, but my bullshit sensor was hypersensitive in college and brothers are always competing with each other, so I noticed right away when he didn't ask. It was one of those details that a younger brother always notices, relishes, and gloats about later on.

—I hope it disappears soon, I said.

—I'm sure it will, he said.

—Yeah.

—Wait . . .

—What?

—What are you talking about? he asked.

—Huh?

—What were you talking about just now?

—I don't remember. The word my brother wouldn't ask me became the word I couldn't remember. It would take me years of excavation before it came back to me during one particular revision of this essay in LA.

—Me neither, he sighed.

We forgot to close the bedroom door. That was our tragic flaw that night. The resinous second-hand smoke, instead of disappearing in our open window, simply drifted into the TV room while Wick and I raided the fridge, piling turkey and ham cold cuts with Dijon mustard on top of cheddar cheese slices, cold fried chicken, mint chocolates, a to-go container of potato salad, and cranberry juice. We returned to the TV room and watched music videos on MTV of the Red Hot Chili Peppers, Boyz II Men, Nirvana, U2, TLC, REM, PM Dawn, The Cure, and Eric Clapton. There were definitely others, but I can't remember them. As we inhaled our food, we cracked jokes and laughed hysterically at Sir Mix-A-Lot videos and Moo and Oink commercials. We were princes of the motherfucking evening.

But then the front door slammed open an hour ahead of schedule. We sat up on the couch, trying to act "normal," whatever that meant, a performance and an intention that was straight-up farcical. The issue was our eyes, which evidently, were totally bloodshot, even though we didn't know it. Also, we laughed for no reason in particular. Mary took off her jacket, lifted her nose in the air and took a dramatic whiff, and walked up to Wick. She asked him about his permagrin that kept spilling on to his lap whenever he tried answering. She asked him why his eyes were red. She asked him why the TV room smelled strange. She probably wondered why his face was puffy. Our collective make-believe was fucking pitiful, so bad it made me snort in laughter. It was obvious we were blazed and obvious we weren't giving up on our performance of normalcy either, even though we'd already lost the battle.

Dad and Mary walked to the kitchen and began whisper-shouting angrily to each other. We snickered under masks of seriousness. We tried to keep out shit together. We tried really hard not to freak out because freaking out and being high were a terrible combination, especially in a hostile environment. I tried to not feel depressed that our joy and freedom had been replaced with tension and drama, but the disappointment lingered around me and stuck to my clothes and skin like a broken sample vial of cologne, the kind I coveted my last year of high school. Eventually, our dad marched into the living room like a prison warden and crouched behind us, resting his arms on the back of the couch. Wick and I were still lost in our charade, convinced we might rediscover our performance of normalcy any second, like finding missing keys in your backpack.

Pops cleared his throat and paused for dramatic effect.

My brother and I looked at each other from the corners of our eyes. Wick's lips trembled. I pursed my lips out of the pain of constraint. Sometimes, there is genuine pain in containing your laughter.

—*Look*, Dad said, I know what you two did you think was *cooool*.

That was his stress, by the way, not mine. Our dad stretched out that word for so long it practically broke inside his mouth.

Dear readers, my brother and I have many flaws, but our desperate search for joy, our loyalty, and our camaraderie, aren't one of them. Before we knew it, we burst out laughing. It hurt too much to hold that laughter inside. After all, laughter is always seeking its own flight.

Pops waited, annoyance masking his face. —Anyway, he continued, you're *not* to do that here ever again in this house. You got that?

—So, I asked in disbelief, you want us to smoke pot out in the *street*, what if we get ar*rest*ed?

—I don't care *where* you do it, but you're not to do it *here*.

The two of us nodded not because we agreed or because we understood (our father's logic was incredibly shoddy), but because we expected nothing more from him. I remember feeling sad that someone who'd experimented with drugs as much as our dad had (dude actually sold weed at one point) would drop this Nancy Reagan shit on us now. At the same time, I learned eventually that my dad had been busy transforming himself for the second act of his life, which became clear several months later when he and Mary returned home tipsy, their flushed faces reeking of highballs and jubilation, Dad announcing in a slurred cadence that the two of them were getting married, which brought up feelings of confusion, ambivalence, dread, and fascination in us both.

Instead of being a point of empathetic connection with his sons, smoking weed became a wedge issue, a chalk line drawn on the sidewalk between his old life in Northern Michigan with a fashion-forward nuclear family, three loved businesses on Front Street, a Japanese mother-in-law, a hapa wife with a small stash of weed in her underwear drawer that I'd found one day snooping in their bedroom (which I thought made her a criminal or a stoner or both), a long personal history with weed (both the smoking and the selling of it), and his new life in Chicago, which became the hard reset of his life as a manufacturer's representative as he took great strides to become a new man—more visibly Midwestern, less metrosexual, less artistic, more conservative, vaguely urban, and slightly more flirtatious with women, his history as the former husband in a mixed-race marriage now wiped clean before our eyes, even though we were the mixed-race part. The act of smoking weed had become a dividing line separating our dad into separate timelines, rules, and identities, only one of which we understood, neither of which we were part of anymore. When he was done telling us the new rules of drug use in the house, Wick and I waited that night until he walked down the hallway and disappeared into the bedroom before we got up from the couch, walked outside in a daze, and plopped down on the stoop. We smoked a cigarette together (maybe two) and smelled the crisp Chicago air. We talked about things we didn't care about and wouldn't remember later on. We processed our disjuncture separately, quietly. There was no place we could go afterwards except inside ourselves, to sleep and to forget, so we sat there as long as we could on the stoop, feeling the wind on our face, wondering when it was exactly that we got left behind something we'd been running away from.

次に/Next:

1. To read about the baby girl LB & Jackson dreamed about but never had, go to page 246 and bring Kleenex.
2. Jackson is the worst kind of Nisei. Don't believe me? Go to page 42 and see for yourself!
3. Don't cry for me, Argentina/you know I never loved Madonna /she's a bad Evita / worse than Tía Conchita (p. 288).

4. Or just turn the p

a

G

E.

12. My Favorite Colors as a Teenager (because It was a Simpler Time before Asterisks)

1. Burgundy*
2. Forest Green*
3. Cream*
4. Navy Blue*

*One of my favorite articles of clothing in high school, *especially* after my parents got divorced—all of us freefalling from upper middle-class blindness to lower-class bluntness—was a cream Polo sweatshirt with burgundy, navy, and forest green stripes and a navy and burgundy coat of arms. I was fucking in love with that thing. Each time I wore it, the day became a sacred artifact, granting me seventeen hours of pedestrian ecstasy. I almost forgot that I was poor, didn't live with my parents anymore, and didn't know where I was going to live after the year ended (spoiler alert: Del Mar, California).

次に/Next:
1. To learn about this whole "hapa business" Jackson keeps talking about, or maybe just to shut him up, let's consider page 296.
2. To learn about Jackson's favorite childhood video games (the non-permutational type), go to page 85.
3. Playlists? Nah, let's talk about ALBUM lists for the post-grunge college student in ALL of us on page 155.
4. (Speaking in my terrible English accent): Or just turn the bloody page, you yank Mc-wanker!**
   **(Shrugging). I know this doesn't make sense. It just felt good to write.

13. A Place to Catch Your Breath, Dream a Little, & Make 折り紙

1. To make an origami crane, follow these simple instructions:
   A. Tear out this page (gently, very gently). You don't wanna disturb the other pages or tear me into pieces.
   B. Now follow the invisible instructions on this page with the understanding that origami is just an operant metaphor of metamorphic mixed-race identity in this memoir.

2. All done? Nice! Now, please follow these simple instructions:
   A. Leave your origami crane on the pillow of someone you once loved.
   B. Take a couple deep breaths and feel your body.
   C. Feed mochi to the crane, being sure to take some nibbles for yourself.
   D. Take a bath with candles, a glass of cold water, & a dream pop playlist (p. 239). Cancel the world for an hour and wait for the crane to disappear.
   E. Take a nap on the weekend and dream of flying paper birds with impossibly long necks, a fairy tale vulnerability if ever there was one.
   F. Hold hands with the person you gave the crane to, maybe kiss their neck.
   G. Never stop feeding your soul with the flesh of the crane.
   H. Daydream like a motherfucker, crane in hand, breath held inside burning lungs.
   I. Catch a sunset, wuzzle with your pet(s), read romance manga, and look for other cranes in the sky.
   J. ~~Eat the crane.~~ Set the metamorphosis free, dear reader!

次に/Next:

1. Che, callate, boludo y andá a manchar una empanada de cebolla y acelga, en la página 288, dale?
2. To learn how Jackson and LB overcame the grief of not becoming parents, please go to page 25.
3. (Argentine) Raindrops keep falling on Jackson's head on page 121.
4. Or just turn the page.

14. Things I Would Love to Forget (but Can't Because They're Too Painful)

1. Being taken to the hospital in 1992, tripping my balls on bunky acid

2. Getting jumped by one of my Loyola Academy classmates for telling him that there was nothing wrong with being gay, that some of my favorite people were gay (still true, by the way)

3. Being falsely accused of impregnating a one-month girlfriend in Chicago (the one I was practice-rapping for in the mirror) and believing her when she said she was gonna get every cent she could out of me and make sure I never went to college. Plot twist: she never apologized after she later realized she was already pregnant when we'd hooked up

8. Being called a *stupid white boy* by a Black driver speeding through the intersection of Clark and Lawrence, which crushed my soul for a week

15. Not being able to afford my grad school tuition at Yale after three semesters and then being forced to drop out, which broke my heart because I deserved to be there

23. Feeling bullied and ostracized by Americorps volunteers, most of them white women who mocked me for dropping out of the grad school I couldn't afford and said that I was (intellectually) slow and told me that no one cared about me or my thoughts and said I wasn't really Asian and forced me to watch in humiliation as one volunteer announced my own acceptance to Notre Dame's MFA program and fellowship as her own good news in a group self-intro so that I'd be too ashamed to repeat

my own news when it was my turn to talk about our future plans, which I'd worked so hard for and which she'd taken away from me simply out of jealousy and spite

44. The day my mom moved in with a strange white guy in a motel and officially separated from our family

87. My mom strangling me as a kid for being late and then beating me up later on until my ass was bruised for disobeying her

99. Feeling incredibly alone and unwanted after I moved to Chicago to live with my dad, only to learn later that he'd almost sent me to Florida to live with my mom, which at least confirmed his prolonged absences and my feelings of being unwanted

111. Picking up empty vodka and gin bottles off the floor (also during my Americorps service) while my brother slept feverishly on a dirty mattress during one of his worst relapses

140. Attending four different high schools in four different years and being the perpetual new kid every single year, with all of its accompanying privileges and disadvantages

325. The look in LB's eyes every night I left her at the hospital for the ten days she fought an infection that killed baby embryo (after the doctor nicked one of her ovarian cysts), which was now endangering her life

852. The fine lines on my face and underneath my eyes that tell me it's all over

1,718. All the amazing girls I cheated on in high school and college because I was a fucking *idiot* and got away with it as the mixed-race pretty boy

994. The time an ex-girlfriend pretended she'd swallowed a bunch of Advil, forcing me to call 911, and then the ambulance

539. My defaulted school loans

275. Saying goodbye to my two cats, Misha and Ali, for the last time without a proper goodbye, never knowing for sure if they knew how much I loved them. A month later, Ali ran away and my ex-girlfriend left Misha with a friend of a hookup, exclaiming, *it was no one's fault,* which is what people say when it's unquestionably their fault

115. Getting in a fight with the same girlfriend mentioned in #275 who wouldn't let me break up with her until she'd called it quits on her terms, the only artist I'd ever dated until LB

50. The feeling of powerlessness and the Asian stigma of being unemployed

34. Listening to 9/11 happen on the radio BBC in West Africa and being the only American in the whole village (I cried into my spaghetti)

7. Throwing Miko, our Siamese cat, into the Jacuzzi as a boy (gomen, ne)

6. Getting into but not going to Vassar (eat it, guidance counselor!), which was the sum of all my high school dreams back then

0. Grinding through academia as an adjunct and knowing my dream of

teaching could end any moment, my life precarious, my education undervalued

次に/Next:

1. To read Jackson's list of favorite cities in North America, go to page 205.

2. To see Jackson and his brother smoking weed, ~~driving up I-5 in a shiny Turquoise Lowrider Impala with chrome, wire-rimmed spinners, listening to *The Chronic*, and drinking 40s with an environmentally friendly steel straw,~~ go to page 50.

3. When teachers treat you like you're dumb and you're smart, you realize the world is stupid (but secretly worry that you're delusional), as described on page 294.

4. Or just turn the Betty Page, you beautiful pin-up bombshell of a reader.

15. Mortality Love Song

1.

According to studio executives and advertising billboards, I didn't matter anymore now that I was thirty. Everything from this point forward was just a series of ego crises exploding in slow motion. Soon, I'd sprout hair in my ears, on my legs and back like a latent Neanderthal, even though my lack of body hair had easily been the most Asian part of my body. Soon, my life would become an unironic sitcom about faded, humbled 30-somethings dealing with stiff mortgage payments, professional malaise, student loans I couldn't pay, and college nostalgia I couldn't slay, always trying to protect my dignity from a society obsessed with adolescence. Soon, I'd become another "sane," chubby adult highlighting ads in the newspaper for things I used to scoff at when I was a teenager, for things I don't even need as an adult: face lifts, hair plugs, penis extensions, mysterious blue capsules that no longer gave me heart attacks, neck liposuction, crash diets invented by speed-addicted anorexics, and permanent makeup to make my hapa eyes pop like a Moé superstar. Maybe someday, I'd read the back of *The Village Voice* to find offices providing legal aid to people seeking political asylum for their asses that clearly didn't have a place here in the West Coast where obesity was always a cautionary tale.

2.

Even though I'd been good at resisting the groupthink slogan that suggested my life was over after thirty, I wasn't completely immune to it either. After all, all I had to show for my life at the age of twenty-nine was a Winesburgian collection of character sketches about New Yorkers in Washington Square that force-fed epiphanies down the reader's throat (eat your heart out, Charles Baxter), a tattoo of three kanji that made my obāchan groan and then mutter, *yakuza, ne,* at the dinner table, and a

Bachelor's degree in a major no one understood (Comparative literature) at a liberal arts college no one knew the location of (Oberlin College) until *Girls* made everyone look it up on *Wikipedia*. There were other things too that made my life feel even less impressive and substantial then, artifacts taken from other worlds with different actors and plot lines, which elicited a series of vivid memories I wanted to suppress more than anything, but couldn't:

1. A dysfunctional, on-again, off-again relationship with one of the most beautiful and pathologically sensitive women I'd ever met in my entire life who might or might not have had borderline personality disorder. Our relationship was so DOA, we used supermarkets (specifically the *toy aisle* of Fred Meyer) and discount Seattle movie theaters to give us the clean plot structure, self-evasion, anesthesia, romantic chemistry, and senseless laughter we could never replicate in our own relationship, even with sex.

2. A letter from a collection agency for loans I didn't even know I'd applied for.

3. Three rejection letters from three PhD programs I didn't deserve to get into without a second foreign language and a more coherent specialization. Ah, details.

4. My old Yale ID from grad school (one of the last school IDs of me with hair, sadly) where I'd left after three semesters because I couldn't afford to finish since Yale's M.A. programs back then were cash cows and fellowships and tuition scholarships were sparse, even with its billion-dollar endowment. In fact, I took out student loans to cover my tuition and rent, living on the $80 I earned each week working at the Sterling Library for food, a gorgeous, retrofitted cathedral designed to Borgesian specifications that almost made me forget my hunger. But I was poor, so poor I couldn't afford all the books for my Modern Japanese History seminar where we read two books every week. I couldn't even afford Sapporo Ichiban ramen. I regularly stole napkins from cafés and created tiny bundles of cheese cubes, baby carrots, and water crackers wrapped in blue crested napkins from the hors d'oeuvre table after keynote lectures by renowned scholars. I slept

on a mattress without a blanket. I called up old girlfriends on the phone and asked shamelessly for money because I was desperate. Sometimes, I went to bed famished. I got back together with the girlfriend in paragraph #1 at least once because I needed food. Sometimes, my roommate, a Spanish Lit PhD student with a tuition scholarship and a big fat stipend who was once my friend, ate my food because he was too lazy to go to the supermarket or buy Japanese take-out next door, a guy who eventually started dating a disgruntled ex-girlfriend of mine from Oberlin who attended Yale too. She still hated me, even years after we'd dated, even after I'd offered her an olive branch in the spirit of grad school and the erasure of undergraduate drama I'd been both a narrative subject and object of, but now, when our paths crossed inside the apartment, she half-smiled like a wounded harpy who had turned my own apartment into her lair. I quietly feared the day they ganged up on me because that's what couples do (but that's another essay in another collection). Whenever I saw R., I cursed my luck. I wished I'd stayed in my old place on Mansfield Avenue before I'd transferred from the Divinity School to the Graduate School, before I lost a way to pay for my tuition, before I fucked everything up like buying a cell phone I couldn't afford and moving into an apartment with someone I shouldn't have trusted and calling an ex-girlfriend in Chicago for food and trying to broker a détente with a spiteful ex who just *had* to date my roommate, of all people. I wish I had stood up for myself after the Graduate School dean sat on my transfer application until financial aid awards had been allocated. Every morning as I brushed my teeth and washed my face in the industrial bathroom light of the apartment, I heard my former friend and my former girlfriend fucking in his bedroom like clockwork, which sounded like window washers squeaking their squeegees against dirty windows. I began to wonder if they intentionally fucked when I brushed my teeth, but I didn't care enough to ask. I was too exhausted to be that self-centered (anymore). The final blow was when my roommate and former friend—un buen tío anterior who used to dance to the Verve and the Red Hot Chili

Peppers in his graduate housing apartment and drink pints of Guinness at cafés with me and crash undergraduate parties on Old Campus without my approval and throw parties later in our always-empty apartment—removed his plates and silverware from the kitchen just to be a dick, leaving me with literally nothing to eat my food with except my bare hands. Instead of staying in New Haven for another semester as I'd planned, I moved to Seattle with the pathologically sensitive girlfriend and then we did everything mentioned in #1 to avoid interacting with each other. My move to Seattle was the beginning of my downward spiral to nowhere, but then I met you, dear reader, in the Pacific Northwest, during my automatic writing art therapy phase, which saved me. That's not hyperbole, by the way, just one jump too far in this essay.

3.

By the time I'd settled into the Pacific Northwest, I began having these awful "epiphanies" all the damn time (hence, my Winesburgian collection of short stories and my defensiveness with Charles Baxter essays), but even the novelty of my gun-to-the-head modesty, even my sudden shift in self-criticism and my recent spate of self-loathing wasn't remarkable, it was just what 20-something guys did when they felt old, and the real burn was that I was still young enough to *hate* life clichés but tired enough that I no longer had the energy to fight every new life cliché that popped up. Staying on the cutting edge of everything I held dear just wasn't worth it anymore. It had become an obstacle course to my sanity, filled with cultural triathletes and savings account mercenaries I could never compete with. I never had a chance. I just didn't know it.

4.

Thirty is a sharpened number with a brutal edge. It did violent things to me. At one point, I found myself muttering, "I'm too old for this shit. I can't be indie about everything anymore. Could I ever?" It killed me that I now bought tea out of desperation at Starbucks and hoodies at Urban

Outfitters that looked like every other English major on the West Coast. Once I turned thirty, I admitted to myself that I had been miserable for much of my 20s, something which was difficult to admit. My adult performance back then deserved a failing grade. Yes, I knew how to be a lit student, a language, culture, and music lover, a passionate lover boy, and a language-driven fiction writer. Yes, I was great at that shit, but I didn't know how to be an adult, how to integrate my collegiate passion projects into the unsexy frame of adulthood ticket punching. I didn't know how to adult, how to be happy and also responsible, and I really wanted to be happy again, the way I used to when I didn't give a shit about anything except sex, books, languages, writing, and infatuation. Crashing into the wall of thirty-something mortality was a rude awakening for someone not yet anchored to the world. Frankly, it should have happened—would have happened—earlier if not for grad school, which is always the final deferment before the first payment of adulthood for every intellectual and artist and writer in America. But no matter how I looked at it, I was a conspicuous failure as an adult. I adulted liked shit. I couldn't score a decent waiting job in Seattle until I lied on my CV and got a job at a French bistro in Lower Queen Anne, I couldn't get hired at a local bookstore after leaving a graduate program at Yale, couldn't get into David Walker's intermediate fiction writing class at U Dub despite my infinite potential (in large part because I didn't have a printer), I couldn't even make a clean break with the girlfriend in #1, which she deserved, if nothing else. I was failing so bad at everything. As a student, I used to be chocolate for the eyes in Chicago. Random Evanston girls used to laugh at everything I said at parties, even when I said opaque bullshit about books I hadn't read, but always meant to (e.g., *Infinite Jest*). Middle-aged women stopped me in the middle of the El to tell me I was beautiful. Young professionals did eye ballet with me on the street. High school girls walked over to me at late-night cafés in the Gold Coast and asked if I had a girlfriend. New Trier girls stopped me at the bus stop in Winnetka and gave me love notes with separate phone numbers and hair descriptions (I never called). College girls giggled when I made passionate arguments in lit class and asked me out on dates after final exams and whispered when I passed them at Evanston cafés, probably high, drunk, or chainsmoking. In other words, I used to be completely fucking spoiled with an obscene amount of female attention, none of which I'd deserved AT ALL, but then again, who does? Beauty privilege is a real thing, my friends, and I only realized this once I stopped being pretty. But for most attractive people I know, the opposite of beautiful isn't ugly, it's invisible. That's what I became after moving to Seattle. Now, in PDX, shit was getting real at the age of twenty-nine. I had to accept my mortality because the evidence was overwhelming and irrepressible, but now gravity wanted to join the party and do crazy shit with my former porcelain hapa skin. And adulthood—that emasculating, eviscerating, sterilizing psychopath— wanted to erase my hairline, remove the glow from my eyes, and carve fine lines into my forehead. I fucking hated every part of the liminal experience of turning thirty even more than the invisibility.

5.

The day a college student in the U-District called me sir, I almost choked on my tea. I'd heard that word before. It was the same poison dart that had once flown out of my own 20-something blowgun at unsuspecting adults when I was a prehipster student at Oberlin who carried a Manhattan Portage satchel wherever I went, smoked after every minor accomplishment, got waylaid by four-hour conversations, and fucked, read, smoked, and wrote in one continuous flow of energy the way only a serial monogamist and lit major could do, high on language, desire, ideas, and pleasure. I skipped (and sometimes failed) my classes to read French novels and books on evolutionary socialism that weren't even required in my seminars. I drank scotch, read the Beats out loud, started writing a postmodern novel, and played chess obsessively with friends, some bitter, others yogic. I pretended I still lived in Chicago even though our college was in the middle of the Ohio cornfields. My college nostalgia was destined to die eventually, I've known that for a while, but my rebirth stalled until I traveled to West Africa, moved to Portland, took my first creative writing workshop, became an Americorps volunteer in Chicago, and then started my MFA. It's better I didn't know how long it would take for me to (not!) work it all out.

6.

When I turned thirty, people started using that fucked-up word, "sir," that poison dart, to describe *me,* not my grandparents who had to chew everything a hundred times before swallowing or my classics professor who probably wore bowties and galoshes to department parties, even in the summertime. No, people were now using this word to "playfully" let me know I wasn't cool because coolness was the prerogative of youth culture. The truth was, college students can smell your age like a Ziplock of skunky kush inside your jean jacket. They just know. They always do. One day, college girls stopped batting their eyes at me. In fact, I *ceased* to exist unless I was grading their essays, but even then, it was my power dynamic and not my body that they were attracted to and it hurt not being sexually objectified like that! Being called sir fucked me up for the simple reason that no one wanted to sleep with a sir unless he was part of the Royal family or rapping about women with large asses in need of political asylum. I had become the tutti-frutti ice cream of the human species: bright, obnoxious, speckled with strange blemishes no wanted to understand, completely ignored by teens but absolutely adored by children, especially those with cavities and color-blindness. Children know prime daddy material when they see it, and even worse, they know it before you do. One day where the sound of hacky sackers groaning in the courtyard, the clicking of lighters and ultimate Frisbee players screaming in the quad, the thump of Sublime and Tribe bass lines blasting out of dorm windows, and the subtle scent of honey and granola rising into the air from a nearby co-op used to be, the place where all those things once rang inside my soul, now I heard the distinct sound of something falling from the sky and it was fucking terrifying. But my feelings eventually shifted, much like my racial identity, and I learned to fold kami into a bestiary of my own imagination.

7.

When I turned thirty, I sighed in gratitude. I turned to my girlfriend at the time (the one who would eventually abandon our two cats and then claim it was no one's fault) and blurted out to that I'd been *culturally demoted.* She laughed. She tried to tell me it wasn't true, but the truth was, I appreciated the reprieve. I liked the new atomic weight of my vote on election day and the right to forgive myself sometimes for the many ways I disappointed myself and my Japanese ancestors. Turning thirty was a disaster. But in the next three years, it also became a landmark: I would volunteer in the West Side of Chicago as a bilingual literacy tutor, then get into my dream MFA program, get more ink on my arms, publish my first short story, complete my first editorial internship in New York, and eventually meet LB, the love of my life. In other words, it was my thirties where I slowly redeemed myself for the litany of mistakes I'd made perpetually in my 20s. In time, I leaned on my flaws instead of hiding them. I began to embrace my identity as an emotional, affectionate, urban metrosexual, a mixed-race/hapa writer, and a linguaphile. For the first time, I told strangers I was Asian and white, something I'd only told girlfriends and close friends. I embraced how deeply flawed I was as an emergent human being, how deeply flawed I would always be. I began embracing my wanderlust instead of erasing it. I tried to accept that I was too sensitive, emotional, passionate, playful, nerdy, and romantic to follow the standard American script of white masculinity. I liked slowing down my life. I liked going for runs in the rain. I liked being in love more than anything in the whole world. I liked buying my own clothes and controlling the visual field of my own stylistic identity. I liked stability, thoughtfulness, passion, and empathy. I liked meditating. I like my mixed-race identity. I loved my Japanese ancestry. I aspired to a personalized spirituality. I stopped feeling obligated to know everything. I stopped being threatened by other people's talents. I found meaning in the cultivation of my own craft, even if most of my writing still collapsed on the page. Sometimes, just the act of writing a short story or a personal essay saved me from myself and the treacheries of this two-faced world.

8.

Turning thirty hurt less after I learned to forgive people, including those in this essay, including myself in this world. The evolution was inconsistent and imprecise, the learning curve incredibly steep and hostile, but eventually I learned who I was and who I wanted to be. I understood there would always be an enormous gulf in between. I learned how to talk about someone without talking shit about them, unless I wanted to talk shit about them. I learned how to protect my idiosyncrasies from the social fascism of conformity, which transgressed my Japanese identity in ways that weren't comfortable at times. I learned to appreciate basic but important qualities in others like honesty and kindness, inner strength and gratitude, empathy and patience. I learned to critique myself without patting myself on the shoulders for my self-awareness. My life as an evolutionary adult wasn't cinematic, but it was real. It was mine. The foibles and the euphoria. The tenuous joy and the Icarian crashlandings. While I did my best to embrace my existential burden like a good Danish cultural critic, I learned I am responsible for my mistakes, but I'm not sentenced to them.

9.

When my girlfriend in Portland gave me the four-track I'd asked for my birthday (to this day one of the kindest and most thoughtful gifts I've ever received), the first thing I did was sit down and write electronic music on my keyboard. Good or bad, it was my music, based on my rules of creation, my flaws hoisted into the air like a declaration of war. As exhausted rain puttered in the streets of Goose Hollow, I vowed to make my life into a concert hall so that I could fill it with my recitals of love, desire, longing, and joy, so I could play through my endless mistakes and rekindle my humanity with every melody. I vowed to build a temple of song to worship the quanta of this fleeting life. I vowed to write and conduct the soundtrack of my life that would be part Phillip Glass, part DJ Krush, part Latin love ballad, and part Balmorhea. I would spend the rest of my life writing short stories and personal essays and language-driven novels and experimental memoirs with a quiet tremor, describing this flawed and heartbreaking and heartbroken world with luscious, vulnerable, and heroic awe. I would craft a trichromatic love story out all the broken objects in my heart and whisper the punchlines of every failed joke because you are my witness now and these are the only primary colors I know how to give you besides my affection, which you never asked for.

次に/Next:

1. To see the (surprisingly white, male Eurocentric) books Jacksons was obsessed with in college, go to page 165.
2. To learn how to spot a hapa (and smother them with love, adoration, and mochi), go to page 296 and make a mixed-race person happy today.
3. To learn about Jackson's childhood refuges, go to page 22.
4. Sometimes, the idea of home is a moving target, like on page 175.
5. Dear High-School-Jackson, we need to talk. Meet me on page 219.

16. ~~Random~~ Eclectic Shit I Listened to in Junior High because I was Nerdy & Complicated & Loved Dancing & was Looking for Love (Like Literally, Not Sexually)

1. "Romeo and Juliet Overture" by Tchaikovsky

2. "Come on Feel the Noise" by Quiet Riot

3. "West End Girls" by Pet Shop Boys

4. "Jupiter" and "Mars" by Holst

5. "Beat Street Breakdown" by Grandmaster Melle Mel

6. "Jump" by Van Halen

7. The "Resurrection" Symphony by Mahler

8. "I Feel for You" Chaka Khan

9. "Silver Cloud" by Kitaro

10. Collected Nocturnes by Chopin

11. "Rhapsody on a Theme of Paganini" by Rachmaninoff

12. "There's No Stopping Us" by Ollie & Jerry

13. "Ain't Nobody" by Chaka Khan & Rufus

14. "Billie Jean" by Michael Jackson

15. "Thanksgiving" by George Winston

16. "The One I Love" by R.E.M.

17. "Ballade #1 in G Minor" By Chopin

18. "Stand" by R.E.M.

19. "Hymn" by Vangelis

20. "Les Divas du dancing" by Phillippe Cataldo

21. "Save a Prayer" by Duran Duran

22. "Kids in America" by Kim Wilde

23. "I Wanna Dance with Somebody" by Whitney

24. "Africa" by Toto (I know, it's a ri*dicu*lous song, but I *still* loved it)

25. "Don't Stand so Close to Me" by the Police

26. "Tainted Love" by Soft Cell

27. "Peer Gynt Suite" by Grieg

28. "Heart of Glass" by Blondie

29. "Lieutenant Kijé Suite" by Prokofiev

30. "Appalachian Spring Suite" by Copland

31. "Photograph" by Def Leppard

32. "Video Killed the Radio Star" by The Buggles

33. "Blue Monday" by New Order

34. "Andante Spianato" by Chopin

35. "With or Without You" by U2

36. "Parents Just Don't Understand" by DJ Jazzy Jeff & The Fresh Prince

次に/Next:

1. These are the idiosyncrasies on page 186 that Jackson (almost) stopped apologizing for once he'd started writing this permutational mindfuck of a memoir.

2. To resist the cult of Maradona, speak in Argentine Spanish, & walk around Palermo Hollywood, go to page 288.

3. To understand how Jackson survived puberty in Chicago, go to page 273.

4. To watch Jackson get totally humiliated in his high school French class (quel trou de cul, toi), go to page 159.

5. Or just turn the p-p-p-page.

17. The Culture Shock of Dancing Atoms

1.

Only travel, love, reading, and art have made me truly vulnerable to beauty and its multiform psychic violence. After all, familiarity on some basic level is immunity. When we're familiar with a specific space, we stopped being affected by it, and this is the only reason why I stop trying to understand what places mean (to the world, to me, to its people) until I'm lost again, until I've become exiled by unfamiliarity, until I've been thrown out of my predictable life by the bouncers of modernism redux. When LB and I returned to Chicago after living in South America for a year and traveling through Europe in youth hostels, I got a taste of the vulnerability and the unfamiliarity I'd craved since my first year of college and it fucking scared me.

2.

I'd always loved the *idea* of not recognizing where I lived or seeing my native land as foreigners did for the simple reason that I've always sought defamiliarization since I was a hapa boy trapped in a beautiful hamlet in Northern Michigan where racial and cultural differences were erased, ignored, or indicted, but where the human spirit was also nourished by clean air, quiet streets, fresh lakes, 31 sakura groves, and Ansel Adams forest snapshots. Walking down Michigan Avenue with fresh and untrained eyes as an adult meant that I could fall in love with my city all over again, it meant I could recreate Chicago into a fresh, subjective, and linear experience of joy and self-discovery again as it once was for me as a seventeen-year-old teenage boy with California tan lines and a briefcase of debate evidence. Seeing Chicago with fresh eyes meant I could recreate its segregated majesty in my soul again, one pothole-filled street, one brick apartment, one half-dead courtyard, and one back-breaking skyscraper at a time like the narrator in Borges's "Circular Ruins."

3.

Sometimes during naps and extended daydreams, it felt like LB and I had been transported back to the melodic din of loquacious, smoked-filled cafés in Paris, the soft blur of Amsterdam bike lanes and its whispering canals, the chilly majesty of the frosting-covered mountains in Geneva's confectionary cityscape, and the opioid sunshine of Sitges where I suggestively licked a popsicle in front of a group of gay Spaniards by accident, LB in complete hysterics. I could see our dusty bed in our two-star hotel in Sol where LB and I made love in the dust-filled darkness after eating photogenic paella at a famous restaurant we'd talked our way into in Spanish and dozing off before being woken up by drunk Madrileños singing '80s rock songs and *Magic Flute* arias in the streets and hyperactive French teenagers racing down the hallways and knocking on the doors of guests. Fous le camp, I'd grumbled. I could see us stuck inside a creaking, scorching old train that threatened to bake us alive as we traveled through the Sahara desert, the dust invading through the open window before we arrived in Marrakech and almost got mugged by Moroccan teenagers in the medina who yanked the map from my hands and tried to charge me €20 for taking us to our ryad against our will before I got into a shouting match in French, LB standing there confused and on the brink of tears, their leader threatening to beat me up for not paying their unsolicited fee, my patience turning into unstable anger before I finally handed him a pocketful of small coins.

4.

Traveling is always simultaneously time-traveling. You're learning about that country's history at the same time that you're exploring its urban spaces, constructing a new historical framework (for you) at the same time you're reconstructing its culture in every street, landmark, and alleyway as you're reverse engineering time itself. It's only because each country's history is new to you as the cultural tourist that the present and the past always collapse into each other, but that's part of the magical blur of travel. Your long-winded strolls through each new city are just a kinetic ethnography, so you walk until the soles of your feet are blistered with historical footnotes.

5.

After returning to Chicago, Zoe seemed worried about our ephemerality, like LB and I were flickering between parallel worlds in Buenos Aires, Paris, Madrid, Geneva, Barcelona, Casa, Marrakech, and Amsterdam like fickle atoms dancing under the scientific gaze of electron microscopes. Sometimes, she curled up on our suitcases in protest. Take me with you, her naps said. Don't leave me alone, her naps shouted. Sometimes, there wasn't enough room in Chicago for all our memories of Buenos Aires. Sometimes, there wasn't enough time in Chicago to rescue every memory kidnapped by the shifting historical frames of the present. My Latin professor in college once said that the present changes the past, not the other way around, an argument I would have embraced if it hadn't come from someone whose scholarship was entrenched in antiquity. But later in life, I realized he was right and I should have studied my declensions more.

6.

In Chicago, the morning sunlight streamed into the bedroom like aerated bourbon. Inside my head, I saw visions of human pyramids climbing into the Barcelona sky, their faces embellished with gold dust, a tiny child clambering to the top to blow a gold bugle like an LDS herald of the apocalypse. I forgot where I was when I woke up one afternoon, but I'd woken up in a cold sweat, afraid I'd slipped into a wormhole straight to Marrakech, counting the seconds until the night blotted out the natural light like a slumlord nailing the windows of a condemned building. Sometimes, traveling felt like a collective hallucination that I stumbled into like walking onto someone else's movie set. Other times, traveling felt like the gradual annihilation of my once-familiar life in Argentina, one sumptuous meal, one Instagrammable stroll, one bucolic train ride, and one exhausted flight back again to an old life that hadn't changed nearly as much as you had.

7.

Though I eventually stopped calling our Palermo Viejo apartment home, it was the last place LB and I were a cohesive design. We had spent the last year living on the other side of the equator where toilets flushed counterclockwise, futból and protests were national religions, and empanadas, asado, and mate were lighthouses for the shipwrecked and the disoriented. In Cap Fed, cafés became small operas, sometimes introspective, sometimes unbearably bright, but always contrapuntal: a social melody with baroque rules of simultaneity. In this mythical and faded city, mate gourds froze timelines, ambient laughter was viral, echoing in almost every street, bluntness slashed etiquette, the sticky winter sky weaved tales of thunder out of unraveled rain clouds and every conversation in the street became dialogue in someone else's short story or bar anecdote. Time in Cap Fed was an emotional force of nature crashing down recklessly on the sad exaltation of every missed sunset. I still think about the used bookstores there all the time with smoke filling my heart.

8.

For the first month back in Chicago, I thought I was back in South America every time I woke up in Lakeview. My mind was sluggish, tortured by nostalgia, and confused by differential sunlight. Chicago was my complex dream catcher, capturing the grainy sedimentation of my unconscious mind, amassing the sensory details of all the places I'd traveled to and passed through that summer. My mind was a mixed-up photo album of confusing experiences that I began doubting, moving closer each day toward the Chicago stockyard again like an almost-broken freight train gaining strength through momentum.

9.

At every stage in my life, I always returned to this working-class city where I became an adult, began college, learned to smoke, became a "writer" first and then a writer second, and daydreamed obsessively about the globe beyond the simulacrum ocean. I spent most of my 20s dreaming about the rest of the world, but now culture-shocked and jetlagged, Chicago became my cradle of infancy again. I loved her as an adult for all the reasons I'd despised her as a college student obsessed with literature, language, and philosophy: the El was filthy, the sunshine broke out into thunder showers without warning, the air was sticky and sultry at night, the Loop resisted transformation, the sidewalks reeked of stale beer, the vegetarian restaurants were ten years behind California, strolls across the Chicago River routinely broke my heart, and there was a feeling of solidity when I walked through neighborhoods made of brick and mortar. Every time I returned, I was forced to create a new relationship with her streets, always starting from a harsh discontinuity, always continuing with a blurry and fierce disfiguration of time, always skimming the instructions of exile, always stoking my intransigent and conflicting fire for sanity, adventure, stability, novelty, belonging, and alienation. There could never be a détente.

次に/Next:

1. "Ciao bachelorhood! Goodbye and Goodluck," Jackson said on page 182.
2. When love is the only salve to a broken heart, look inside medicine cabinet #99.
3. Jackson did WHAT on page 230? That boy was cra-zy (but clearly not crazy enough).
4. To read Jackson's favorite playlist from junior high, go to page 73.
5. Or just turn the . . . you know what.

18. Shit My Parents Used to Do That Embarrassed the Hell Out of Me but I Give Them Props for Now that I'm Older than They Were

1. Taking me to the supermarket dressed in tight kelly-green sweatpants and a Japanese leather jacket with enormous shoulder pads that made him look like he was a robot and a football player (Pops)

2. Going to work dressed in a miniskirt, fishnet stockings, and Tina Turner wig (Mom)

3. Hiding schwaggy weed in their underwear drawer (Mom)

4. Going to work for Halloween dressed up as a samurai (Pops)

5. Walking up to me while I was in the middle of asking out a girl named Sara after a school dance (Mom)

6. Hiding softcore porn in obvious places in the closet (Pops)

7. Getting drunk with strangers in a restaurant in Puerto Vallarta and then cackling at their dirty jokes in order to show her family what a great time she was having while Dad became suddenly sober and just replied with comments like, "Yeah, that's right" (Mom and Dad)

8. Making Jackson Pollock t-shirts with white Haynes tees, toothbrushes, and acrylic paint in the backyard, then selling said t-shirts at their store on Front Street. Later, wearing said t-shirts at supermarket along with

tight kelly-green sweatpants and Japanese leather jacket with enormous shoulder pads (Pops)

9. Announcing in front of all her hot female customers that she wished my brother and I were gay because *we're such handsome, well-dressed and sensitive boys* (Mom)

10. Dragging my pouty ass to a Huey Lewis *and* a Tina Turner concert at Castle Farms (Mom and Dad)

11. Shooting free throws like a jet-propelled ballerina (Pops)

12. Having the courage, the strength, and the selfishness to move to California without thinking about her teenage sons (Mom)

次に/Next:

1. To learn how Jackson built a shrine out of his own trauma, go to page 232.
2. To read about the first time Jackson got sick and nostalgic in Africa, go to page 33.
3. What were the great authors of the world Jackson was devouring in high school? No fucking idea, but JACKSON was listening to THIS SHIT on page 159.
4. Or just turn the page.

19. The Age of Aquarius

One of the kindest things my dad ever did was teach me how to become a koi in a fresh-water lake. I was almost a teenager back then, my body already unrecognizable and uncountable. I was relieved that summer camp was over and ecstatic about the metempsychosis of junior high where students evolved into different (and sometimes, higher) versions of themselves, shedding their childhood like silk cocoons. There were a few orphaned weeks of summer vacation left. The sun had already lost its venom when we went for a swim in the tepid lake, the sky a fluorescent vapor. My family had driven to a beach near Glenn Lake for a picnic. I'd never learned to swim, so I avoided the deep end of lakes because they were an unknown and suspicious state of being. A secret hiding place for delirious piranhas, otherworldly jellyfish, and maybe dead bodies. After watching me doggy paddle, my father called me over.

—Hey, come here, he said with a wave of his hand.

I side-stroked to the deeper part of the lake and stood up next to him.

—You wanna learn how to swim?

—No. Yes.

—This is what you do, he said, making a prayer sign with his hands that would one day come to symbolize Shinto prayers and yoga salutations for me twenty years later after we stopped talking to each other. —Then you close your eyes and kick your legs and move your arms.

It sounded too easy. The truth was, I hated getting water inside my nose, but the air smelled like the end of the summer and my body was changing its syntax every hour. My tween lesson in metamorphosis would have been easier if I'd had gills, X-ray vision, and a magical shell made of moon dust. My tween lesson in metamorphosis would have been easier if I'd had cyborg mecha arms, b-boy toprocking skills, and an audiophonic memory like an Austrian prodigy, but I was just a boy disengaging from boyhood, dreaming of a futuristic Tokyo, remembering my last bike ride through a thunderstorm. Soon, I'd be wandering through the existential limbo of junior high. Soon, I'd be a seventh grader lost in another timeline of tiny metamorphoses and chrysalic identities, only some of which I'd control and even few of which I'd understand.

Standing in the freshwater lake with my changed and changing body, my skin wet and cool from the lake, my farmer's tan glowing in the dusk, the wick of summer almost snuffed out by the growing winds of autumn, I put my hands together like a future Shintoist in prayer, took a huge breath until I'd swallowed the dead sunlight inside my diaphragm, and then dived into the lake's warm membrane, my skinny body slicing through the water like a spotted koi. I closed my eyes and paddled furiously as if to escape a giant explosion. When I crowned the lake with my head, I looked back at my dad to see if he'd witnessed my transformation from wimpy teenager into steroidal goldfish. He stood ten feet away, nodding.

At any other time in my life, I would have cried for such rare and exotic approval from him who'd always been so emotionally unavailable and so focused on his business at the cost of my own encouragement, but that first swim had changed my relationship with my body, mutating fear into a fabulist moment of self-creation. I learned that time sped up and slowed down in every breath, the qi humming through my changing body until there was nothing left in my veins except the jet fuel of adolescence.

次に/Next:

1. Ready for a döner sandwich? They sell that yummy shit on page 133. Just saying.

2. To read about the things Jackson misses, go to page 92.

3. At the Postmodern Café, we'll fragment ANY narrative or system of knowledge, gua-ran-teed! Come find us and enjoy one of our many overpriced, self-aware macrobiotic dishes, just off the I-180.

4. To go on pilgrimage in Azerbaijan with Jackson, go to page 211.

5. Or just turn the pageeeeeeeeeeeeeeeeeeeeeeeeeeeeeeeeeeeeeeeeeeeeeeeeeeeeeeeeeeeeeeee
eeeeeeeeeeeeeeeeeeeeeeeeeeeeeeeeeeeeeeeeeeeeeeeeeeeeeeeeeeeeeeeeeeeeeeeeeeeeeeeeeeeeee
eeeeeeeeeeeeeeeeeeeeeeeeeeeeeeeeee   eeeeeeeeeeeeeeeeeeeeeeeeeeeeeeeee
eeeeeeeeeeeeeeeeeeeeeeeeeeeeeeeeeeeee   eeeeeeeeee   eeeeeeeeeeeeeeeeeeeeeeeeeeeeeeeee
eeeeeeeeeeeeeeeeeeeeeeeeeeeeeeeeeeeee   eeeeeeeeeeee   eeeeeeeeeeeeeeeeeeeeeeeeeeeeeee
eeeeeeeeeeeeeeeeeeeeeeeeeeeeeeeeeeee   eeeeeeeeeeee   eeeeeeeeeeeeeeeeeeeeeeeeeeeeeeee
eeeeeeeeeeeeeeeeeeeeeeeeeeeeeeeeeeee   eeeeeeeeeeee   eeeeeeeeeeeeeeeeeeeeeeeeeeeeeeee
eeeeeeeeeeeeeeeeeeeeeeeeeeeeeeeeeee   eeeeeeeeeeeeeeeeeeeeeeeeeeeeeeee
eeeeeeeeeeeeeeeeeeeeeeeeeeeeeeeeee   eeeeeeeeeeeeeeeeeeeeeeeeeeeeeeeeeeeeeeeeeeeeeeeeee
eeeeeeeeeeeeeeeeeeeeeeeeeeeeeeeeee   eeeeeeeeeeeeeeeeeeeeeeeeeeeeeeeeeeeeeeeeeeeeeeeeee
eeeeeeeeeeeeeeeeeeeeeeeeeeeeeeeeee   eeeeeeeeeeeeeeeeeeeeeeeeeeeeeeeeeeeeeeeeeeeeeeee
eeeeeeeeeeeeeeeeeeeeeeeeeeeeeeeeeeee   eeeeeee   eeeeeeeeeeeeeeeeeeeeeeeeeeeeeeeeeeee
eeeeeeeeeeeeeeeeeeeeeeeeeeeeeeeeeeeeee   eeeeeee   eeeeeeeeeeeeeeeeeeeeeeeeeeeeeeeeee
eeeeeeeeeeeeeeeeeeeeeeeeeeeeeeeeeeeeeeee   eeeee   eeeeeeeeeeeeeeeeeeeeeeeeeeeeeeeeee
eeeeeeeeeeeeeeeeeeeeeeeeeeeeeeeeeeeeeeeee   eeeeeeeeeeeeeeeeeeeeeeeeeeeeeeeeeeeeee
eeeeeeeeeeeeeeeeeeeeeeeeeeeeeeeeeeeeeeeeeeeeeeeeeeeeeeeeeeeeeeeeeeeeeeeeeeeeeeeeeeeeee.

20. My Favorite Video Games Growing Up: Atari 2600 v. Arcade Games

1. Pitfall (Atari): 1-0
2. Frogger (Atari and arcade): 2-1
3. Tron (arcade): 2-2
4. Space Invaders (Atari and arcade): 3-3
5. River Raid (Atari): 4-3
6. Donkey Kong (arcade): 4-4
7. Video Olympics (Atari): 5-4
8. Galaga (arcade): 5-5
9. Pole Position (arcade): 6-5
10. Tetris (arcade): 7-5
11. Dragon's Lair (arcade): 8-5
12. Defender II (Atari): 8-6
13. Pac-Man (arcade): 9-6
14. Kaboom! (Atari): 9-7

Winner: Arcade games!

次に/Next:

1. Jackson's favorite colors as a teen dreamer, all on page 56.
2. Buy your copy of the *North American Jet Setter's Guide to Imaginary Itineraries* on page 205.
3. To see Jackson praying for rain in West Africa, go to page 105.
4. Or just turn the page.

21. Carry the One Inside Your Heart

1.

My first Christmas Eve in Chicago was also my first taste of excommunication, hibernation, and subtraction. In an alternative world where I had the dad I thought I wanted, he would be in the kitchen shaving succulent pieces of ham with his electric slicer, singing Bing Crosby jingles in a burgundy cardigan and sipping on rum and eggnog, happy to spend time with his boys, excited about us being together for the first time since the divorce, but our dad was conspicuously absent that night, eating dinner with his new girlfriend and her massive Croatian family while (Chad)wick and I were a decimated tribe, sprawled out at our apartment in Little Vietnam. We watched TV and ate Chinese takeout like pariahs. We felt spry and rejected. We felt small and erased. To avoid blaming ourselves for our loneliness, we curled into strange fetal shapes on the dirty sleeper, holding our breath like a chorale.

2.

Wick and I dipped our chopsticks into the dregs of moo shu pork, watching TV on the same Sony Compact that used to be in our parents' bedroom on top of their dresser, back when we were a tenuous nuclear treaty guarded on a hill in a hamlet. Our former life in Northern Michigan had never been idyllic, but the time-lapsed concrete stains of Uptown and our disconnection as a family made it feel that way. Before the divorce, we avoided each other with parallel hallways, parallel worlds, and parallel soundtracks. Our parents transmogrified the family store on Front Street into their first child, Chad escaped to his odd clutter of jocks, bible-thumpers, nature lovers, and white preps, and I sought consolation in livid Beethoven Sonatas, MTV videos, the 8-bit realities of Atari and PC video games, and a rash of incurable crushes on girls who could shatter the

86

universe with a starry-eyed gaze aimed directly at my heart like a celestial shiv. In some abstruse and accidental way, we were a family in Michigan if only in our daily language. Or if nothing else, we were the opposite of what we became, which was nothing. I was naïve enough as a teenager to think our dad was going to rescue us from that massive crater that the divorce had caused. I was naïve enough to forgive him when he didn't.

3.

I knew this tiny TV in the living room. I preferred it over all the leftovers from our old life in Michigan. This miniature box of circuits and tangled wires had witnessed everything first-hand leading up to the silent countdown of the divorce: my parents' arguments about accountants, invoices, and dinner etiquette (going to the bathroom during dinner, yes or no?), their sustained wrestling match over conflicting interpretations of parenthood, the ditches they plowed into the wet earth of our minds to serve as trenches later on in their asymmetrical warfare, and the slow detonation of every failed diplomacy. That small TV in Chicago contained every state secret my parents had. As a boy who wandered into the negative space of the house continuously, as a boy who routinely slipped on his own crushes with manga heroines and raced towards thunderstorms in the summer, I found the little Sony TV both comforting and quizzical. I used to watch Saturday morning cartoons on it, wearing Transformer Underoos and my brother's stiff cotton bathrobe that reeked of acne medication. Like my obāchan, I felt stifling loyalty and love for the smallest denominator even if, even when, it didn't love me back.

4.

After the divorce, Pops inherited the small TV, along with the house on the hill and two sons. Our dad wasn't sentimental the way we were. Eventually, he sold the funhouse, moved to Indianapolis for two years, and started a new Midwestern sitcom out of our ashes. At the time, my brother and I assumed we were part of the crossover. We assumed because we're his sons that we'd simply transfer to his new life like ones being carried from column

87

to another in simple emotional arithmetic. It was years later in Little Vietnam while we ate Chinese food from to-go boxes on Christmas Eve that I realized my father would never carry the one inside his heart. Always the pragmatist, he had left us in Michigan along with his failed marriage and his liquidated business, rounding up the numbers inside his head to simplify his life. But the math was infinitely more complicated for us.

5.

After Dad sold the house on the hill, 1528 South Union Street became a museum of nostalgia like all the other dead objects in our broken life in Northern Michigan. Our house became a place of cold and private beauty stored in the cellars of our collective memory. Without it, we became refugees of cultural mythology, spinning unreliable tales of a war we had survived but never seen. I spoke to speak about the family breakup to complete strangers at cafés in Lakeview who didn't know me when I belonged to a stable world with a familiar script. Our family, our Elysian backyard with the peach tree and the mulberry tree, the house on the hill, our parallel hallways, my weekly trips to obāchan's trailer after piano lessons, every single remnant of our small-town life became inflated metaphors of conflicted longing. My Kawai piano, soiled by moving trucks and ten-date girlfriends, had bruises from my former life as an aspiring concert pianist. The only surviving objects in our Chicago apartment from the old world were the dirty sleeper and the tiny Sony TV, which was too small, had too few buttons, and worked like a dream. It was nothing like us. We didn't deserve simplicity.

6.

Chicago was numb and cold like a cadaver. As Wick and I flipped channels on the tiny TV set, we stopped on one channel with a yuletide log on the screen, a synthesized version of *Jingle Bells* playing in the background. The night dragged its paralyzed limbs down Clark Street. The piercing cold air outside slapped the windows like gang taunts. Everything about our first Christmas Eve in Chicago was surreal: the mysterious absence of snow, the muted authority, our parents' old TV in the fireplace, the five buttons on the remote control, Dad spending Christmas Eve without us. Wick and I learned how to divide and subtract invisible numbers. We learned about the fuzzy math of two sons from a voided marriage. We learned that having two parents who lived thousands of miles apart from each other didn't make you an integer, that having a father didn't necessarily make you a son.

7.

For the rest of the night, we watched TV in the half-furnished apartment tucked away in Little Vietnam like something in a salad roll. We destroyed the food with our appetites: Chinese food, old white wine, distilled expectation. We devoured moo shu pork from take-out cartons, our hands turning into claws, into weapons of sensual redemption. We devoured our dinner and watched that fake log burning on the screen in the fireplace. We pretended the log was there to rekindle our trampled morale, but the TV was *always* in the fireplace. It wasn't a holiday gesture, it was simply the last orphan in the family wake.

8.

After we threw our chopsticks on the coffee table, we reminisced about our dad's holiday care packages he'd left in the TV room, how we'd grabbed handfuls of chocolate-covered espresso beans, opened a first and then a second can of colorless pâté, spreading the bourgeois cat food on top of slices of smoked cheese, and popped double-chocolate-dipped-cranberries into our mouths like antidepressants. That Christmas Eve, Wick and I gorged ourselves on laced Chinese food and old memories until we were sick to our stomachs. Our appetite became our collective protest against absurdity.

9.

At 11 o'clock, lead-footed zombies clunked up the staircase. The front door slammed open and Dad and Mary stomped into the apartment, out of breath, slightly drunk. Their bellies were convex (probably from eggnog and Zagreb veal cutlets), their faces ruby-red and squeaky like waxed grapefruits.

—Hey hey! she said, the smell of wine distilled into the air.

—Hey Mary, we said flatly.

—Whaddya guys doing? Pops asked rhetorically.

—Watching TV, I said.

—Well, um, wanna go to midnight mass? she asked. We could all go together.

Wick and I shrugged our shoulders, wiped the hoisin sauce from our lips, turned off the television set, and put on old sport coats over wrinkled button downs. We borrowed '80s ties, frock coats, and silk scarves from the mysterious archives of Dad's closet. Inside the Jeep Cherokee, we looked deceptively like a family, which moved and angered me. My brother and I gave each other the same look of ambivalent fury.

10.

At Mt. Caramel Cathedral, Handel's "Hallelujah" hovered in the nave like cirrus clouds. The musical notes were frozen in the rafters, communing with glum icons and frosted stained glass. The chorus was ethereal in exactly the way I wanted to feel just then, twenty minutes from the unspiraling of Christmas day. The priest's prayers were all in Vatican Latin—the Gs were all soft, not Caesarian as I'd learned in Latin class. Parishioners held votives in their hands like tiny Kendo swords. The air was luminous, like a series of solar systems orbiting in slow motion around the burning pulpit.

11.

I was a high school student and a paint-by-numbers atheist at my Jesuit prep school, so I was used to resisting Catholicism, but as we marched down the church steps afterwards in mock congregation, the bells chimed from campaniles. As we walked to the car, our heels made wet crunching sounds in the fresh powder. The whispering snow evaporated in my breath like elementary particles, like pieces of shaved ice and disintegrating hymns. I felt entombed in the transcendent beauty of that moment, however transitory. For a few seconds of reprieve, the math of every injustice was frozen on my tongue, but it would never survive the burn of the fever of the dream.

12.

Distracted by the cold beauty of the whispering snow, the spectacle of those luminescent candles, and the hard song of the bells, we lost our courage to be angry as we so often did with him because we wanted to believe desperately in his secret love for us, because we wanted to believe desperately in his love for our shared history together, a love that was hypothetical and mythical at worst and clumsy and incommunicable at best, a love that could somehow wipe away our infectious state of not belonging, which he was both the cause and the catalyst at different times.

13.

As snowflakes spiraled down from the filleted sky, their surrendering sacred geometries melted on my flushed face and turned to droplet kisses on contact. Going to midnight mass was a conscious act of remastering, an insolvent retelling of our relationship with him that would quickly default. But for one night we savored the aroma of the lie of the fairytale. The erratic wind and verbose snow buried us alive in unspoken words, erasing our footsteps like untouchables.

次に/Next:

1. To read about living in Buenos Aires during the rainy season, go to page 121.
2. To see the different religious stages that Jackson went through, go to page 257.
3. To read about the things Jackson's parents used to do that embarrassed him growing up, go to page 80.
4. Or just turn the goddamn page, bruh.

22. Things I Miss (Some, Terribly)

1. ~~Shopping at The Grove, breakfast burritos in DTLA, strolls through Silver Lake, Vegan Big Macs in Hollywood, strolling through the 3rd Street Promenade, hikes in Griffith Park, vegan cheeseburgers in Los Feliz, iced Oat Vanilla Lattes in WeHo, and watching movies at Cinerama. Okay, fine, I miss LA!~~

2. Having long hair, which really softened my face

3. Collecting fallen leaves in the Traverse City Commons

4. Being a college student

5. Fried Chicken, beef ramen, and omelets with Jarlsberg cheese

6. Listening to the BBC and Radio France in Burkina Faso

7. Walking through San Telmo at dusk

8. Spending days listening to Sigur Ros on repeat at Notre Dame while writing *Amnesia of June Bugs* ~~now available at 7.13 Books~~

9. Obāchan chasing me around the house with a broom when I messed up her hair

10. The organic optimism and simplicity of childhood

11. Driving to Leland with the fam and eating fried smelt at the Bluebird

12. Walking in the rain on a dirt road in Interlochen with a girl I'm crushing on

13. Going to bed without brushing my teeth (gross, I know)

14. Dropping acid and listening to the Cocteau Twins on repeat

15. Having sex all weekend long (I mean, who even has that kinda time now?)

16. Sleeping for fourteen hours straight after crashing at 6 am

17. Related to #13, #14, #15, and #16, living without consequence, which no one deserves, but everyone flirts with

次に/Next:
1. To take a break, dream a little, and make some origami, go to page 57.
2. BEST DAMN DREAM POP ALBUMS EVER, come at me, bros! on page 239.
3. To snoop inside Jackson's satchel while he's sleeping, go to page 119.
4. Or just turn the page.

23. The Day I Lost Rock 'N' Roll

It was 2003 and America had finally come undone. The day I arrived in Paris, American forces had just invaded Iraq. Two days later at the Père Lachaise cemetery, I lost rock 'n' roll for good. On my cemetery map, there were black dots for the tombs I'd already visited—Chopin, Fauré, Rossini, Colette, Molière, Balzac, Delacroix, Modigliani, Edith Piaf, Pissarro, and Oscar Wilde—but for some reason, I couldn't find Jim Morrison's grave. Surely, that meant something. As a music-loving, French-speaking, pop-culture snorting American, I expected a big red dot for this dude, even though I realized how ethnocentric that expectation was. If nothing else, the makers of this map knew that people all over the world went on pilgrimages to see his grave, so why not make it easy for us? But God bless French egalitarianism: American rock stars have the same black dots as French poets, Italian artists, Polish composers, and flamboyant British novelists, which is as it should be.

As I clenched the torn cemetery map in my hands, cursing at the recalcitrant wind, a clean-cut guy in jeans and parka with cropped hair walked up to me, his arm wrapped around his girlfriend's neck like a clumpy scarf. He was handsome and put together in that slightly refined, European sort of way and she was a knockout with prominent cheekbones and caramel-latte-colored eyes. I shook my head, as if to shake the cobwebs out of my brain. —Excusez-moi, mais est-ce que vous avez un plan du cimetière ? he asked with a slight German accent.

—Bah oui, I said, do you wanna take a look? I'd been standing on a tiny path, struggling to keep the map open. The wind was straight up bullying me. Qu'est-ce que vous cherchez? I asked.

—I'm looking for Jim Morrison's grave, he continued.

—Moi aussi, I said with a smile. I glanced at his girlfriend for confirmation and she smiled. She was tall and slender, even more stunning than her distant abstraction, and she had crumbs on her cheeks, a detail I found especially charming. I smiled back, turned towards her boyfriend, and tried again to open up the cemetery map. A violent gust of wind punched through the wrinkled paper. I held on to the edges with clenched fists, turning to the other side. Jim Morrison: N9.

—C'est là, I pointed, you wanna walk there together? I asked. He nodded, grabbing her hand. As we walked, we continued chatting in French. At the Chemin Lesseps path, our conversation came to a halt. We took a sharp right and continued until we noticed a flock of tourists taking pictures and laying flowers on top of an unadorned grave, and somehow, we just knew. We walked into the center of the assembly to a tombstone that said JIM MORRISON. The weird thing was, there was nothing on top of the grave: no controversial statue of a couple fornicating, no mosaic tribute to The Doors, not even an engraved album cover. The only thing I saw were two bent steel wires pointing in different directions like the antennae of an extinct species. Evidently, there used to be a bust here commemorating the God of Rock and Cock, but someone had jacked it. It was probably one of those acts of defiance that sounded cool when you were drunk in Paris, like, *dude, let's go steal Jim Morrison's bust*!

I turned to the German couple. Their mouths were open wide in disbelief. I shook my head and raised my eyebrows in frustration. Look, I wasn't a huge Doors fan. I only knew the lyrics to a few songs and even then, it was all chorus, but so what? This seemed sacrilegious. Jim Morrison deserved more than a few steel wires. We all did. The confused throng of people arrived, lighting cigarettes, and taking pictures to prove they had witnessed the absence of reason. It was 2003 and nothing made sense.

The German couple took a few snapshots and then we walked away together through the cemetery. —C'était affreux, he said to me. I agreed. It was horrendous. We tried to talk about The Doors, but neither of us knew that much about Jim Morrison, so we stopped fronting because what was the point? I'd say we were casually interested at best, but personally conflicted as to whether the defiling of someone's memory really mattered to people who had no deep understanding of what had been taken in the first place. It wasn't our dream, wasn't our generation, our love was so far away, it felt insincere though it wasn't. We talked about the Doors songs we could remember, about the songs we could still sing, to borrow a line from Charlotte Gainsbourg, we talked about strangers becoming less strange through music and language, even one that wasn't ours, which is as far as we got, but still closer than I'd expected.

We walked through the sprawling cemetery in silence until he finally asked me: —Alors, d'où venez vous? I'd been waiting for this question from the beginning. I got this question in Paris every day in 2003: *where are you from?* It was a simple question that at any other time would have been uncontroversial, but that day, a compilation of conflated headlines flashed through my head: *President Bush Declares War on Iraq, American Troops Attack from the North and West, Chancellor Schroeder and President Chirac Form Antiwar Alliance.* I paused for a second, considered the repercussions of my answer. Friends of mine backpacking through Spain, Southern France, and the Swiss Alps, had claimed they were Canadian, a gesture I found cowardly and self-ashamed as if Europeans didn't understand what a political minority was or couldn't distinguish between Americans that traveled and those that wore tinfoil hats and spoke in conspiracy theory. —*Des États-Unis*, I answered. For a split second, his eyes lit up, expanding into orbs in the brisk spring air. I looked at his girlfriend whose eyes remained soft and unchanged, realizing suddenly that she didn't speak French, that we'd been having a conversation without her the entire time without my knowledge. He whispered something into her ear in rapid German. For a millisecond, her eyes became wide like satellite dishes.

—I see, he said, smiling politely.

—Where are you from, I asked, even though I already knew the answer.

—D'allemagne. The conflation of real and imagined headlines continued in my head: *Hundreds of Thousands Protest American Invasion in Paris, Antiwar Protests in Twelve American Cities, Contre la guerre, pour le peuple irakien, Irak en chaos, El Agresión del gabinete bush se pone más fuerte, American Prisoners of War Displayed on Iraqi Television, Why We Will Win, American Warmongering: A Five-Part Series, War on Terrorism Expands to Iraq.*

—Paris est une belle ville, he said, pausing to translate.

—Oui, c'est vrai, I said in agreement. *Protests Sweep through Spain, France, Germany and Britain, 90% of Spaniards Condemn Iraq War.*

—Are you staying in Paris for a while? he asked.

—Just seven more days, I said with a sigh. *British Troops Invade from Southern Iraq, the Importance of a Rapid Victory, What Bush Has to Lose, The Unfolding Humanitarian Crisis in Iraq.*

We talked about the joy and the burden of being a foreigner in France, laughing about the small things we could share for fifteen minutes in a world butchered by gunpowder narratives. In the back of our minds, our countries' histories of bloodshed were an unspoken twinge of conspiracy, a hungry specter dancing between our words. As the soft spring sunlight ate through the dense foliage, smiling through our pores, we talked about traveling. Our connection as two foreigners in Paris felt small but authentic. Finally, because I couldn't hold it in anymore and I feared we might say goodbye too soon, I told his girlfriend about the crumbs on her face. Little pieces of day-old bread clinging to her prominent cheekbones. The man laughed and told her in German. She blushed and wiped the crumbs off with the palm of her hand, a self-conscious smile pressed into her lips. I laughed. They laughed with me. For one second, the three of us were a concert of goodwill that the world desperately needed.

We passed the eastern gates of the cemetery and stood on La Réunion Street, an irony that I properly ignored.

—À la prochaine, mon ami, I lied, shaking his hand gently.

—See you next time, he repeated in French, smiling.

—Auf Wiedersehen, I said, smiling at the woman who wore her lunch on her face.

—Bye bye, she said in English.

We looked at one another for a few more seconds and then walked in opposite directions. In my head, I knew that Iraqi villages were being crushed into a fine flour of human bone, protesters were marching in the streets of Paris, Berlin, Madrid, London, New York, and San Francisco, conservatives were boycotting French imports, French Fries had been changed to dumb-as-fuck-sounding Freedom Fries, the French Press accused America of political chauvinism, humanitarian agencies prepared relief supplies for a catastrophe we'd caused in order to make Americans feel safe again (and Americans never feel safe, even with all their guns, SUVs, megachurches, and segregation).

I strolled for a little while through Paris and then stopped to turn around. The streets looked fresh in the filtering sunlight. In the distance, I looked at the couple as they held hands, walking into the sunset like in old Westerns. The golden rays of dying light were slowly dissolving their thin bodies until they were fuzzy around the edges like a memory out of focus. I folded my map and walked until I came to a busy street. Several blocks away, I heard the fife and drum of protesters and I turned the other way, far away from the lunacy of war and its inevitable remapping of the soul.

次に/Next:

1. To read about the time Jackson fell in love with a black and white lamp (which is every bit as absurd as it sounds), go to page 271.
2. To learn about the things Jackson wanted to be growing up, go to page 47.
3. Find your own North American besties on page 205.
4. Can't get enough of French Trauma? Go to page 159 to see where it all started for Jackson and watch a 10th grade pretty boy get destroyed by his French teacher!
5. Ou, juste tournez la page, mon pote.

24. Not Done with the World

After five rounds of in vitro fertilization, LB and I didn't have the funds to be parents anymore. We cried all the time. Avoided Facebook. Held our dogs too tight. Watched baby elephant videos. To escape the wormhole of grief, we bought tickets to Prague we could barely afford. Our sadness flickered like a ghost in our peripheral vision. In Old Town, we smiled. Licked the rain from each other's lips. Kissed on Charles Bridge. Wrote graffiti declaring our love. Held hands on the tram. Ate soup that warmed our bones. Somehow, we were not done with the world.

次に/Next:

1. To learn about the things Jackson once believed had magical powers, go to page 37.
2. Shame! Shame! Shame! (or not) on page 186.
3. To see what makes Jackson so emo, go to 103.
4. To feed the elephants and free them from the circus of the fucking world, go to page 294.
5. Or just turn the page.

25. Piano Lessons

CZERNY: Mrs. Kurtz had one linked aphorism: don't play the Mozart Sonata until you've practiced Bach first, and don't start the Invention until you've finished Czerny. The truth is, you gnash your teeth when you trudge through Czerny's thick yellow book because he didn't write songs, he wrote *exercises*. Your fingers glide up and down the piano for a bloated hour, fighting cramps and tricky finger positions, and for what? All that time and you haven't played a single note of *music* for your obāchan. She sits at her kitchen table that extends outward in a moment's notice, its surface, an archeology of spilled TV dinners, canned peach accidents, and a historiography of Paul Klée paintings made from grease stains and dribbled apple juice on fake wood linoleum. She lights a cigarette and listens to you play. Sometimes as you practice inside her trailer that's half a mile from the Traverse City airport, you jump ahead to Bach anyway, especially when a plane roars through the sky. You know you'll do anything as long as she stays at that table and listens to you play. You pretend she's waiting for you to play Mozart. But the truth is she loves you because you fill her living room with music.

BACH: You feel slightly guilty that you just violated Mrs. Kurtz's cardinal rule, so you play the Invention extra-long this time. You even start off slow, trying to hear each new voice repeated in the echo chamber of middle and bass registers. You wonder: does the piano get sick of the same song? Did Bach have a bad memory? Maybe he forgot he already used this melody before. Maybe you should add some of your own notes for flourish, of course. Your fingers trip over the keys. In the piano cockpit, you see the disjointed head of Mrs. Kurtz. You're making her angry. But when you turn to your obāchan, she sits in silent admiration, puffing away at a new Benson & Hedges. You switch from Moderato to Allegro while Mrs. Kurtz shakes her finger at you. Her eyes slowly cannibalize your counterpoint. Bach didn't include specific tempos in his inventions because he wanted you to make your own decisions. You even believe that for a second. Every time you sneak a peek at the kitchen you know there's something right about the sharp little mistakes you're collecting in your hands like fresh fingernails.

MOZART: This is your obāchan's favorite composer. Sometimes, when your fingers throb in mutiny, or when Mrs. Kurtz makes you drink her lemonade—lemon water is what it really is—you skip to Mozart without looking back. You know this is the biggest violation of all besides not practicing, of course, or spitting out lemon water onto Mrs. Kurtz's pink polyester pants. It feels good to be rebellious and faithful at the same time. You feel like you're skipping to the apple crisp square in the TV dinner obāchan makes you for lunch. Since you can't get away with it at dinner, you revel in it at the piano. Obāchan's trailer is Oz, it's Switzerland when your parents' bickering begins violating international law, it's a safe space with Hershey bars in the butter dispenser and Pringles in the cabinet. As you play the Sonata from the top, sometimes she opens up the windows so her neighbors can spoon your errant melodies, so they know she has a music box for a grandson. Other times, she hums along with you, boiling water for her ocha and sticking two TV dinners into the oven. She gives you the Hungry Man fried chicken dinner even though you'll always be her grandson when you play the piano. You love each variation as a sovereign moment. Brahms and Rachmaninoff weren't the only composers to palm old books of Haydn and Paganini in their sleep. This moment together means everything to you, the way you remember her, even now, watching you from that sticky foldable table of hers, her wrinkled face softened by cigarette smoke and filtered sunlight that pours through threadbare musty drapes. You cannot separate your Saturdays from this woman, nor your fingers from the piano. The only time you don't feel lonely is when you play Mozart. It's the only time you can accept your mistakes and (almost) forgive the cancer that ransacked this woman's body like a violent fugue.

次に/Next:

1. To watch Jackson get his feelings hurt, go to page 103.
2. To see Jackson spending time with his mom on Christmas, go to page 17.

3.   To learn about Jackson's favorite colors as a teenager, go to page 56.

4.   To get transported to a completely random chapter, go to page 241←I actually just asked LB to pick a number between 1-74 (sound familiar?) and she picked Chapter 63, which, as you know now, is on page 241, so off you go with your little pre-roll nostalgia!

5.   Or just turn the page (careful, sharp objects on the next page).

26. Word Daggers That Still Make Me Bleed After All These Years

1. I hate you.

2. Salut, tubabu!

3. I don't trust you.

4. Stupid-ass white boy!

5. But you're not even Asian.

6. Jackson, no one cares what you think.

7. You're cringe-worthy, amateur, and childish.

8. This story is vomit soup.

9. This novel is like *Crash.*

10. I feel that your novel [about mixed-race identity and APIA masculinities] will have a limited readership.

11. Stop being a pussy and grow a pair.

12. I hope that you guys bring Dengue fever back to the States so that everyone in America dies.

13. Today, on Mother's Day, your mother died.

14. Your name is Jonathan.

15. [Teenage girl pointing you out to her friend]: Eww, gross.

16. Another arrogant male writer.

次に/Next:

1. To read about the first time Jackson got sick in Africa and became nostalgic, go to page 33.
2. To read Jackson's favorite words to say out loud, go to page 173.
3. To watch Jackson daydreaming, go to page 190.
4. Interested in the construction of hapa masculinities? Yeah, me neither. Let's go to page 207 instead and ditch this kombucha stand. Who's with me?
5. Or just turn the page.

27. A Small Misunderstanding About the Rainy Season

After three months in West Africa, I learned to lie to myself. I told myself I was used to my clothes glued to my skin. I told myself I was used to the nodules of sweat rolling down my spine like ball bearings making a jailbreak. I told myself that I'd probably experienced every phase of sunstroke, every stage of dehydration, near-dehydration, and afternoon delirium. I'd pretended it wasn't shocking anymore when my tailored short-sleeve shirts felt like paper cement, that wiping sweat from my brow and upper lip were simply the normal way to begin a sentence when talking to villagers in Djibasso. I'd practically written a hand-written letter of congratulations to myself for embracing the sweltering, dizzying hot mornings in the oppressive Sahelian heat on my bike ride to the local *collège* where I taught English to middle school students. Eighteen kilometers from the Malian border, I lived in a desert that was sautéing my brain (an image amplified by my malaria prophylaxis)

After I'd settled in my teacher's house, the villagers taught me both in lifestyle and in local proverb that there was nothing to do from 10:00 am until 3:00 pm except stay out of the sun's trajectory. My only choices were to sip laced gunpowder green tea with the villagers, read the same Zola novel again under a swaying mango tree (*La Bête humaine)*, and write letters to distant friends in America who lived in an alternative world with air-conditioning, plumbing, 9/11 hysteria, and clean tap water that didn't give them cholera when they swallowed it. My choices in West Africa always began and ended with me lying down on a natte outside in the shade underneath my hangar or listening to the BBC and Radio France on my broadband radio or gazing at overfed clouds pass by sluggishly like brides stumbling out of fat huts.

I walked to the Thursday Market in my village, which was bustling with conversations in Bwamu, Jula, French, and Arabic. The smell of dirty yams and pungent body odor, overripe fruit, fresh pagnes, and fried dough was a giant face-slap. I bought bananas, cucumbers, and a canned pineapple (all great luxuries for me) along with two coconuts and a half a dozen eggs, some of which were bound to be fertilized or full of blood.

As I walked back home, Disco the cassette clerk walked up to me. —Bonjour, J., he said, smiling.

—Bonjour, Disco. Ça va? I asked.

—Oui, très bien, merci.

—Génial.

—Bamusodo? he asked, switching to Jula.

—Akanye, I said, mother is fine.

—Facè do?

—Akanye, I lied, even though the last time I'd heard from my dad, he'd written me a letter saying how disappointed he was in me for dropping out of Yale without bothering to find out what had happened or why I was living on $80 a week working in a Borgesian dream library or why I owed my landlord money after my financial aid ran out.

—Ça c'est bon. Et tes cours? he asked, switching back to French.

—Pas mal, I shrugged.

—I hear you read books under the hangar, he said, flashing decayed teeth that reminded me of ODB however briefly.

I nodded. —Disco . . . is this weather hot to you? Doesn't it seem *particularly* hot today?

—Chaud? he asked, confused.

—Oui, chaud.

He shook his head. —Non, il fait beau comme ça.

I patted goodbye to him on the shoulder as I'd seen so many villagers do. Close to my cement house with the tin roof, I wiped my glistening forehead, I wiped my sticky arms, and I wiped my moist temples again. My lips were covered with beads of sweat, my grimy neck caked with a wet and fragrant dust that would be hard to wash off. Maybe, my body was actually crying. Maybe, sweating was simply the way my pores grieved over the theft of precious fluids. As I passed the last aisles of commerçants and merchant kiosks, produce stands and fabric booths, the carrot-colored dust stuck to the hair on my toes and hid underneath my nails, blowing into my mouth. I eventually passed the Koranic elementary school and the beaten down mosque when I saw a Burkinabé man bundled up in a puffy winter jacket on his way to the marketplace. I stopped in shock, my mouth wide open, before continuing on. Once I'd reached my cement house with the tin roof, I buried my eggs in the dirt and put my groceries inside a metal box away from recalcitrant flies and fist-sized spiders before taking a long and indulgent bucket bath outside behind my compound walls, the lukewarm water trickling down my clammy skin in all the places where the dust clung tenaciously in the crevices of my skin. Never was I more conscious of the precious value of water than when I lived in the Sahelian desert where water was proverbial, seasonal, rationed by distant wells, and often poisonous to drink uncooked, always requiring bleach and a rolling boil before it could touch your lips. I might have been the only person in my village wishing for the rain to rescue me from the draught, the only adult in the Kossi province who probably dreamt of chilled mineral water and sloppy baths in clawfoot tubs and the persistent mist of Seattle winters and waffle cones jammed with pistachio Gelato on Mott Street. I was definitely the only person in my village rushing home with no place to go except inside my head.

次に/Next:

1. To learn about how Jackson and LB survived the most traumatic episode of their relationship, go to page 25.
2. To learn more about Jackson's lexophilia, go to page 110, because who doesn't love some good 'ole fashioned love of words in the age of Trumpian anti-intellectualism?
3. For readers who've had to redefine their home throughout their life, this short essay on page 175 is for you.
4. Or just turn the page & read about video games, you crazy little otaku!

28. Some of My Favorite Video Games (In No Particular Order)

1. Deus Ex, Human Revolution & Mankind Divided
2. Fallout 3, Fallout New Vegas, & Fallout 4 (pretty much everything except 76)
3. Mass Effect 2 and 3 (but absolutely not Andromeda!)
4. Skyrim & Dishonored
5. Heavy Rain
6. Borderlands 2 & 3
7. The Last of Us Remastered
8. Uncharted 2: Among Thieves
9. BioShock Infinite
10. Wolfenstein: The New Colossus
11. L.A. Noire
12. Final Fantasy VII, X, XII, XIII, & XV
13. Flower
14. Life is Strange
15. Pokémon Go (at least until I started walking into strangers and almost got run over in DTLA by another psychopath in a SUV)
16. Persona 5
17. Detroit: Become Human
18. Valkyria Chronicles
19. Animal Crossing: New Horizons
20. Mario Kart 8 Deluxe
21. Watch Dogs 2
22. Legenda of Zelda: Breath of the Wild
23. Night in the Woods
24. Nier Automata

次に/Next:

1. Which languages does Jackson hope to study some day? Answers on page 210!
2. To learn about the things Jackson once believed had magical powers, go to page 37.
3. To see memory collapsing into narrative historiography, consider page 141.
4. To turn the page, just let your fingers do the talking, buddy.

29. Snagged in an Old Butterfly Net

1.

In Portland, Oregon, I got a call from a friend of a friend. She worked for an immigration lawyer and one of her colleagues needed a French interpreter in a pinch. The asylum lawyer, a refugee who I'll call Yacoub, and I all met once to go over a few things in his family history and adapt to each other's accents. On a second level, Yacoub and I were listening to words we already knew but couldn't always recognize in each other. He had a Mauritanian accent and like most West Africans, he rolled his Rs. Most French speakers claimed I had a Belgian or Swiss accent (whatever that meant). As we spoke, we became victims of dialect, urgency, and defamiliarization, but we pushed on with our flawed cultural exchange because his life depended on it.

On the day of Yacoub's asylum interview, we met in the lobby of the INS building. The air was stagnant like in every government building, filled with the weight of human words, confessed and unspoken, official and unwritten, stamped and erased. After all, this federal agency was a de facto dictionary of American citizenship, defining Americanness in the sense that what was called American and what wasn't (i.e., who became American and who didn't) was continuously interpreted and redefined here, not by linguists, philology scholars, or grammarians, but by civil servants carrying suspiciously thin folders that reduced human struggle to bullet points. Above the X-ray machine, the dual portraits of Bush and Cheney practically snickered at me. There could have been dialogue bubbles coming from their mouths that said, *Good luck kid. This country isn't a free ride and we don't give a shit about Mauritanians, unless they bring over a corporation.* I grabbed my satchel from the X-ray machine and took the elevator to the 9th floor, my feet tapping the ground to break up the silence. As Yacoub's translator, silence meant loss and loss meant deportation. For both of our sakes, I vowed to fight that silence and defeat my own self-consciousness to the very end, so that I could be the advocate he needed. This moment forced me to reconsider the power of my own words, a leitmotif in my life and in this memoir.

2.

Eight years earlier, I'd spent the summer between semesters working on a coming-of-age novel and several pieces of nonfiction. My mom mentioned my prodigious output to my brother, who got annoyed and blurted out that my writing was "just a bunch of words." That slogan became forgotten artillery ordnance in a proxy war of identity, language, and vocation until the first explosion. The delayed violence of those words was disguised to me until the exact moment I tripped over them unwittingly. For seven years, whenever I started seeing myself as a writer, even for a brief moment, I'd hear his barb again and then witness the world around me detonate into rubble. The fact that Wick and I have been extremely close since forever somehow didn't diffuse the explosiveness of his words because I was too vulnerable to criticism and I feared failure. I was sensitive to his dismissal because my writing career had always been suspect at best and aspirational at worst. It was only after a stint in the Peace Corps and a series of volunteer gigs working with refugees that I learned the power, the necessity, and the redemption of language, the way it could change your life and help you achieve cultural reincarnation in America.

3.

At my liberal arts college, I'd been working on a maximalist bildungsroman called *Letters from a Pyromaniac* about a college student (of course) who left America, fell in love in Provence, became a famous writer, and wrote his family and friends long, serpentine letters of love and nostalgia to placate his own expat guilt. It took me four years to write that monstrosity of sadness and longing. To this day, I've never revised *Letters from a Pyromaniac*, but it helped me understand that I was a "language-driven" writer who found redemption in language. At the same time, I was incredibly sensitive about my shortcomings and deeply insecure about my manuscript: had I actually written a novel or was it just *a bunch of words*? Considering the long and tortured war that America has waged on intellectuals, writers, and rhetoricians, my self-reproach was inevitable. During creeping moments of nauseating insecurity, artistic futility, and impostor syndrome, I begged book-loving friends and theory-smart girlfriends to read sample chapters to see if I was wasting my time. Maybe, this is just the nature of insecurity: skilled at deflecting positive feedback, magnetized to totalizing self-criticism, sadomasochism, and self-loathing.

My brother's barb wasn't meant to go in that deep, but it did only because I didn't know how to remove it. I knew then just as I know now that he was just calling me out, which is what siblings do. Ultimately, though, his reasons for saying what he did didn't actually matter once they entered my bloodstream. Criticism, by its nature, can be a slow-acting neurotoxin of the self and of the cultural imagination that destroys everything from the inside. For most of my life, I felt as if I had no right to reimagine my past through the prism of my own words, and yet language was sometimes the only friend I had in my 20s. Language helped me interrogate and embrace this country as a site of narrativized trauma, racial complexity, class evolution, historical violence, polyvocality, existential reimagining, and cultural hyphenation. Language became a good luck charm to ward off the cult of binary thinking and a hidden password to open up the secret spaces of my own hapa identity. That kind of magic was an unassembled power for me.

4.

In grad school, usually at cafés or walking around campus, I meditated on language, which I saw as a suspension bridge, connecting but also conforming to separate cultures and ethnicities like the English my obāchan spoke with her thick Japanese accent or the English words she peppered into her Nihongo every time she called her sister in Ōsaka. Language always wears the clothes of its speaker, shaped by their unique speech patterns and linguistic idiosyncrasies. Language is a cross-cultural love story of chatty merchants, violated verb conjugations, insolvent loan words, and forgotten Latin declensions. Language is a giant swingers party where slang swaps partners with grammar. Language is an hourglass of human culture, a vivid ekphrasis of the physical world. As a grad student obsessed with philology, Japanese novels, foreign languages, and etymology, these flirty metaphors of language were exciting to me because they made invisible things feel visible. Constructing new metaphors for language inside my head helped me catch tiny insects in my too-big butterfly net. And yet, even these thoughts got swept away with a single slogan: *Just a bunch of words.* Every time I heard it, I got the chills. My companionship in words, my ideas about language, all disintegrated into phonemes until there was nothing but the sounds themselves.

5.

In the Sahelian village of Djibasso, where I taught English to middle school students in Burkina Faso as a Peace Corps volunteer, I spoke so much French to villagers, students, and colleagues at the local *collège* the first two months that my head throbbed. After months of language training and years of studying French at uni, my French was fluent, but unnatural. I kept translating my thoughts in English into blocks of idiomatic French, instead of letting my French pour out naturally and imperfectly as I do in English. My fear of fucking up French was preventing me from speaking it freely because I had a problem letting go of my identification with my own linguistic craftmanship. In my 4<u>ème</u> and 5<u>ème</u> classes, I spoke French like I was trying to harness it into a long sword to slay the awkward silence and darting glances inside the classroom. Never in my life was I more convinced that I was just a bunch of words than in my first months in West Africa where every moment was weighed in the units of language, both its conspicuous absence and its unpredictable abundance. There were so many words I didn't know in my village where local languages like Bwamu, Fulani, and Jula competed with French (the colonial lingua franca), so being able to define myself as just a bunch of words, especially in French, was the highest form of cultural prayer, really, for a person contemplating his weight and his worth in the units of language.

6.

It was 10 o'clock in the morning and I was drinking wine with Jules the surveillant, who had lured me to a local buvette to show me les gens du coin (the locals), only to find out he wanted me to buy a round of old and stale wine before lunchtime. He was talking passionately about how much he wanted his daughters to go to college. He wanted to see them succeed in a way he never had. I took a sip of the old boxed wine and winced, interjecting comments whenever he paused to breathe. My French that day was particularly clumsy and odd-shaped. I couldn't pluck the right words from my mind and harness them into an honest sentence so early in the morning, but I knew they were dormant inside me, had always been inside me since adolescence when I studied French in high school, snagged in an huge butterfly net of memory, sound, and language, gagging at the sound of le Bretagne. Someday, maybe tomorrow, maybe next year, the words would eventually come out right, even if I had to return to the States to catch all of them with a flick of the wrist.

7.

Inside the interview room that was both an interrogation cell and a seminar room, perfectly balancing spaciousness and austerity, muted wood desktops and suffocating minimalism, I swallowed the dust mites in my throat and sat down. It was so quiet in there you could hear yourself breathing. The INS officer walked slowly inside the room. His greeting was cordial and warm, but also superficial and restrained. He reminded me of a divine bureaucrat in Kafka's castle. After making small talk, the officer opened up his too-thin folder pierced with its own bullet points. The warmth in his face clicked off and the asylum interview began. Over the next three hours, he asked Yacoub questions that were so heavily nuanced and so deeply personal and invasive, my job changed from interpreter to biographer, from mouthpiece of the state to amateur eidetic. It was as if both men were trying to condense an entire relationship into one conversation so they would never have to speak again. As I began translating their mediated dialogue like a spiritual medium, my mouth overflowed with experiences I'd never had before, details of places I'd never seen, and questions I'd never posed.

My role as cultural translator forced me to wear the mask of both the INS officer and Yacoub simultaneously: a two-way mouthpiece and intersection for their personal tragedy and blunt interrogation, emotional devastation and forced empathy.

As I retold Yacoub's story in English about being hauled into trucks by Mauritanian Arabs where he later escaped to a Senegalese refugee camp, I began slowly understanding that diction had existential and political repercussions for certain people in certain circumstances, especially non-white ones. One careless sentence, one mistranslation, and one conflated antecedent could ruin his life forever. I could accidentally annihilate this man's American life and erase his American family by misunderstanding the very things I once believed were both academic and irrelevant (except in lit seminars). Suddenly, tone and syntax, phraseology, idiomatic expressions, grammar, double entendres, Senegalese slang, speech utterances, class performance, point of view, irony, implicit argumentation, and figure of speech could all change the meaning of his life, set it on its head, and radically alter its definition in both a cultural and ontological sense. This interview came down to a few key words that could change this man's destiny. I needed my words to be the right ones.

8.

Yacoub continued reciting his life story to me in French: he'd met an American woman he loved. They had a daughter who knew nothing of his old life, working as a "boy," a servant in an upper-class home in Dakar. This linguistic power to frame, exonerate, and humanize Yacoub's asylum narrative was something I didn't want, but was forced to accept anyway. The power of language was dangling before my eyes like a golden bough in a Roman fairytale. It was insane pressure. It was unjustified power. The whole world glowed in the reflection of every polished word. If Yacoub were sent back to his village in Senegal where his father was enlevé, Yacoub would be enlevé too. That's what he wanted me to tell the INS officer. Enlevé: to be removed, taken, kidnapped, or made to disappear. It's an awful word because it means all of those things at once, but you have just one shot to

115

save a person's life when you translate his injustice, which is the injustice of the injustice.

As a translator, my job was to help these men understand each other in a way that language, by its very nature, is constrained from doing well. After all, the spaces between words, the holes inside them, are an entire galaxy unto themselves, separating peoples and cultures. Words constitute our first and last attempt to digitize reality through syntax, the way we create Tibetan sand art out of breath, sound, and phoneme. And when language fails—as it does and as it will—we become allergic to human intention. How could I possibly harness this flawed process of translation when no language could survive its own cultural vivisection forever? How could I help these men understand each other (one Black/one white, one refugee/one US citizen, one outsider/one insider) if the conditions for their communication were predicated on the unstable fault line of a destabilized and moving object like language?

On the other hand, was there anything more human in the whole cosmos than language? So infinitely complex, always the mouthpiece to infinite abstraction, always permutated and permutating, always misused, violated, and disrespected, always metamorphic and static, potential and kinetic, yet always time-traveling between stuck and fluid meanings. There is something strangely noble and absurd about language, the way we try to do justice to this fleeting and ineffable world through the portraiture of our own words despite being sabotaged by the very prisoner we seek to liberate. We are our own creation.

9.

By the third hour of the asylum interview, I was exhausted, and I wasn't even fighting for my life. Understanding someone, trying to be understood, and trying to learn all of the unique ways in which people use language to tell stories about themselves is an exhausting but necessary exercise in human empathy. Words would never capture the penumbra in Sacré Coeur or the smell of fresh pains au chocolat in a Latin Quarter bakery that Yacoub probably flew over on his way to America. Words would never replicate the intensity of Kandinsky's color symbolism and Buddhist thangkas or unleash the smell of wet grass and fresh soba noodles in a Tokyo yatai or recreate the lyrical melancholy of a Billy Holiday ballad or the tiny percussive thuds of shattered glass in a Los Angeles hit and run.

Words, like their inventors, have serious limitations and those limitations define the inventors in tragic and fatal ways. Yet, despite its intrinsic fragility, promiscuity, and ambiguity, language is a clumsy bomb we drop on our own primordial state of helplessness to gain the upper hand in our communication with the void. We use language for wedding vows, song lyrics, stop signs, and divorces. We use it to declare war, incite riots, read verdicts, canonize fables, and demonize celebrities. We use it to persuade, provoke, and seduce readers. We use it to coerce, incite, and demoralize enemies on the Popular Front. We use it to seize control of political scandals and create new ones. There's something noble and absurd about the imperfections of language. Maybe, we like its fatality, musicality, and mutability. Maybe, we admire its elasticity, pluck, and indestructability. Maybe, we see ourselves through our own creation. Maybe, we want to construct an alphabetical divinity in words so that our mouths become the saviors of our bodies, because the elusive nature of communication offends us. Maybe, the beauty of language should be weighed in its own units of impossibility. And maybe, language is the perfect placeholder for our failed immortality.

10.

Inside the INS room in the early afternoon, it hit me that the wrong words could condemn a Mauritanian refugee to a Senegalese dungeon, but the right ones could baptize his second child or piggyback the high F in our explosive national anthem when the singer sings the word "free."

Words could commute Yacoub's death sentence and anoint his American wife with the name of a Mauritanian tribe. Words could be a cultural arsenal for a generation of new immigrants stuck in the stockpiles of unassembled language. Words could be the mouthpiece of white supremacy speaking over and rewriting the struggles of the subaltern as so many political revisionists have done in the past. With a little love, pruning, and proper revision, words could even become material witnesses of our own trauma as they had been for this man seeking a better life in a country distrustful of words (and the people who used them). Words could incarnate pain but also heal pain by converting readers (and INS officers) into witnesses of history, by turning all of us into guerillas of cultural exchange and defenders of public good. My own discovery of the immanent power of language was also my technique for forgiveness. I forgave my brother by understanding the responsibility and the power that always comes with speaking the unspoken in the police state of unspeakability. I learned that silenced people were always worth fighting for. I learned that words (my words, your words, their words) were the only chance we had to save this damaged world from itself.

次に/Next:

1. To understand Jackson's reverse nostalgia for a city he's never lived in, go to page 241.
2. To see how Jackson scored on the "How Japanese Am I Anyway?" Quiz, go to page 42.
3. Fuk Sppelling! Am I right? Sure I am, especially on page 253.
4. To read about Jackson searching for Jim Morrison's grave in Paris, go to page 94.
5. Or just turn the page.

30. Things Inside My Black Satchel on 23 January 2014

1. 3 black sharpies (2 regular, 1 retractable)

2. A half-eaten almond bar in a Ziplock bag

3. A small blue lock I don't have the key to, which feels way too symbolic

4. Stolen stationery from The James Chicago Hotel (which they charged me five bucks for) with the address of the Iowa Short Fiction Award written in blood-red ink

5. A fluorescent green index card from LB that still makes me cry. It says:

I Love you ♡

I Love you ♡

I Love you ♡

6. A weathered copy of Gary Shteyngart's *Absurdistan* (Obie represent!)

7. An oral hygiene kit that includes: 1 box of smart picks, 1 emergency toothbrush with protective cover, and 1 travel size container of toothpaste

8. A Starbucks gift card that one of my favorite students gave me three years ago, which I still treasure and am afraid of finishing

次に/Next:
1. To read about some of the crazy shit Jackson did to "understand his reality," whatever the hell THAT means, go to page 230.
2. To read about the first time an Argentine boy stole Jackson's cell phone, go to page 45.
3. To learn about how Jackson redefined "home" after he fell in love with an insect and moved back to Chicago, go to page 175.
4. Or just turn the fucking page because YOLO and also FOMO.

31. The Psychoanalysis of Rain

Since the first downpour of the rainy season, my body has been craving sleep in Cap Fed. Like a teenager surrendering to a twelve-hour coma every Saturday, my mind created fictional, alternative worlds without broken sidewalks, flash inflation, political protests, battlefields of dog shit, white women tourists looking for Argentine dick in milongas, and armies of porteñas in tight dresses elbowing their way through the congested sidewalks of Microcentro and flinging away unsolicited piropos from random men. In Argentina, my dreams traveled more than I did, circumnavigating the globe, exploring the space in and between continents. During our first winter in July in Palermo Viejo, sleep whispered to me to undress as the rain broke into sustained laughter, streaming down the windows, rolling off the rooftops, splashing tiny umbrellas entering and exiting tachos. Sleep told me to let my guard down and surrender to her clumsy psychoanalysis, to experiment in self-hypnosis. As the rain fell down in a hard cadence, tiny puddles invading our bedroom through the balcony door, sleep told me to close my eyes and let go, to surrender and forget as the electric images of rain-blurred signs of Buenos Aires whirled around in circles in my head like a color-streaking carousel.

When it rained in Buenos Aires, my need for hot showers, cranked-up space heaters, and soft fabrics became a primal anthem. I obsessed about Thai curries with scorching chilis, coconut milk, and lemongrass. I obsessed about LB's aromatic empanadas filled with fried potatoes, onions, and pungent, gooey, sharp cheeses dipped in chimichurri sauce. I obsessed about my next glass of Malbec cultivated in a Mendoza vineyard that would stain my teeth, accelerate my sleep, and warp my judgment. I obsessed about still-warm chocolate chip cookies that collapsed in my hand and streaked my fingers. I obsessed about mate that made my intestines glow with soft qi and retrieved energy. I could have filled a small canyon with my thirst for the life we'd created together in South America, for the life we had chosen just as the 2008 Recession jabbed America in the ribs.

The persistent chattering of rain on the windows took me back to when my adolescence was an accident, when R&B singers sang songs on the radio about heartbreak, pain, and cruelty, when you could sing along without knowing the lyrics and fall asleep in the middle of a thunderstorm in an empty house and still feel optimistic about your own celestial configuration in the cosmos. I spent so much time in Buenos Aires listening to Mazzy Star, Soda MC, Corinne Bailey Rae, Natalie Walker, Nitin Sawhney, Dido, Kevin Johansen, Los Enanitos Verdes, Arcade Fire, Juanes, Asobi Seksu, Estelle, Carla Bruni, and Blonde Redhead as the rain became an obsessive riff for the drumbeat of the city. I listened to sad music, much of it dream pop, until it wounded me and put me in touch with my emotional reality, until I could shed the dead weight of my teenage nostalgia. I told myself that everything was an idea once, even a song. I reminded myself that all ideas, even great ones, fell apart, especially those rendered beautiful by the exiled sun and rendered profound by longing and distance.

South America's children were probably all born nine months after the biggest rain spell of the year at the apex of cuffing season. When the air was a scorched grey gloom, when the marbled clouds looked like gruel sticking to the rafters of the sky, and when the dark clouds purged themselves onto the broken streets of San Telmo, the only thing that made sense was to make love, gobble down alfajores, and drink mate, releasing our complex sadness into the apartment in Palermo Viejo like an essential oil diffuser. LB and I had to create a new methodology of desire inside our cramped apartment and reconnect our orphaned bodies for every day the winter melancholy loitered the streets like last-call buskers and the rain plucked the clean plot lines from our dreams like vultures of experimentalism.

The saddest days in August were the days I forgot to protest my dead life back in America, practically begging for my expat life to devolve into madness as an honorable pretext to return to a country I missed, loathed, loved, and didn't understand, even though it had always been plagued with spiritual sickness, class stratification, systemic racism, gun violence, and dead-end mythologies of becoming and enduring. Making out with LB as the rain crept underneath the balcony door to the foot of our bed became an incendiary act of self-destruction and self-affirmation. I felt the gentle arousal of a thousand lights turned on inside our bedroom like an electric grotto for the dispossessed, every button inside my spine clicked on by the soft warmth of our kisses that seemed to say: —Not yet, mi amor. Once more, mi amor.

次に/Next:

1. Jackson? You there, buddy? If you can hear me, blink one hundred and ninety times.
2. To read about the things Jackson would like to forget (but won't), go to page 59.
3. Corporal punishment: good or bad? You decide on page 232.
4. Flight #133 from New York City to Istanbul is now boarding.
5. Or just turn the page.

32. Books I Was Obsessed with in College

1. Franz Kafka's *The Castle* and *The Trial*
2. Mikhail Bulgakov's *Master and Margarita*
3. Shusaku Endo's *Silence*
4. Luigi Pirandello's *The Late Mattia Pascal* and *One, None, and a Hundred Thousand*
5. Simone de Beauvoir's *Les Belles images*
6. Fyodor Dostoevsky's *The Brothers Karamazov, The Idiot,* and *The Possessed*
7. Robert Grudin's *Book*
8. Leo Tolstoy's *War and Peace*
9. Ryū Murakami's *69* and *Coin Locker Babies*
10. Goethe's *Faust*
11. Henry Miller's *Tropic of Cancer* and *Quiet Days in Clichy*
12. Ernest Hemingway's *A Moveable Feast* and *A Farewell to Arms*
13. André Breton's *Nadja*
14. Mikhail Lermontov's *A Hero of Our Time*
15. Sembe Ousmane's *Gods Bits of Wood*
16. Banana Yoshimoto's *Kitchen*
17. Rainer Maria Rilke's *Letters to a Young Poet* and *Duino Elegies*
18. JD Salinger's *Nine Stories* and *Raise High the Roof Beam, Carpenters* and *Seymour: An Introduction*
19. Jack Kerouac's *Visions of Duluoz* and *Dharma Bums*
20. Phillip Sydney's *Defense of Poetry*
21. *The Marx-Engels Reader*
22. Gertrude Stein's the *Autobiography of Alice B Toklas*
23. Friedrich Nietzsche's *The Genealogy of Morals* and *The Antichrist*
24. Alexander Pushkin's *Eugene Onegin*
25. Voltaire's *Candide*
26. Paula Kamen's *Feminist Fatale*

27. Reinaldo Arenas's *Before Night Falls*
28. Virginia Woolf's *A Room of One's Own*
29. Kurt Vonnegut's *Slaughterhouse Five* and *Breakfast of Champions*
30. Vladimir Nabokov's *Lolita, Despair,* and *Invitation to a Beheading*
31. Tayeb Salih's *Season of Migration to the North*
32. Umberto Eco's *Foucault's Pendulum*

次に/Next:
1. Polyglot's Delight, a popular dish at Café Two Hundred Ten.
2. To see Jackson turn thirty, go to page 63.
3. A New Indie Classic of the Absurd: Pomos, Models, & Dead Cats, on page 133!
4. Or just turn the page & grab a bowl of miso soup, ne?

33. Obāchan in a Cup

1.

My hapa family was a case study in class decline. It was a slow slide from the upper middle class down to the sandbox of the lower middle class (and beyond). After my parents got divorced, we took turns living in poverty like it was some radical social experiment, but regardless of who was poor, we always celebrated Christmas on the dinner table. Our gifts were modest, laser-targeted, and basic: *War & Peace, The Brothers Karamazov, 69,* and Little Prince calendars, stacks of socks, three-pair sets of boxer briefs, a wool sweater with burgundy fringe, bundles of incense, boxes of Turtles, and booklets of lifesavers. Occasionally, someone threw in tan sheepskin slippers, a shitty drum'n'bass CD for my lame electronic collection, a cheap juicer for my brother, a kid's turtleneck covered in squiggly lines for obāchan's 4'10" frame. Once, there was even a tacky marriage proposal written in Times New Roman block letters on white paper for my mom, which made me cringe, both the font and the pretense. But all these things were exceptional. The highlight of our holidays was always the food.

2.

Our dinners were sumptuous, miraculous, and multicultural: Sukiyaki and osushi one night, Yorkshire pudding and rosemary lamb the next, a real death blow to my college vegetarianism. One holiday with Mike (Mom's second husband), it was New Zealand clams, unagi, Waldorf salad, and shrimp shumai. Five years later with her third husband, it was vegetarian taco salads or miso shiru, ocha, and goma-ae. My mom had a legendary ability to reify homemade spaghetti and soy meatballs out of an empty fridge. The next evening Wick and I might discover sashimi plates on the dining room table the size of NBA basketball courts. As a family, we never had enough money to eat well for Christmas dinner *and* tune my Kawai piano. My mom never made enough money to help me get fillings for my cavities, but with credit cards, we could celebrate the imperfection of our class nostalgia and perform miracles together on the stovetop that transformed tabletops into Bloomsburg exhibitions. Creating art for art's sake, my family combined elements of texture and taste with the mechanics of color theory. There was a flower arrangement to our entrées, a harmony of light and darkness inside the dining room, a small ceremony for the chilled chickpeas and sun-dried tomatoes, crisp Arugula salads, haunting ginger slices and incinerating Thai soups, that was uniquely Japanese in spirit and decor.

3.

Our appetite was the way we survived each new boyfriend our mom invented in her laboratory of isolation, the way we coped with each drinking relapse my brother suffered on the holidays until he finally came clean. Food was consolation for each new wave of disappointment, self-destruction, and heartbreak. We were a family still consumed in the self-corroding memories of small-town Michigan where we once lived together in an alternate world where I used to translate obāchan's orders at Big Boy's during lunch even though she was speaking in English. We were a family that had learned to sublimate its sadness into its sensuality, we transformed our hunger for affection into the things we could not put into words, into the things we could not consume, into the things we couldn't swallow whole.

4.

My family had always been a loud and passionate mess and obāchan was the quiet ballast. Her habits never changed. She made miso shiru and instant coffee almost every day of her life in America. She called her sisters every Japanese New Years. She drove to Mrs. Kurtz's house for piano lessons and then to Tom's supermarket every single Saturday. When my mom finally talked obāchan into moving to Southern California with her, she died three years later of lung cancer, leaving behind a cultural heritage I'm still skimming with a soupspoon.

5.

Today, my lunch made me feel closer to my obāchan. I ate medium grain rice with wasabi furikake, unagi, and miso shiru. As I ate these things, I thought instantly of her laugh. The way her eyes disappeared, eaten up by a wet brilliance that mirrored a full lacquer bowl. I thought of the last week of her life, when Wick and I fed her things she could no longer swallow just because she wanted to taste this fleeting world one last time. We stuck tiny slivers of unagi and spoonfuls of miso broth in her mouth. And when her eyes wrinkled at the corners, we dislodged fragments of tofu and eel from her gums like fearless dental assistants. It didn't matter that she couldn't swallow anything anymore except the sunlight coming through the blinds. We understood how food redeemed even the weariest spirit for a moment. Food was the only thing we could take for granted in a family of translators, escape artists, shipwrecked swimmers, and circus freaks.

6.

As I stirred the foggy broth in my bowl, I felt close to my grandmother. Miso was my comfort food, my séance, my tool of prophecy. Somewhere between the tiny islands of bean curd, the powdery clouds of fermented soybean paste, and the small reefs of wakame lay obāchan's legacy, hidden in the metaphysical flotsam of my family. We were like a group of shipwrecked refugees, swimming to a warm shoreline before the light disappeared behind a cloud. We were always swimming, it seemed, lapping back and forth from the shipwreck to the island. We'd always been a family of brutish swimmers, stopping just to taste the sun melting on our tongues like unelected children of the brine.

次に/Next:

1. To read Jackson's list of celebrity crushes, go to page 198.
2. To learn about Jackson's favorite childhood video games, go to page 85.
3. To read about the things Jackson's parents used to do that embarrassed him growing up, go to page 80.
4. Or just turn the page.

34. My Best (Read: Worst) Pranks

1. Wrapping LB's burrito in a paper towel where I'd drawn a picture of a cow with X's for eyes and a dialogue bubble that said: *Please don't eat my baby*!

2. Propping a barrel filled with water and shaving cream with my friend Alex against the door of a poet who made out with both of us at different times and tried to play us against each other, woke me up in the middle of the night to buy her alcohol I'd never agreed to, slipped poems underneath our door we didn't ask for, and walked around campus like she was an IRA member her senior year. After we'd propped the barrel against her door, we knocked and ran like hell. This is one of the only pranks I feel bad about, but I'll tell you what: she could write the fuck out of a stanza and I still look for her name in the poetry section of bookstores. I hope she's still writing

3. Sticking garlic cloves, stuffed animals, and potatoes inside LB's lunch bag when she's not looking

4. Convincing my friend, Shaps, was who visiting us in Argentina, that LB and I were members of an ecumenical nudist vegetarian society that required all guests and members alike to attend prayer sessions in Spanish and perform naked menial labor in the courtyard in the sun. He almost cancelled his ticket

5. Logging onto Shaps's open Facebook account on my computer during his visit to Buenos Aires and then enrolling him in every erotic massage club available, leaving messages like: *I'm feeling really stressed out and could really use a "release," if you know what I mean (wink, wink)*

6. After LB told me what to engrave on her Shuffle (to be honest, she was crazy vague), picking something way more interesting. When she unpacked her iPod, the engraving said, *como caca,* which translates as "just like poop" and also "I eat poop" in Spanish porque yolo y ¿porqué no?

7. Throwing dirty underwear, Zoe's toys, and cold water into the shower while LB showered

8. Hermetically sealing a nesting doll sort of Christmas gift for an ex-girlfriend with masking tape that took her forty-five minutes to open. When she finally unwrapped the last layer (a tiny, quadruple-knotted shopping bag), she discovered a pair of her missing granny panties, an old packet of powdered pesto from our cabinet, and a mysterious plastic lid I'd found on the kitchen counter

9. Completely rearranging the studio apartment of a Japanese ex-girlfriend. When she returned home (I wasn't there to witness it), almost every object had been moved either to a new location or rotated 180 degrees. I'd also moved her stuffed animals to the closet, placed the colander on top of her TV like a little hat, bundled her silverware and hashi (chopsticks) into small piles in the fridge, and created a path with connected paper towels from the kitchen to the window, her shoes marching to her bed

10. After we'd been dating for two months, hanging LB's bras and Zoe's toys from the chandeliers to greet her when she got home from work

11. Convincing a bunch of family friends at an Easter dinner in Suttons Bay that my brother was a secret Republican, which led to nonstop harassment the whole night

12. Doing performance art for a whole year when I lived in French House at Oberlin College by convincing everyone that I was a diehard Maoist, even though I was way too bougie for that shit. I even put a picture of him on my front door with a real cigarette superglued to his mouth

13. Telling a girl at Tank (a student co-op at Oberlin) that my name was Jehoshaphat. When she talked about me to other students, no one had any idea who she was talking about

14. Going to a restaurant with my friend Jacose and pretending I was an exchange-student whose German just happened to sound pornographic (e.g., using words like *cockundbutten, shitzenfacen, Herr Crapstein, bigdikimyourassen)*

15. Giving my family inappropriate Christmas cards. I sent Pops a Christmas card of two naked dudes embracing since he'd said homophobic shit to me more than once. I also gave my mom a *Happy Bar Mitzvah* card for no particular reason and Wick a card addressed to his favorite Black uncle celebrating Kwanzaa because family. Once a multicultural urban liberal, always a multicultural urban liberal

16. Signing LB up for bible study mail correspondence because Christian soldiers must fight their dirty wars

17. Signing up Wick for the Depends undergarments sampler because he's an emotional sharter

次に/Next:

1. To read about Jackson's favorite video games right now, go to page 108.
2. WANTED: Hapa Spies [clap clap]/are judging you/they're judging your every groove/on page 1-9-3.

3. What do you want to be when you get older, Jackson? Before he never stops talking, go to page 47.
4. Or just turn the motherfucking page. Sorry, I'm a little salty about these revisions RN.

35. Lost in Alphabet City

1.

It was another halcyon day in Traverse City that people "up north" took for granted every summer. The windows of my mom's house were jammed open like a vandalized school bus, a soft and fragrant breeze blowing gently through white lace curtains that swished in the air like old wedding gowns. The summer perfume of wet grass and fertilized earth passed through the house like an ecological séance, evoking primordial mud and complex foliage. I was sprawled on the couch like a quintessential complit major, taking a break from my novel, lost in a daydream of grad school seminars and future solitary strolls I hoped to take around a future Ivy League campus, when the phone rang like a mysterious chime. Our house had been silent all week. I'd spent my entire summer up to that point devouring books on my summer reading list and slaving through GRE study guides, hoping to cram thousands of polysyllabic words into my brain that I had missed during my late bloomer education. Each night as I fell asleep, random Latin-based words and truncated excerpts from recent passages dribbled into my mind's eye, forming a linguistic mobile around my head that spiraled into misaligned sentences. I walked to the landline phone and picked it up skeptically when Alex, my best friend from college, invited me to Turkey to spend part of the summer with him. He said that if I bought my plane ticket to Istanbul, the people he was staying with (family friends, he explained) would pay for everything. Two days later, sick of vocabulary lists and Eurotrash novels, I took a Greyhound bus to New York City, exhilarated, nervous, and confused about the collapse of summer and my vanishing mobile of words. My head felt sparkly clean.

2.

The bus was somewhere in the middle of New York State when A., the woman I'd been talking to for five straight hours, fell asleep on my shoulder. She was returning to Hoboken from an ashram. I was heading to Port Authority to take the JFK Shuttle. She suggested we meet up once I'd returned.

A month later after I returned to New York from Turkey, I called A. and we talked briefly, but she never returned my calls again, which saddened and confused me. After my epiphany on the flight to Istanbul, she was the perfect person to talk to about the spiritual self-discovery of travel. As I left a second message on her answering machine, I thought about how we can say something and completely mean it in that moment and still pretend afterwards that our words had no weight or obligation or consequence later on, shifting the power of our own language until it collapsed under our feet. I thought with some guilt about N., my brilliant college girlfriend, who had insisted on having an open relationship this summer (which I'd hotly contested). I thought about how different New York felt after traveling through Turkey than it had after a month of novel binging in Northern Michigan. During my first week back in America, I had a passionate one-week relationship with T., an ex-model, who had a septum piercing before it was fashionable and a holster for a wallet, which New Yorkers tried not to stare at. One night inside T.'s apartment, her roommate, who was one of her model friends from their former life in Tokyo, played Digable Planets' *Blowout Comb* on the stereo, an album I would listen to obsessively twelve years later in grad school as I wrestled with my own dissertation prospectus and thought hard about my own racial identity as a hapa writer searching for my own critical and creative language. I remember sometimes feeling overshadowed by their shared history and my ephemeral presence in their lives in NYC, which I knew was going to end the instant I left New York. I was envious that they'd lived in the motherland where my mom and obāchan had been born. I felt swallowed by the smallness of my history and my connection with them.

One evening after eating sushi and having drinks at a small bar in Tribeca, T. showed me one of her go-see portfolios. For a second, I thought

I was looking at another woman, her beauty reimagined through a Vaseline lens. The night before I left New York to return to Traverse City with a Turkish rug and a chai set I'd bought my mom in Istanbul, T. and I went to Cooler, a bar in the meat packing district, where I saw three awkward aspiring pomos from Oberlin whom I'd never talked to. They looked conspicuously insecure, affected, and self-conscious, dressed in too-short navy-blue pants and cheap plastic frames. They fooled no one, not even themselves. When I told T. that my school was invading my reality, she suggested we walk up to them and fuck with their performance. She suggested we culture shame them for pretending they were above the very thing they were clearly outside of. I felt a momentary burst of affection for her loyalty but chickened out since even trolling Oberlin hipsters meant euthanizing summer vacation. After we went back to her apartment, we fucked twice that night with unspoken urgency. The next day, I sat on the Greyhound with my brother. I blasted The Prodigy's *The Fat of the Land* and Underworld's *Second Toughest in the Infants* on my Discman and daydreamt about Mediterranean beaches on the Turkish coast, archaeological ruins, rock and roll bars in Istanbul, dancing French girls at the Foça Club med, walking through WWI trenches in the Gallipoli peninsula, late-night police searches in an expat's apartment (the walls covered in blue chalk), shoe polish boys and cherry juice vendors assaulting me in the streets, and the Call of Prayer blaring from the Aya Sophia. I thought about the promises A. didn't keep, about the aggressive urgency of every kiss that T. and I gave each other in bed, about my evolving obsession with Malai Kofta after eating lunch with my friends, Lisa and Raffaele, at an Indian Restaurant on East 6th Street. As I thought of my open relationship with N., I tried to decide if I'd cheated on someone. I tried to decide who the victim was and whether part of faithfulness was simply circumstance or just sheer luck.

3.

Three and a half weeks earlier, Alex and I were walking through a bustling outdoor market in Istaclâl Caddesi as Europop break beats shook the windows of tiny boutiques, old men drank chai from tiny glass cups, playing backgammon, and smoking. There was a counterpoint of frying onions, clouds of sweet paprika and mint yogurt sauce, spiced lamb meat rotating on Gyro spits and chicken grilling for döner sandwiches while 20-something Turks dressed in tight pants and button downs clinked beer glasses at rock and roll Bars and Nirvana and Led Zeppelin blared from old stereo systems. Street waifs polished the shoes of businessmen who sang into their cell phones. Old women in hijabs held hands with their nieces dressed in miniskirts who smoked cigarettes and carried Louis Vuitton knockoffs between painted fingernails. The call to prayer suddenly reverberated from the Sultanahmet, Yeni, Blue, and Aya Sofia mosques like a stadium announcement. Alex and I navigated through Taxsim as cars tried futilely to penetrate the throng of gregarious Turks and wide-eyed tourists, both of them stuffing the streets with excited conversation, sales pitches, Koranic proverbs, cigarette smoke, come-on lines, insults, and laughter. The air was filled with Turkish words I didn't have time to study, the Latin alphabet committing mutiny against my brain, the linguistic mobile inverted above my head.

4.

Alex and I walked down the narrow cobblestone streets to Çihangir, passing from behind a dead cat whose eye was enlarged as if it had been strangled or run over. I yelped too late. Alex shrugged his shoulder as if to say, *yeah, it happens.* This was the first time I got lost on this trip. I felt overwhelmed with fatigue, joy, and culture shock. I felt culturally interstitial, caught between the open windows of Northern Michigan, the never-ending corridors of JFK, the pile of Eurocentric, male novels waiting for me near the staircase in the house up north that smelled of wet grass, and the omelet and kielbasa my mom had made for me before tucking away her sadness in the folds of her bathrobe. I was stuck between the slow world of the insatiable reader traveling the world in every book, stuck in the penumbral cobwebs of memory, haunted by the family we once were (and the family we never were) inside that house, the unconquerable silence of that summer in a small town, and my long bus ride across the rolling green meadows of New York with A., who'd just returned from an ashram, fallen asleep on my shoulder, asked me to call her, and then ignored me once I called. I thought about my brilliant college girlfriend who'd demanded we have an open relationship in case she fancied a bloke in England, the nervous breakdown and subsequent epiphany I had on the flight to Istanbul, all the details of my incipient summer scattering through my head like a fallout of ash after a massive book burning in the former colonies, the cultural amnesia starting with a great hypnotic flame and ending with the streets covered in burnt philology, the letters of the Latin alphabet twirling through the air like tiny whispers.

次に/Next:

1. To see Jackson playing piano for his obāchan, go to page 100.
2. To see the damage of an absent father, go to page 207.
3. To see Jackson and his brother getting in trouble for smoking weed, go to page 50.
4. Or just turn the page.

36. Fave Songs in High School

1. "Please, Please, Please, Let Me Get What I Want" by The Smiths

2. "Sadeness" by Enigma

3. "More" by The Sisters of Mercy

4. "Michèle" by Gérard Lenorman*

5. "Motownphilly" by Boyz II Men

6. "Smells like Teen Spirit" by Nirvana

7. "Trouble Me" by 10,000 Maniacs

8. "Thanksgiving" by George Winston

9. "Crazy" by Seal

10. "Losing My Religion" by R.E.M.

11. "Wicked Game" by Chris Isaak

12. "Né en 17 à Leidenstadt" by Jean-Jacques Goldman*

13. "Smooth Operator" by Sade

14. "Love" by The Sundays

15. "Here Comes Your Man" by the Pixies

16. "The Confrontation" in Les Misérables

17. "Get Up Off of Your Knees" by The Housemartins

18. "Driving Your Girlfriend Home" by Morrissey

19. "I Will Always Love You" by Whitney

20. "Nothing Compares 2 U" by Sinéad O'Connor

21. "Friday, I'm in Love" by the Cure

22. "Right Here Right Now," by Jesus Jones

23. "Real" by the Tiger Lilies (Okay, this isn't actually the name of the band or the song, but a friend lent me this tape that I can no longer find and I haven't been able to locate this song on Google either, believe it or not, but the lyrics are something like, "if it's real, you say it's real, then why can't I touch it?" Hivemind, whatever you do, please don't research this for me and then tell me on Twitter at @jacksonbliss, whatever you do)

24. "Oscillate Wildly" and "Stretch Out and Wait" by The Smiths

25. The Tempest, Pathétique, Moonlight, and Appassionata Sonatas by Beethoven

26. "Vogue" by Madonna

27. Anything by the Cocteau Twins

*Both songs were included in a mixtape that my close friend, Sébastien, made for me my senior year, which became one of the soundtracks of my time at Loyola Academy where I read Sartre, Frankl, and Hugo on the Evanston Express, studied Latin vocabulary on the bus, and peoplewatched on the red line, formerly known as the A train.

次に/Next:
1. I WANT YOUR WORDS, JACKSON BLISS. Okay, fine, you can have them on page 173.
2. These were the safest places for Jackson as a boy, on page 22.
3. To learn about Jackson's love of language, go to page 110.
4. eg apeh tnrutts ujro.

37. The Transfusion of Yukiyo Kanahashi

1.

The English word dementia is derived from the Latin word *demens*, meaning "out of one's mind." Taken apart, *demens* is composed of two words: the prefix *de*, meaning "away, down" and the noun *mens*, the Latin word for "reason, mind, intellect." This is the story of how language and memory fall apart but never disappear when you break them down into tiny little pieces.

2.

In the final year of obāchan's life, photography was an important motif of the beautiful dream and the fleeting world. My Japanese cousin, Eikichi, took a bunch of photos of my grandmother's final trip to a Buddhist temple in Ōsaka. The photos are painful to look at because—with one exception where my obāchan is laughing a joyless laugh, her eyes closed—there's no laughter in her face at all, no exuberant sparkle in the temples like before. They are exactly what I expect of Japanese family photos: people glued by tradition, cemented by hierarchy, weighed down by honor and gravitas. The photos are also powerful for the simpler reason that my obāchan is barely there in the 浮世 (ukiyo). Her face is supernaturally pallid like a poisoned moon, her lips are crushing the line between them. Her eyes are unsettled and overpowered by exhaustion. In at least two photographs, while Aunt Shizuko looks straight at the camera (you), obāchan is looking off into the distance as if she can't bear to look you in the face. Maybe, she didn't know Eikichi was taking her picture. Maybe, she stopped caring. Maybe, she no longer knew how to pretend she was okay. In another photo, obāchan looks incurably sad, the saddest, in fact, I've ever seen her in my adult life. Her eyes plead for more time. They seem to mourn the inevitable great blur of life and death, speaking in the language of loss and subtraction. Her eyes are the war orphans of the invisible war taking place inside her

141

body. You are her witness now. You are her casualty. In still another photograph, obāchan's mouth is half open like she's groaning. If you look long enough you can see the emotion hemorrhaging inside, the quiet slowly bleeding out. The agony on her face isn't just the pain of the broken body or the mutiny of the cells. It looks like the pain of not knowing how to hide your pain anymore. The utter collapse of 頑張る, the Japanese verb of perseverance and determination spoken before every enormous challenge and battle, invoked even in the face of annihilation. When these three pictures are put together, her face tells a story of suffering and exile, they tell the story of permanent loss, how she lost her own country, way of life, language, and family once she moved to America, how age and disease slowly pilfered her memories fifty-eight years after Japan surrendered on board the USS Missouri. In these pictures, obāchan looks like she keeps finding the same wound inside her with every self-examination, the same returning paradox. Despite her visit to Nippon and the ambient details of staccato Buddhist chants, ringing bells, long-winded Japanese honorifics, despite the lingering smells of kamaboko, senbei and overflowing good-luck incense in the background, she looks mortified. Her face is not a silent pain at all, it's a grievance she shares with the viewer by accident, as if tripping and falling on your heart. This is the story of how the particles of my obāchan's soul slowly dissolve into the atmospheric mesh threads around her like a bleeding silkscreen in the camera's eye.

3.

I spent most my life piecing together her story, and even more time waiting for the scraps to cohere, but one day I finally understood the truth about my obāchan: part of her died when she left Japan as a young woman. During the American occupation, Japan nationalized its shame, handed over its army and its right to self-defense, and ignored the crimes against humanity it was both a victim and also clearly a perpetrator of. Meanwhile, a new constitution was translated from English to Japanese (making Japanese laws essentially foreign), making clean-cut GIs power brokers for a country they didn't understand or love, after hundreds of thousands of civilians perished in the Tokyo firebombing, which my grandmother survived by jumping into the river and holding her breath. After America's inhumane radiation experiment in Hiroshima and Nagasaki, Nippon lost its emperor, its national narrative, its urban landscape, and its own physical memory of itself. In that post-war chaos, my obāchan worked in Yokohama as a seamstress when she met my grandfather, a racist American soldier who was a stubborn drunk, an amnesiac, and a future sex offender. This is the story of how Japan lost the innocence it never had again and the story of how my grandfather died of cirrhosis of the liver at an American army base before I was born, killing himself before I'd have the chance to, a kamikaze without honor or sake.

4.

The word dementia is also a cognate of the Latin infinitive *demēre*, meaning "to take, cut away, withdraw, subtract or take away from." Medically, dementia is considered a chronic cognitive disorder, often caused by injury or disease to the brain, resulting in severe or partial memory loss, mood swings, strong personality shifts and conflated recall, sequentially, spatially and temporally. This is the story of obāchan's loss of reality, the abduction of her own narrative arc by the serial killers of memory, all of them.

5.

Someone might accuse me of biographical revisionism by writing this essay, but I saw what I saw in Eikichi's photos in much the same way that obāchan knew what she knew when she looked away from him. In each photograph, my obāchan is both present (as pain) and invisible (as joy), as if part of her is already taking a field trip to the spirit world. Soon after she returned to California, she began coughing inexplicably, even worse than before, which went on for days, then weeks, until the months stuck together like magnets. Slowly, she lost weight until she was gaunt and bony. Her face turned sallow, her smile lines and crow's feet cut deep into her skin from dehydration. Her appetite dwindled, satisfied by morning coffee, rice, a bowl of miso shiru, and a miniature version of my mom's dinner. Eventually, she saw the doctor and learned that she had stage-4 lung cancer. The doctor gave her the death sentence: two months, three at the most. I was in Portland, Oregon, walking to a restaurant when my mom told me obāchan was going to die. I fell apart, my stitching became unstitched. I bawled in front of complete strangers on the sidewalk, a stranger to myself. After her death, I looked at obāchan's pictures of Ōsaka again and felt haunted by her haunting, her spirit floating back and forth from her body like a mercurial guest. The light in her eyes in every photograph was fading, her energy weak and sluggish like a brownout in a once-dazzling city. Even during her last visit to Japan, you could see that cancer had taken over her radiant sparkle, her eyes now filled with the self-knowledge of the dying and the damned. This is the story of how prophecies sometimes work backwards, telling you what already happened.

6.

Once, I had a girlfriend in 8th grade. She stood me up the last day of the semester when I was going to give her my Christmas gift—a teddy Bear in a fake fur coat, veil and satin bow called Lauren BearCall. That Christmas, after I told obāchan my story about my flaky girlfriend who forgot to meet me on the last day of class before Christmas vacation, obāchan just shook her head in disapproval. You were once in a relationship, I protested. No, she countered. She told me it was bad to have a girlfriend. It was better, she explained, to not be in a relationship at all. No hurt, she said. Better not to be in relationship, she explained. This is the story of a Japanese American woman covering up her trauma from her hapa grandson who would one day write a memoir to excavate (her) ghosts.

7.

Both etymologically and medically, dementia involves the loss of stuff. In most cases, it's the loss of rational cognition, almost always including a nuanced definition of personality subtraction, the removal of some quintessential aspect of the self, much like an excision of the spirit. In other words, the person we know (or used to know) isn't completely there anymore: she's on a leave of absence, a cognitive exile. This is the story of how my grandmother inhabits two worlds at the same time, shuttling between the Church of the A-Bomb and the Island of Sakura, flashing between identities and continents in every complex chemical reaction in her brain, traveling in the space between neurotransmitters and the half-life of memory, which always corrupts with time.

8.

Once my brother and I began taking over hospice duties for her, I started reading brochures for end-of-life care. In one brochure, it said that family members should show pictures of the dying person's life to help them digest the richness and the fullness of their lived experiences. With the right reader, every life was a rich bildungsroman. I grabbed every musty, floral-themed album in my mom's apartment in Leucadia, led obāchan over to the couch by the hand, and then sat down together with her. Photo by photo, page by page, album by album, I replayed her life back to her: おばあさま, this is you in Paris with Mom and Dad. Oh, she said, surprised. This is you in London, I said. She nodded like London was playing hide-and-go-seek with her memory. Grandmamma, this is you in Hong Kong with Mom, I said. She bent over the photograph, looking for faces she understood. This is you in Ōsaka, I said. Oh, Ōsaka, she repeated, like a word charm. This is you playing the piano at Mrs. Kurtz's piano recital, I said. In three hours, we soared through her life at blinding speed, splicing a lifetime achievement montage that seemed to pass right through her like a clear soup. I was devastated: this was her life in snapshot, collapsing into snippets. She'd had a brutal adulthood that got better over time, but now she didn't even remember what she'd overcome: a sexually abusive husband, a world war, a destroyed country, a broken-up Japanese family, an estranged and abused daughter, and the institutionalized racism and xenophobia of small-town America. She was the very definition of a survivor, and what's worse, she no longer knew it. Intellectually, I was also envious: obāchan got to relive each seminal moment of her life over again, for the first time, every joy her first joy, every sublime moment an eternity, and all the pain, suffering, separation, and grief she'd experienced since Japan became a radical experiment of radiation, democracy, cultural translation, and historical erasure, was now wiped clean. This is the story of how Platonic knowledge is joyful recollection because traces don't disappear. This is the story of how memory degeneration can be both morphine and character assassination.

9.

After their mysterious marriage, my grandfather wanted his Japanese wife and his hapa daughter to move to American as soon as possible. He didn't want them to become "Japs," even though both of them already were and he would never be. Nothing scared him more, in fact. Despite the fact that he was the foreigner and couldn't understand them when they spoke to each other in Nihongo (the first language for both of them), my grandfather banished them from their homeland, sending my mom and then later my obāchan to Kingsley, a small town in Northern Michigan, to rid them of their sickness called 日本人のあたし (Japanese Me). This is the story of how an estranged gaijin in Japan (estranged from Yokohama, estranged from his own family in Washington state) turned his hapa daughter and Japanese wife into foreigners in America who would remain stuck in the spaces between cultures, languages, identities, and stories forever.

10.

Part of the cultural definition of dementia is predicated on the notion of an unchanging self. Americans, in particular, have a monolithic view of the human personality. We pretend that each person has a single overarching self that controls all ancillary traits and characteristics. When we deviate from this monolithic personality superimposed on us from the outside, we're described as "fake," "fronting," "trying too hard," and "phony," all words used to describe people who aren't "real" because they're not consistent. Sociolinguistically, what is "real" in America has become synonymous with what is true, legitimate, and authentic, even though humans can't agree on what reality is for the simple reason that it is an interpretation of our subjectivity, so elusive, so protean and ontologically promiscuous, like a consort of false idols and imaginary worlds. The binary line separating reality and fantasy is a false one, but this is exactly how reality is supposed to be—impossible to locate, impossible to delimit. This is the story of how we oversimplify the war maps of the self in order to avoid the battlefield of identity, in order to not step on the landmines of contradiction, which are everywhere.

11.

One of obāchan's last conscious projects was an album book of photographs she'd curated herself. Unlike the clean, well-divided, and linear picture albums I'd shown her after reading a hospice pamphlet, her final album was a masterpiece of fragmentation. In it, she had rearranged pictures of her life that often went backwards and upwards chronologically, laterally instead of sequentially. Often the pictures followed a circular, often a dizzying trajectory that always returned to her hapa family and her trailer in Traverse City, Michigan and her American life as a seamstress for upper-middle-class conservative white women that smiled when she spoke because her accent overpowered her words like an angry dime-store perfume. They smiled because she was cute, which is sometimes the opposite of real. By looping through time and space, obāchan's picture narrative returned again and again to her (hapa) grandsons she used to chase around with a broom and prepare somen noodles for in the summertime and drive to Mrs. Kurtz's house in a subdivision for piano lessons and sit, often for hours inside her own trailer, smoking Pall Mall 100s and listening as butchered Mozart and Beethoven rose up from the altar on her piano, the notes spilling out the windows that were opened wide for all the neighbors to remember. Witnesses to my half-butchered sonatas, all of them. This is the story of how one woman resisted the cult of linearity by bending her memories into chainmail.

12.

The day I realized my grandfather had raped my obāchan was the day I realized I was capable of imagining terrible acts of violence. As a committed Buddhist, I'm ashamed by this confession but the rage smolders inside me like mnemonic napalm. One day when we were eating TV dinners and watching TV, she told me: he made me do things I not want to do. Her confession returned to my mind when I read about paper gods forcing ink mortals to do awful things in Ovid's *Metamorphoses*. It wouldn't even surprise me if her sexual assault was the way my mom was born, the reason my obāchan married a drunk, stubborn American soldier who took away her childhood with an occupation that was physical, geopolitical, emotional, and psychic. This is the story of how a Japanese woman married an atomic bomb to protect her family's honor from detonating (a family that later forced her to sign away her inheritance once she became the cultural property of America) like an honor marriage with a rapist.

13.

In America, we treat dementia as an incomplete version of the former self, even when it's a result of insufficient oxygen to the brain by metastasized lungs as in her case. We view dementia as raving, possibly schizophrenic (but absolutely lunatic) alternative identity that has hijacked the person we used to know. Dementia is always the enemy, not our cultural insistence that who we are doesn't change through time or the illusory construction of the das ego invented by European psychotherapists to chart the human mind into recognizable modes of identity, behavior, and performance. The problem is always when we deviate from something that may not even be real, not the deviation or the transgression itself. Dementia is a sort of mundane metempsychosis, a change or shift in human souls from one body to another, but what if it isn't the subtraction of the self but the self's own multiplication and reflection? What if dementia is not the cognitive haunting of who we once were or the perversion of how people once knew us but our most emancipated version of our self, freed from the constraints of rationalism, narrative, or repeatability? What if obāchan on her deathbed was not an abridged version of her former self but a completely unfiltered and unfettered version of who she'd always been inside? The Yukiyo Kanahashi I knew had a permanent accent and a shrunk-in-the-dryer vocabulary. She was unfaithful with definite articles. She stressed the wrong syllables, making them sometimes unrecognizable to native speakers. She also did other things with language that were unique: all dogs were doggies, my brother's name became an exclamation and then a warning with the slightest shift in intonation, hamburgers became "bah-gas," my dad's name became a swear word, and the word sakura could be a holiday, a flower, and a song, depending on the language she spoke. I loved the English-speaking version of my obāchan, but that was just an excerpt of a larger body of work, a shrink-wrapped version of herself suffocating under a layer of cellophane. Her English, her Americanness, were both performances just as my Japanese, mixed-race, and hapa identities were. At times, her English was almost a racist caricature of herself. Her Japanese, on the other hand, was the uncorking of the impossible bottle. When she spoke Nihongo to her siblings on the phone every New Year's Day, our house became a concert hall of repackaged stories, translated, annotated, and emended for our protection. This is the story of obāchan's dementia as both an act of defiance of western (linear) time and also an expansion (concert) of who she used to be before yellow people became lab rats for the Manhattan project.

14.

When she moved to America, Japan froze in time. Her photo album of dementia was distinctly diachronic, looping continuously in a temporal helix that crossed wires and became knotted often, the form and content of her past changing with every frame, every row, every page, working out a new permutation of memory, each fresh (non-linear) narrative traveling back and forth, up and down, contracting and stretching. Obāchan's memories of Japan, on the other hand, were devoutly, distinctly synchronic. While her life in America continued to progress in the changing of presidents—Eisenhower-Kennedy-LBJ-Nixon-Ford-Carter-Reagan-Bush-Clinton et al.—Japan was stuck in the Showa period for good, its doctrine of racial superiority and the sins of Nanking only casually erased by the blunt force of Enola Gay's urban liquidation, the Battle of Midway, and the occupation of the emperor's throne by toe-headed hakujins who didn't speak a word of Nihongo, and didn't know Shinto from shindo (the Japanese words for earthquake, depth, progress and elasticity). Was it her attachment to a lost childhood, the bloodshed and the amorality of war, the erasure of nationalist narratives of violence or simply the implosion of

Hirohito's personality cult that made my obāchan cast such a sweeping spell on her homeland, the land of the sun-origin stuck in suspended animation, frozen at the exact place where civilian blood flowed profusely? This is the story of how Japan became a cryogenic prison of history and a tourniquet of melancholia once my obāchan('s soul) passed the international timeline.

15.

To me, my white grandfather was a ghost, a toxic presence symbolizing a life vacated and surrendered from the inside. But to my mom and to my obāchan, he was once all flesh and booze, moving from Pennsylvania military base to German military base like a picaresque war antihero. He was alive just long enough to earn a Purple Heart, become an alcoholic, create a family from the mud of catastrophe, and then abandon it once he became weary (sober) and his hands began to shake. When I was an adult, my mom confessed to me that he had molested her too, usually when he was drunk enough to be a human Molotov cocktail, every cigarette a potential explosion. For the second time in my life, I felt a hot anger rising inside of me like a projectile. This is the story of a war criminal decorated for his battle wounds and violence, which would resonate through every one of us after his fatal battle with the bottle.

16.

An implicit assumption in both the medical and the etymological definitions of dementia is the idea that what we lose mnemonically is worth keeping, but what if what we held onto was the source of our trauma. What if selective memory is both a manifestation of trauma and pain, and also the psychic recreation of it, an emotional salve to the military science of trauma, one bandage for every teeth mark left by history? What if dementia proves that the entangled strands of culture, narrative, psychology, and memory, are actually knotted and triple-tied? What if dementia proves that all human beings are actually multiplicities (mirrors) of themselves? This is the story of how delirium and conflation become a joint project of self-multiplication, especially when reality (promiscuous, subjective, impossible to locate reality) murders the songs of your childhood.

17.

Language is a blurry photograph and communication is simply a broken camera lens, making our album books of reality just crude translations of translations. In grad school, my desire to learn Japanese was related to my desire to freeze American time and thaw Japanese time. Speaking Nihongo was an ekphrastic gesture, my way of painting (resurrecting) Japan using unfaithful honorifics, crooked kana, giant kanji, and broken copulas. A gift just for obāchan on the landline. My secret hope was that Japan would thaw in her heart and stay frozen in mine. It would be my way of holding on to my obāchan, the way I choose to remember our culture before the details became thin and too focused. This is the story of how Japanese was both a way to connect with my grandmother and also bring Japan back from the graveyards of pop culture in my fam.

18.

When my brother and I got in a car accident in the family Subaru, I was in grade school, holding manga in my hand that my obāchan had picked out for me a week before in Japan. Though I have a scar on my cheek and another one on my scalp to this day to prove that explosions aren't just the syntax of fire bombings and racist war crimes against yellow people, I survived, the rest of my body unscathed. The doctor told my mom later that if I hadn't been holding the manga in my hand (the thick, pulpy pages acting as protective spirits from land of the sun-origin), I might have died. Or been disfigured. That car accident proved that my monolithic self has never ceased being threatened since the day I realized I was a hapa performing a white person hiding an Asian person. This is the story of how Japan saved my life from narrative monomania or cultural duality.

19.

As a writer of both fiction and creative nonfiction, language is how I slow down time and shed the words that I have carried around with me like the bodies of dead baby birds. Writing is also my project of memorialization. I write so that the reader is forced to do the remembering for me. After all, writing is aesthetic delirium, a diachronic synesthesia of person, language, and event that infects the reader with narrative dementia for historical events they couldn't possibly remember, entrapping them within a textual wonderland. In this essay, I'm wandering, always wandering through the leviathan of details and coincidences. I'm exposed, already infected by the unstable neurotoxins of memory, sickened by the lyrical (cyclical) passages of this memoir. This is the story of how a writer (reader) leaps over the canyon of amnesia and finds his lost obāchan hidden somewhere in the library stacks of his own memory where every word is waiting to be sewn into a coherent story that falls apart at the seams when you hold it up against the light or disappear into the wasteland.

20.

During the last year of her life, obāchan recreated her own island of the sun-origin. She read tiny Japanese novels that she bought at the San Diego Kinokuniya tucked inside the Mitsuwa supermarket on Kearny Mesa Road. My mom got Nippon TV installed on their cable box so my obāchan could watch Japan in real time, leaping over fifty years of suspended animation with a push of a button. This is the story of how we create nations, mountains, and cities inside of ourselves that are not simulacra, but perfect imagined worlds, more perfect than the original design.

21.

Supposedly, the last sense to go is the hearing. On her deathbed, as her forehead was burning up, I crawled in my obāchan's bed and thanked her again for her fierce love, endless strength, generosity, and devotion. I whispered one final thing in my primitive Japanese into her ears: おばあ さまは、私たちの光です。 Grandmama, you are our light. You are our light. This is the story of how I tried to help her cross to the other side, a world I prayed was full of butchered Mozart Sonatas, Ōsaka festivals, the smell of kamaboko, and senbei frying in the background and good luck-incense rising up, the tendrils of smoke painting sakura branches in the sky.

22.

When she died, my obāchan was completely out of her mind. Dementia, after all, is the travel between the self, beyond the self, and around the self until there is no self left, or until there are too many selves to reconcile. The day before I left California, I was sitting at a café with Wick, reflecting on my obāchan, focusing all my attention on her as I opened up my portable Japanese-English dictionary which I'd brought to help me speak with her when her English collapsed into rubble. I had probably creased the page myself days before without knowing, pressing my hands firmly on the spine in case of emergency. Even so, these are the kanji I found on that page as I was thinking about her, just as I was replaying the last minutes of her life in my mind: hieru, "to grow cold," higashi, "east," hikitoru, "to take care," hikō, "flight," and most importantly, hikari, the kanji for "light." This memoir is the story my obāchan didn't want to tell anyone, the story she kept telling me in excerpts of encoded trauma, the voyage I wish I could forget, and the story I was destined to assemble and retell in a way that only I could, written in the lyrical (cyclical) style she would have forbidden and also demanded of me. This is the story of my obāchan's deracination, self-multiplication, and also her return to the motherland told in the prophecies of a travel dictionary. This is the story of my memory of her memory, transposed into a series of (im)perfect and flawed translations, a project of narrative multiplication, the lyrical disorder of a damaged (artistic) brain, and an honest permutation of memory. This is the story of how a memoir can be a blood transfusion, giving sustenance to every version of her life she forgot and every version she left untold.

次に/Next:

1.   "America isn't that self-aware, Julie Delpy insisted, "and neither are you."

153

"That's true," I stammered, "but I'm self-aware enough to know that my celebrity crush for you is all in my head and that the cycle of irony never ends."

"Ta gueule!" she shouted. "Les choses imaginaires sont réelles aussi."

"So is my self-aware list on page 198."

She pulled out a Gitanes and stared out the window, blasée and hurt.

2.   To see all the places Jackson has lived, go to page 38.

3.   To witness the awe of Jackson's pranking genius, go to page 129.

4.   Or just turn the page.

38. My (Hella Long) List of Favorite Albums in College, Thanks in No Small Part to a Fraudulent Account With Columbia House For a One Lisa Gonzalez, Who May or May Have Not Ordered Twelve CDs and then Disappeared from My Life Forever Once the Promotion was Over

1. *Midnight Marauders* by Tribe Called Quest

2. *Strangeways, Here We Come,* and *The Queen is Dead* by The Smiths

3. *Laid* and *Seven* by James

4. *I'm Your Fan: The Songs of Leonard of Cohen Compilation*

5. *Siamese Dream* by The Smashing Pumpkins

6. *Deep Forest* by Deep Forest

7. *(What's the Story) Morning Glory* by Oasis

8. *Cole Porter Songbook*

9. *The Majesty of the Blues* by Wynton Marsalis (thanks again, Columbia House)

10. *The Dark Side of the Moon* by Pink Floyd

11. *Bona Drag* and *Vauxhall and I* by Morrissey

12. *The Best of Duke Ellington Compilation*

13. *Reachin' (A New Refutation of Time and Space)* by Digable Planets

14. *Kime Ne* by Özlem Tekin (bought in Istanbul)

15. *Four-Calendar Café* and *Victorialand* by Cocteau Twins

16. *Kind of Blue* by Miles Davis

17. *Come from Heaven* by Alpha

18. *MiLight* by DJ Krush

19. *The Miseducation of Lauryn Hill* by Lauryn Hill

20. *Headz 1-2 Compilation* by Mo' Wax

21. *Dummy* and *Portishead* by Portishead

22. *Second Toughest in the Infants* by The Underworld

23. *Formica Blues* by Mono

24. *The Score* by The Fugees

25. *Complete Piano Quartets* by Johannes Brahms

41. *Tidal* by Fiona Apple

次に/Next:

1. Lessons in Mental Colonization Starring Dead White Guys on channel 165.
2. Jackson's Love Song for Chicago exclusively here at Studio 273.
3. Linguaphiles (you know who you are), your support group has been relocated to room #210.
4. O.J.T.T.P.

39. Fuck Brittany and Her Stupidass Peninsula!

It was the dreaded week of oral reports on the French provinces. For fifty minutes every day, our lives became a broken-down elevator stuck between floors. As the 10th grade pariah and official pretty boy in a French class of 12th grade conjugation robots, senioritis-infected slackers, and part-time Francophiles, most of them already gone emotionally, daydreaming about the manifest destiny of drunk college hookups in cold industrial dorms and the rabid cultural tribalism of Big-10 football, I was reminded of my social exclusion and grammatical shortcomings almost every day. Mrs. V., my French teacher, hated my ass and I hated her right back. She used to call me *François le pénible* whenever I raised my hand. *Francis, the Pain in the Ass.* Trump had nothing on my high school French teacher when it came to coining demeaning, childish, and sticky nicknames. This class made me hate French, which was hard to do. The day Mrs. V. finally called out my name like a judge in a federal courthouse, I walked to the front of the classroom, holding my scribbled notes in my hands like a deflated life preserver on a sinking ship as students licked their lips in anticipation of blood sport. I swallowed hard, took a deep breath, and began my report on Brittany that was heavy with crossed-out typos, insecure cursive, and mistranslated idiomatic expressions.

—Le Bretagne, I began.

—Non! she interrupted, —it's not *le Bretagne,* it's *le Bretagne.*

—That's what I said, I protested.

—Non, you said *le Bretagne.*

The truth was, my French teacher and I had history. Every time I entered the classroom, I actually cringed. Sometimes, she snarled at me. We shared our antipathy like the joint custody for a child born from a drunken one-night stand. Being young and immature, I blamed her for our sparring, mostly because she was an adult but also because I was just a hapa teenager stumbling my way through a series of little earthquakes she didn't understand or care about. My parents had just gotten divorced, my mom had abandoned me and moved to Southern California, and I'd been ejected from the only artistic utopia I'd ever known at Interlochen Arts Academy, which had been the single greatest and most life-changing experience of my life, at least until my dad refused to pay the remaining 40% balance after my scholarship was increased twice my sophomore year to cover 60% of tuition and room and board, so now I was stuck in the very public high school I'd been trying to avoid. For me, Traverse City High School was a space of social distortion, enormous cultural conservatism, white beauty standards, and invisible economic determinism, all of which felt suffocating. Some students hated me simply because their hatred carried over from 8th grade, some hated my long, honey-colored hair, my green eyes, my illegible heterosexuality, and my incipient metrosexuality, some hated my obsession with piano, and some just hated my high school manga orientation with the world. Sometimes, I felt deeply and irrevocably alone. Sometimes, I wished my parents had thought about their kids just a little bit (more).

I looked around the room in dread and disbelief. —Fine, le Bre*ta*gne.

—Non! she declared. You said, *le Bretagne,* again but it's *le Bretagne.*

—But those are the same words!

—No, they're not.

I looked at my classmates for sympathy, but they were all laughing or smirking themselves to death, relieved to be dodging the shooting squad I'd walked into. I glanced at the door and then back at my report in my clenched hands. I hadn't even gotten past the fucking title yet.

—All right, I sighed slowly, le . . . Bretagne.

—Non, c'est pas ça !

—This is getting ridiculous. I'm about to leave.

—Fine, *leave,* she said, but you won't pass this class.

—Le Bre-ta-gne, I said, exaggerating every syllable.

—Non!

Finally, I just straight up ignored her and kept reading until I was finished with my shitty report on Brittany, a French province I didn't give a fuck about anymore, and then I sat down, my face bright like an overripe pomegranate. I fought back tears of anger and humiliation, ignoring the palpable of schadenfreude by every white guy in the classroom who wanted the 10th-grader shot down from the impressionistic sky. I refused to give my teacher the reaction she wanted because I knew the class was waiting for it. I refused to give her the satisfaction of unleashing my sadness into the world, but in my heart, I hated her for transmuting such a beautiful language into such a blunt and violent thing, something French teachers were uniquely skilled at doing parce qu'ils détestent leur propres vies de merde.

Three months later, I was standing in the breezeway with two upperclassmen. With graduation right around the corner, they reeked of dissolution, their souls already halfway to their future college campuses, their lips half-open in anticipation of their first college hookup. When our conversation switched to our French class, one guy confessed:

—Man, when I get to MSU, I'm starting French all over again.

—Yeah, me too, the second guy added. —All I know how to do is fucking conjugate verbs.

And then it hit me: I wasn't the only motherfucker who'd felt lost in our class. I'd felt like a grammar flunky the whole year for having to teach myself the past conditional, the future anterior, and the subjunctive, just to catch up with my classmates. I was the club-footed klutz in that French disco, the whole class moving in sync to songs I'd never even heard of, their shared knowledge like a dance routine I'd never learned. Thanks to Mrs. V.'s draconian pedagogy, I lost the breathless joy I'd once had trying to speak French as a teenager, a language I'd been idolizing since puberty, always smitten by its dramatic cadence and syntactical musicality, always intrigued by its mysterious diacritics whenever I skimmed copies of *Le Monde* at the local bookstore. But in tenth grade, French became a gateway drug to self-loathing I couldn't hide from my classmates. French became a sanctioned act of sadomasochism in the high school foreign language curriculum. French became a disciplinarian's whip and a trophy of the bourgeoisie. A castle too elusive, too high, and too daunting for me to scale.

It would be twelve years until I finally became fluent in French after studying French lit in college and becoming a Peace Corps volunteer in Burkina Faso teaching English to junior high students. It would be fourteen years before I visited Paris for the first time, drank wine every night, and walked around Montmartre at night singing '60s R&B songs and smoking for the first time in years with P. and V., my new French friends. The classroom couldn't and wouldn't be the matrix of my French proficiency.

In college, Pops and I got out of his old Jeep Cherokee carrying cardboard boxes and Target supplies to my dorm room at Oberlin College. I was moving into *La Maison de la Francophonie* (or French House for short), one of seven language houses on campus. A month later, Alex, my new roommate, and I threw a poor student wine and cheese party. We invited friends and other Francophiles (mostly from French House) into our divided double where we drank cheap Cabernet Sauvignon and nibbled on pedestrian Camembert. Everyone was chatting in French, dancing to Europop, and smoking cigarettes near the window to avoid setting off the fire alarm. For the first time in my life, I talked for hours in French with Alex, our friend Nicolas from Strasbourg, and Béa, my French girlfriend from Nouvelle Calédonie, who I was crazy about (until I wasn't). After a few glasses of red wine and a little soft kissing, my French was an emancipated canary. My grammar was still deeply flawed and I still made a shitload of grammatical mistakes when I spoke, but I could speak it. After a month of advanced French class and living in partial immersion, my French was decent. Certain thoughts just burst out of my mouth like air bubbles before I figured out the right object pronoun or contemplated the right verb tense. My mouth was forming a newly passionate relationship with French, one I'd dreamed about in high school, back when I needed it to rescue me and transport me from the grammatical apartheid of tenth grade French class. In college, French became the stuff of Rimbaud, Nina Simone, and Dada, Françis Cabrel, Apollinaire, and Marguerite Duras, it became the "Sanctus" of Fauré's *Pavanne* and the raining businessmen of Magritte. It became an existential modality I'd never learned as a teenager but had always identified with along with my Japanese ancestry.

Being part French was frankly easier because there was already a word for that ancestry in Northern Michigan, there was prestige to being something that white people understood, which was themselves above all else, but there was not a word in English for someone who was mixed-race and part Japanese, there was not a word for someone who looked white but was also the son of Japanese immigrants on his mom's side. Speaking French became one way I could both embrace and defy the rules of my whiteness by speaking something beautiful that Americans could identify but not understand. French was also the way I subverted rules of gender performativity in America: if I spoke French, if I looked French, then I was allowed to fall in love and be passionate about movies and literature and art and philosophy and music and coordinate my Naf Naf sweaters with my Girbaud jeans and have a stud in my left ear and microwave Chicken Cordon Bleu and consider my personal style. I was allowed to have joie de vivre. Later, French would become my connection to the rest of the world, the linguistic toolbox allowing me to communicate with strangers on bush taxis to Ougadougou, advocate for Mauritanian refugees in Portland, meet a Québecois couple in Baja California, learn about a Senegalese taxi driver's life in South Bend, order a local Chardonnay off the menu in a Lyon bistro, ask directions for the port in Marseille, and eat vegan Chinese food in Paris. The French I spoke that night at our party in French House was the French that had been stuck inside my heart since I was an emo-romantic teenager. For the first time, I was speaking French with my lips and my hands, with my mouth, my wine-stained teeth, my brain, and my sex. As we toasted one another, our glasses clinking like a music box, I danced to James's *Laid* and sang The Smiths' *Cemetery Gates* to Béa and argued with Nicolas, my whole relationship with French slowly changing once it became a living cultural artifact instead of a tortured game of make believe. Later that semester in the computer lab, I stumbled on photographs online of Brittany's prodigious peninsula and Breton women dressed in traditional hats that looked like eraser heads and flying nuns. I learned that the Breton language was endangered and that Brest was a major naval port in France. I couldn't decide whether I cared. The truth was, I had no desire to visit Brittany. In "Le Bretagne," French was the language of stillborn daydreams, linguistic paralysis, and emotional inquisition, but here in northern Ohio and later in Djibasso and Paris and Geneva and Brussels and Aix-en-Provence, French became an old song that I found the courage to sing after too much wine and the right audience, the mic burning my hand like acetone.

次に/Next:

1. Climb up Azerbaijan's Besh Bar Mag and eat dirt cookies on page 211.
2. To see Jackson learn how to swim underwater like a baby koi, go to page 82.
3. Page 155, that's all.
4. To see which worods that Jacksoknk smisslleps the most, go to page 253.

THE VICIOUS CYCLE OF IRONY

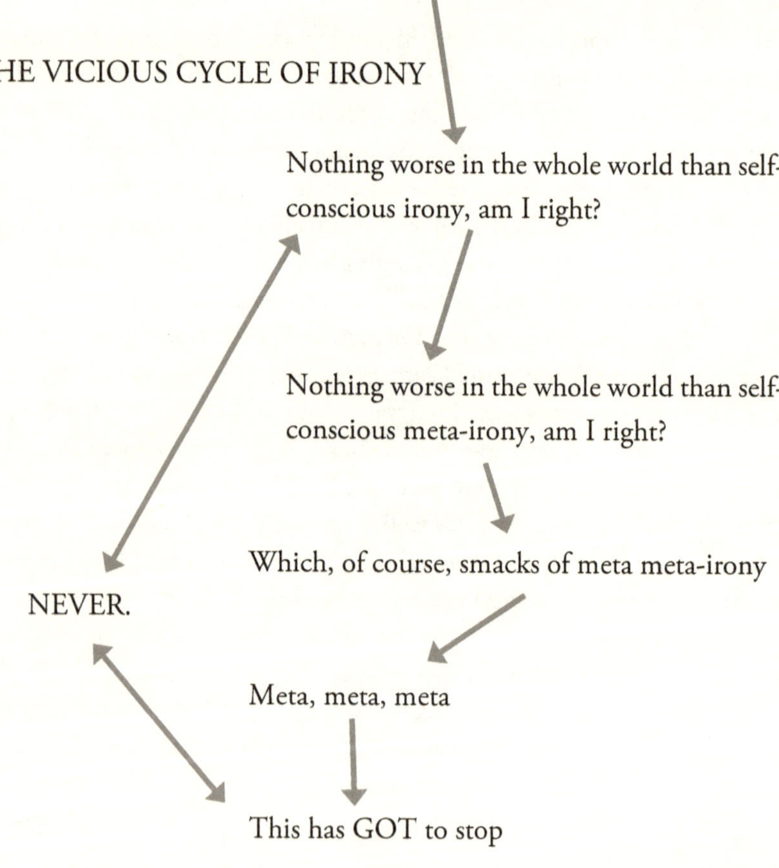

40. The (White, Male, Eurocentric*) Books That Changed My Life in High School

1. *Les Misérables* by Victor Hugo (I wrote my AP English thesis on this tome, secretly afraid that the musical was better.)

2. *Fathers and Sons* by Ivan Turgenev (introduced me to nihilism, which blew my ass away, and also confirmed that the coolest characters always die young, so, I dunno, maybe coolness is overrated.)

3. *Catcher in the Rye* by J.D. Salinger (taught me the value of stylized writing, coming of age narratives, psychological contradiction, foiled authenticity, but also the way we as a society ignore implicit male trauma.)

4. *The Stranger* by Albert Camus (the first French novel I ever read, and also my introduction to Camus's peculiar type of existentialism, which I found dark and brooding.)

5. *100 Selected Poems* by E.E. Cummings (made me want to become a poet and the son of a Latin-speaking preacher, his poems still influencing the way I hear language.)

6. *The Sound and the Fury* by William Faulkner (inspired a heated argument about stream of consciousness with J., a girl with bangs in my Honors English class, our fights becoming so heated, that eventually we started dating, fell in love, and then I lost my virginity to her. After I moved to Chicago, she fucked a dumb jock in a hot tub, which broke my heart because it was so fucking cheesy and so

devolutionary after what we'd experienced together, which is why Faulkner reminds me of losing my virginity, falling in love, breaking up, and then getting erased by bad high school movie clichés.)

7. *The Great Gatsby* by F. Scott Fitzgerald (made me think for the first time that I might be a historical refugee, born in the wrong era and the wrong generation until I realized that there were no PoC in the novel and I would have been erased in Nick's narration.)

8. *No Exit and 3 Other Plays* by Jean-Paul Sartre (confirmed my suspicion that existentialism is a just a handgun for 17-year-olds trying to be European intellectuals by smoking, copping attitude, and arguing about things they don't really understand, especially when they read coming-of-age narratives with stylized voices telling stories of implicit male trauma and foiled searches for authenticity.)

9. *A Portrait of the Artist* by James Joyce (taught me about spiritual epiphanies, literary ambition, and the joys of dialectical plot structure. Also made me want to read Thomas Aquinas in Latin.)

10. *Crime and Punishment* by Fyodor Dostoevsky (where I learned about the power of narrative crime fiction and also discovered that I had morals after all, which surprised me.)

* I blame the Western Canon for colonizing the literary imagination in America and I also blame Harold Bloom for cheerleading the Western Canon (which needs no cheerleading) but ignoring every single Black, African, or African American author except Achebe and Thiong'o.

次に/Next:
1. To read Jackson's lyrical essay about memory, storytelling, and the (kinda heart-breaking) passing of his obāchan, go to page 141.

2. To read about the first time Jackson became sick, fetal, and nostalgic in Africa, go to page 33.
3. Go on a15-minute hajj of Azerbaijan, exclusive on Channel 211.
4. Or just turn the page on the Western Canon and read some goddamn James Baldwin or Toni Morrison or Audre Lorde or Toni Cade Bambara, will'ya?

41. Liberation From the Luminous Flux

I learned through trial and error (i.e., extreme dehydration and public humiliation) that the best time to go biking to the Malian border was right before the sunset became a salve for every scorched object in Djibasso and right after the rabid sunlight broke its fangs against the hard crust of twilight. Once that militant star in the sky had begun shedding filaments of desperate flame into the solar system and the African horizon had finally drowned its greatest prodigy again, I would jump on my mountain bike and peddle west as fast as I could on the dirt road to Tominian, Ségou, and Bamako, just as the liquid darkness spilled into the sky like shodō calligraphy ink.

There was a system to my bike rides: I'd prepare a salad of twice-washed and twice-sanitized tomatoes and local onions (when they were available at the Thursday Market at le Grand Marché), imported olive oil, some red-wine vinegar, and a bunch of herbes de Provence that I'd bought at an overpriced French supermarket in Ouaga as my reward for biking twenty kilometers through the darkness and not dying in a pothole or stung by a scorpion or run over by a UN Range Rover. My salad waited patiently for me in two Mondrian-colored plastic bowls, which protected my food from exploding insects, stinging flies, and catcalling mosquitoes, some of which were *sure* to be carrying typhoid fever, anthrax, yellow fever, or malaria.

Three to four days a week, while villagers gathered in front of *boutiques* to drink tea and condensed milk or meet at local buvettes to nurse bottles of orange Fanta or SoBBra, I'd bike through the solitary dirt road that went from Nouna all the way to Tominian and beyond. When I returned home drenched in sweat and gilded like a glowing creature of radioactive dust, I'd wave at the villagers I knew (Disco the cassette merchant, Mamadou the tailor, Henri the gendarme) as I pedaled to the silent refuge of my compound, the music in my MiniDisc player still splashing my ears. My sweaty body throbbed with dwindling vitality, the fatigue slowly seeping into my bones like a warm fog.

Biking in West Africa was how I let go of myself and relinquished my American rules of life. Biking was my technique for silencing my mind and reconnecting my adult life as an education volunteer to my childhood imagination, back when I had dreams of racing in the Tour de France and standing on the champion's podium in a champagne-drenched yellow jersey, surrounded by skinny European models and dipped in patriotic ticker tape. I biked religiously on that reclusive dirt road because it was a form of hypnosis, going on forever like a familiar jukebox song on repeat. No matter how far I pushed myself to reach Mali, I never reached the border, always turning around shortly before I reached it, making the road seem both borderless and infinite. At dusk, I was one of the only villagers leaving Djibasso who wasn't carrying an amphora on his head or riding a bush taxi. I was the only person in my village trying to time travel to my childhood on a green mountain bike.

When I got home each night, my heart was the tempo of a R & B ballad. I would take a bucket bath after my infinite bike ride, eat warm bread delivered by my favorite shop owner, and inhale a perfect salad protected by a tiny UFO of plastic bowls. In Djibasso, simple things nurtured me whenever I felt unspeakable loneliness, which was often: after surviving another hot and phlegmatic day, macerated by sun and suffocated by sandstorms, I found solace in each simple salad, drawn to the taste of healthy food and the forgiving darkness. Holding warm bread in my hands, listening to the BBC and La Radio France on my broadband radio as I dipped the still-warm bread into the olive oil, red wine vinegar, and lemon juice at the bottom of my salad bowl, were consoling gestures, practically religious. There was emotional comfort in protecting certain daily routines during la saison pluvieuse, when roads turned into brown slop or disappeared in the torrential rain and small lakes formed inside compounds. Sometimes, these daily routines were almost enough, but often my nostalgia and my loneliness crept up on me on the most beautiful nights when the moon projected a milky blue halo onto every hard surface in the village.

One evening when the sky was a thick and heavy tar, I walked out to the terrace, pulled my petit bois table close to my canvas chair, turned on the radio, and began eating my salad. It was a like a Beethoven string quartet in my mouth. When the door to my compound creaked open, a little shadow approached. Only the whites of her eyes and her teeth helped me see her in the pitch of night.

—Bonsoir monsieur, the shop owner's daughter said.

—Bonsoir, I said, ça va ? I asked.

—Oui, ça ba. Her phoneticized French hinted at academic exclusion, suggesting she wasn't allowed to attend the local *collège* like her brothers, where French was the language of instruction. —Boici le pain, she said, handing me a little black plastic bag.

I grabbed the air blindly before touching the bag. The bread glowed in my hands. I pulled out a CFA coin from my pocket and then grabbed hard candy from the table and placed them in her hands delicately like I was handing her a flimsy secret.

—Merci beaucoup, I said, —tiens.

She smiled, her teeth radiating in the soft light of my kerosene lamp. —Au rebois, monsieur, she sang, waving at me. I didn't see the wave, but I felt the motion in the air. I smiled anyway. I understood the importance of gestures even when they were only for us. That's why they're called gestures, because we do these things to call witness to the symbolic nature of our own fleeting existence. My life as an English Teacher in West Africa was my own professional gesture. Many of my friends didn't understand why I left America and the truth was, after 9/11, I didn't either.

Time in Burkina Faso was always dodging my butterfly net, always changing its trajectory and speed. In America, there wasn't enough time to reach my full potential as a human being, but in West Africa, time was a dead insect: first uncatchable and then lifeless. On days when I wasn't teaching at the *collège*, I wrote self-indulgent, Proustian letters to friends who didn't have time for my Waldensque reflections. I played solitaire on the concrete patio with an incomplete deck of cards, which seemed like a blatant metaphor for insanity. I biked to the Malian border that only existed on maps. I reread long-winded novels in French underneath my hangar and rationed out butter cookies for the month. I reheated leftover spaghetti and listened to Nick Drake obsessively on my tape player like an English fanboy. I drew abstract, Kandinsky-inspired murals on the inside of my cement and tin roof house with pastel-colored chalk until my body was caked in the sweat and the dust of the earth tone palette. My solitary life in Djibasso was quiet, slow, and lonely, but it was also simple. Sludgy. Redolent. Sweltering. I dreamt eidetically because I had the time to and dreaming always requires so much hard drive space in our souls. Now, there was space in my mind for memory, travel, and color. With the exception of the call-to-prayer battle that took place every morning between the two neighborhood mosques, located twenty sandal-steps from the compound gate, time wasn't universal, linear, or objective anymore. Without the ringing of cell phones and landlines, without the philosophical delay of mirrors reflecting back my daily existence, without electricity or plumbing, without the chronicle of cable news or the internet (I could only read my emails when I took a bush taxi to a cybercafé in Nouna), time didn't exist because there was no way to measure it, no way to defy my own biorhythms, there was no way to track the way time leaked into the cultural groundwater of my consciousness or accelerated into the night sky. Time was just a theorem of the industrialized mind, a useless paradigm invented by the age of automation to replace circadian rhythm with the luminous flux.

Temporal distortion happened every day in Djibasso. Sometimes, especially on the weekends when it rained all day, time disappeared, eroding like the dirt roads to the Malian border, and when time existed, it existed as a specter, encapsulated on the radio and repeated in Burkinabé idiom: ça va aller, an expression attesting to the permeability and cyclicity of time, to the redundancy and the continuity of human existence. If time existed, it existed in the gradations of my own sweat, in the stretched-out shadows of my gaunt and damp body, in the purging of precious calories during infinite bike rides to imaginary borders, it existed in the lunar frequencies of milk blue haloes on the concrete terrace in my compound. Time was the emotional cycle of one Nick Drake tape, the number of times I asked villagers about their family in Jula or explained the same English grammar rules to my students in French or took a bucket bath with a blue plastic cup and baby shampoo or soaked vegetables in chlorinated water or forgot my Mefloquine to avoid cerebral malaria, the number of times the volcanic sky brought tears to my eyes as I biked through the African bush aimlessly and wiped mango pulp from my chapped lips in the aloe sunset and craved a woman's voice inside my head and craved a woman's smell on my pillowcase and fantasized about air-conditioned cafés in bustling metropolitan cities and prayed for the plum reprieve of twilight every mid-day. If time existed in Djibasso, if it was possible for time to exist at all in a village with spotty electricity, broken generators, cassette vendors, and three-year-old calendars, then it existed in the biorhythms of the body, in the quotidian arcs of the solar prodigy, and in the clumsy hand-painted clouds stuck forever it seemed, in the African sky like stage props for an undigested paradise.

次に/Next:

1. To learn about the things Jackson once believed had magical powers, go to page 37.
2. Game on, motherfuckers, on page 108.
3. If eating could make him skinny, Jackson would eat EVERY FUCKING THING ON PAGE 180, but that's not how any of this works.
4. Or just turn the page to some spoken words.

42. Words I Really Love to Say Out Loud

1. Che!

2. ~~Boo~~ (currently out of fashion due to the pandemic)

3. Construction

4. Bah, non . . .

5. I love you

6. Yooooo!

7. ~~だから、ね?~~ I wrote this hoping it would be completely true by the time I published this memoir and instead, I stopped saying it all because I never get to speak Nihongo anymore since I haven't found a residency program in Japan for emerging writers, LA traffic is horrendous, so Little Tokyo might as well be in another state, and also, traveling is hella stressful right now, so flying to Japan will have to wait. Sigh

8. I'm a professor and a fiction writer

9. She's a pediatric nurse. [pause]. The best kind

10. Fucking (adverbially speaking)

11. Es un quilombo

12. Motherfucker

13. Dope

14. Rad

15. My mom was born in Yokohama

16. ¡Qué boludo!

17. C'est un frimeur

18. Hapa

19. Kaput

20. ~~Ninja, please!~~ (okay, I actually never say this, but I put it in my wish bank anyway)

21. C'est de la foutaise!

22. ~~Pasa que~~. ~~Es que~~. Pasa que

次に/Next:

1. At a DTLA café, she noticed a racially ambiguous, metrosexual guy with a Japanese sleeve and a nose ring, sipping his ~~almond~~ oat latte and lost in thought. *He's probably visiting page 190*, she thought to herself. Reader, she was correct.
2. To take a break, dream a little, and make origami, go to page 57.
3. Why schools are failing our children, a Fox News Exclusive at ten on Channel 294.
4. To bike to the Malian border with Jackson as the sun sets (sounds almost romantic, doesn't it?), go to page 168.
5. Or just turn the page.

43. When Home is Not a Verb Chart

1.

In 2007, I went back to Traverse City to see Leigh and Barbara, two good friends of mine I hadn't seen since college. I hadn't seen Northern Michigan in ten years and hadn't lived there in seventeen. After a short Amtrak ride from Chicago to Grand Rapids, I took a taxi to the Grand Rapids Inn, located paradoxically in Wyoming, Michigan. Inside my room was a floor dryer blowing on the sopping wet carpet and the unmistakable smell of old water. I called LB from a nearby Pizza Hut and lamented over the cheese I was about to eat and the wet carpet in my motel room. After I returned, I inspected the mattress, the pillowcases, and top sheet for bed bugs, King James bibles, and cum stains (i.e., Americana). I turned on the TV absentmindedly and watched the US team beat up on Venezuela in the FIBA Olympic Qualifiers. As I fell asleep, I suddenly thought, *Fuck, I hope it wasn't the toilet that overflowed on the carpet.* I have a history of thinking the absolute worst thoughts before I fall asleep: do I have malaria, are my neighbors serial killers, does she talk with a German accent during sex, did I lock the front door, did I leave the stove on, was that sarcasm, was that shade, will I ever publish a book, and now, does my carpet contain fecal pathogens?

2.

The next morning, I hitched a ride with my friend Angie, who was returning from a wedding down state with Bill (her boyfriend) and Lydia (her daughter). I sat in back with Lydia and told her jokes that didn't make sense. Lydia kept plopping her feet on my lap, even though Angie told her not to. I bribed Lydia with skittle gum and kid talk, which worked for a while. Halfway to our destination, Angie started speaking to me in French so we could speak freely (and also because that was our thing in college, speaking French, and nothing was more consoling than being able to speak

175

French again after a long and twitchy withdrawal). We caught up on two years of lost time while her boyfriend pretended to read a Stephen King novel in the passenger's seat, hanging on to our every word. To be honest, it was uncomfortable AF, but every option was flawed in some way. I felt for him. I knew what it was like to be the outsider. There's nothing shittier in the whole world than meeting someone who knew your partner before you did because their friendship (or whatever the hell it is that they have that threatens you in its vague emotional symmetry) predates you and makes you the youngest person in the room, emotionally speaking. Lydia kept putting her feet on my lap and smacking her gum with not a care in the whole world, even though she got yelled at. I envied her insouciance, which was actually the word that'd come to my head at that moment because of the contact high of speaking French again with my friend who definitely didn't have enough people to share her love with. Neither did I, honestly.

3.

I walked from Leigh's house around town and then downtown, all two blocks of it. So much of Traverse City was exactly as I'd remembered it, even though everyone warned me it had changed so much:

1. The Boardman River was still placid and brown.
2. The town grid was still smaller than a day planner.
3. The Park Place Hotel (where I used to play piano at the Top of the Park and get drunk on free scotch) was shorter than I remembered, but still charming.
4. Grand Traverse Bay was still hidden behind the streets.
5. Paesano's was still serving the same pizza slices for lunch.
6. Glenn Loomis elementary school looked exactly the same and my kindergarten playground was still covered in woodchips and mulch.
7. The Thirlby Football Field (where I used to walk in circles with my friends in junior high to talk to girls

in the shadows of the stadium) was still surrounded by an ugly industrial metal fence with rusted barbed wire that looked like it belonged in a government waste storage facility. This was the place where I ran into a beautiful Native girl with flirty eyes named N. who was my first crush in 8th grade before she made out with one of my friends and then stood me up after I'd brought her a bear dressed up like a Noir Femme Fatale called Lauren BearCall. Thirlby Field was TC's public square for teenagers, the place where my friends and I went after smoking weed in a cemetery together, experiencing the merged dilation of drug time and adolescent time, the place where I once watched a high school soccer game on a beautiful fall afternoon with my high school girlfriend (Lupie), suddenly wondering why I'd stopped playing it as a boy and what I was doing back in public school after the refuge I'd found at Interlochen Arts Academy, a school I missed every single day of my Sophomore year.

I walked around Traverse City for hours, replaying my life, remembering every palpitation I felt in the hallways of junior high, remembering every moment of racial alienation, erasure, and suffocation, remembering every microaggression against my obāchan, every racist comment made against Asian and Black and Native people, remembering every moment of intense childhood joy, euphoria, and isolation, every instance of teenage anxiety, infatuation, and betrayal, every adult moment of collapse and estrangement as a mixed-race writer and multicultural, urban liberal. During my visit, stuck in the rabbit hole of time lost and time regained as a full-fledged adult now revisiting the geography of my longing, alienation, and shame, it hit me that the idea of home, like gender, had never been a stable category for me, always shifting, always redefined against my will as my parents moved around the country in search of parallel worlds where they were different people with different partners with different families living in different worlds. Home for my family was a shifting space, it lacked the stability, the love, and the indestructible sense of belonging I wanted. Maybe, this was why I was so terrible at sticking around and defending my mistakes. Maybe, my idealization of stasis was based on my own inability to cultivate it in my own life. Maybe, the idea of home had never been geographical. Maybe, it wasn't a noun. Maybe, home was something we created with calloused fingertips and utility belts, a feeling we conjugated inside ourselves like irregular verbs for unfinished love poems we were too shy to read out loud. Maybe, home was the blurry storytelling of a too-sweet mojito you had with your friends in LA or a city mural covered in ball bearing raindrops. Maybe, home was the address of the eyes of the woman I adored, gazing at me in a soft narcotic daze as an IV drip blew away the fire ants collecting in her body after surgery. Maybe, home was the qi I felt in her pulse as I held her hand. Maybe, home was a narrative vulnerability of the brokenhearted. Maybe, home was the mosaic of my shattered heart as LB sobbed in my arms after baby embryo died and we were forced to say goodbye to the family we never had, her eyes melting in a fondue of lost words and severed worlds. But maybe, home was the cradle of Zoe's warmth on her pillow and Gogo's tiny head sleeping in her crouch, maybe it was a perfect late-night drive through Lower Wacker listening to Aqualung or a muted café in Wicker Park where every self-conscious hipster turned into a scruffy blur before our first kiss erased every line of music that came before us.

4.

As LB and I talked about moving to Barcelona or Madrid or Paris or Buenos Aires the following year, our home would not be a fixed or synchronic space in our memory. It couldn't be a protected space of teenage nostalgia that I held on to like an operatic placeholder. Home was not a pause button or a linear plot line of humble beginnings and urban ascendance. Home didn't have to be the lake you swam in for first time like a koi or the bed you woke up in after a febrile dream. Home didn't have to be the emotional GPS of your family drama or the prefab subdivision that drenched you in familiarity. Home didn't have to be a memory we pinned down with patient and strong arms like trained psychiatric wardens. Home could be the flash and the snare of a perfect thunderstorm outside our window, the primal warmth of our bed that we shared together, the comforting weight and scent of the duvet, a soft cocoon for us in a storm of new beginnings.

次に/Next:

1. To learn about Jackson's favorite colors as a teenager, go to page 56.
2. Friendship and tea in an Azerbaijani village, all on page 211.
3. Jackson apologizes for (almost) nothing and frankly neither should you, on page 186.
4. Or just turn the page if you wanna know me, homie.

44. Foods I'm Kinda Obsessed With (aka Nom Nom at Your Local Restaurant)

1. Any and all types of Japanese noodles, especially soba, udon, and sōmen

2. Liquid Gold from Press Brothers

3. Club Sandwiches with tempeh bacon

4. Spicy ~~Pad Thai~~ Pad Si-Io at Ruen Pair

5. Khao Soi soup with veggies at Pailin Thai

6. Lemon and Chef #2 Rolls from Sushi Enya in Nihonmachi

7. Vegan Reubens and Jalapeño Poutine at the Chicago Diner

8. Spoons of peanut butter whenever and wherever

9. BBQ twists and Macaroni 'n' Cheese from Soul Vegetarian

10. Hazelnut cutlets (RIP, old friends)

11. Badass OG Breakfast Sandwiches (actual name) from Locali

12. Cruzer's BBQ vegan chicken pizza

13. Soul Bowl from Native Foods

14. Juice blend of apples, lemon, ginger, and carrots

15. Nacho fries with jackfruit carnitas from Next Mex

16. Dark Chocolate (always, always, always)

17. Unagi-don

18. Big Macro Burger with seasoned fries from M Café (please get rid of the gluten!)

19. LB's homemade cupcakes and banana bread

20. Vegan Pho from Loving Hut

21. Mangos, strawberries, and blueberries, just whenever

22. The perfect falafel with hot sauce (hey!)

23. Jackfruit vegetable biryani and Dahl from Dishoom

24. The Machu Picchu and Aztlan raw food bowls at Living Foods

次に/Next:
1. Jackson TOTALLY loves these cities and would visit them every year if he were rolling in it, but since he's definitely not, think of page 217 as, you know, a list of magical items in a page of magical thinking.
2. To see Jackson sweating his ass off in Marrakech, go to page 189.
3. Oh, take a break, dream a little, and make some origami on page 57.
4. Or just turn the page.

45. The Bearable Heaviness of Being

1.

After LB and I fell in love, I routinely ignored her hints about marriage, flicking them off my sleeves like old breadcrumbs. She was a decorated marriage veteran, wearing an invisible Purple Heart from her first marriage after her ex-husband cheated on her like a dumbass. I also had my own laundry list of issues with marriage:

1. DOMA is profoundly discriminatory and same-sex and trans couples should be able to marry whoever they fuck they want.

2. Historically, marriage has been an act of tribal consolidation and class protectionism, connected to property rights and the ownership of female bodies.

3. Social conservatives have been using straight marriage to rally single-issue voters forever (just ask Karl Rove). Therefore, every new straight marriage reinforces a complicit discrimination against non-straight couples.

Then, there were these reasons too:

4. I don't want to doom our relationship with impossible expectations.

5. Marriage devolves into companionship with diminishing bennies, so why complicate something as simple as love?

6. Marriage is slow-motion asexuality, so why sublimate our sex life for a formulaic daydream?

7. Marriage kills romance, so why ruin such a beautiful thing for such an impossible ideal?

8. Marriage is a baby boomer obsession and Gen X/Millennials can get down or disengage whenever they want without labels or fixed categories.

9. Self-aware people should question any and all types of cultural inertia like marriage, heteronormativity, family, boring lovers, or insipid professional identities.

I still find these arguments compelling in many ways, but something changed inside me when I was getting my PhD. My friend Lisa was giving me a ride after Aimee Bender's workshop. We were somewhere in K-town when I realized I didn't have to get married for all the fucked-up reasons I hated marriage, I could get married for all the reasons that redeemed it, but only if I thought it was worth redeeming. It seems so obvious now, but it wasn't obvious back then. No one told me I could define marriage however the hell I wanted to. When I opened the front door of our Hollywood apartment, I ran over to LB, gave her a big hug, and declared: —I love you and I think we should get married, boo. Sometimes, I wish I had waited until after I'd written a love poem before asking her, sometimes I wish I'd planned an elaborate Bollywood marriage proposal with Shah Rukh Khan and Anushka Sharma lookalikes dancing in the background, but I was poor AF, wanted us to keep things simple, and kinda embarrassed about my volta face.

2.

LB brushed off my comment and warned me not to joke around with marriage. She said she'd wanted to marry me for so long now that she'd given up hope. She said Latinas don't play with marriage, so if I valued my life at all I'd stop joking. I laughed and told her I meant every word. I told her I wanted to spend my life with her and that it was only now that I understood the way couples could shape marriage into their own creation: a collective Galatea project of passionate love, bedrock friendship, unfinished personal growth, and group evolution. Also, health (insurance) is kinda romantic.

3.

A month later, we drove to the Beverly Hills courthouse and got married with tears streaming down our faces. We called our shocked parents to let them know that the impossible had happened. We went to Urth Café in West Hollywood with friends and ate vegan chocolate cake and drank green tea. Two days later, we flew to Tokyo for our honeymoon and visited as many Shinto shrines and Buddhist temples as possible. We thanked our ancestors, the kami, and the Buddhas for bringing us together on Myspace.

4.

In some mystical way, marriage feels different to me. It's this beautiful weight that prevents me from floating up into the nebulous sky like a weather balloon and ultimately, crashing back down to earth from every vision quest and daydream binge. It's this awareness that my decisions will always have ripple effects, that nothing I do will remain unknown eventually. It's this sacred knowledge that we will always find each other in the historical riot of amnesia, violence, and paroxysm, even if the world collapses into chaos, a global pandemic infects the planet (oops, too late), and the streets of LA burst into apocalyptic flames like an obsolete literary genre. Marriage is this tiny promise I've made to myself and to the universe to be better than I actually am. It's a promise of well-intentioned deceit and a permanent aspiration of self-overcoming. Marriage is the mirage of an island in a sinking world, which is why the idea of living without LB, the love of my life, engulfs me in a spiraling meltdown of sadness and grief. I know there will never be enough time (or solid land or a large enough cosmological dictionary) to express every majestic thing I feel for her when she looks at me with her melting chocolate Peruvian eyes, the splintered afternoon sunshine haloing her face like a hijab crafted from star light.

次に/Next:

1.   To read about the things Jackson misses, go to page 92.
2.   We asked Jackson to tell us his favorite cities in the whole world. Here's what he said on page 217:

    1. Tokyo ←So fucking predictable!

    2. Paris ←Again, so fucking predictable! This dude is a straight-up narcissist!

    3. ????

3. Wanna get sunburnt in Marrakech? Interested in the Naturalist School of Observation? Nah? Tough crowd, man. Okay, how about we meet halfway on page 189, gentle reader?

4. Or just turn the page, home fry.

46. Things I Used to Be Ashamed of, (but Have Made Progress With)

1. *My belief in ahimsa (non-violence)

2. Not worrying about not "looking" Asian enough to claim I'm part Asian

3. Not "being" Asian enough to claim I'm part Asian

4. Being moved by kindness

5. My love of and connection to animals

6. My shaved head (which makes me look more hardcore than I actually am)

7. My expensive taste in jeans

8. My itinerant lifestyle (and constant return to the Midwest)

9. Not making sense

10. My consummate metrosexuality

11. My contradictory love of jazz, classical music, house, dream pop, and hip-hop

12. My runner's thighs, which used to be biker's thighs, which used to be soccer thighs

13. My vulnerability to the people I love

14. My propensity for lists (-)

15. The gazillion girlfriends I've had in the search for true love

16. (Not) always having my shit together

17. Being a lightweight when it comes to drinking

18. My obsessions, some of which have defined me in the best ways possible

19. The (absurd) joy it gives me when younger women flirt with me (I apologize for nothing)

20. Not having an Ivy League degree

21. My unwillingness to give up on the things I believe in

22. Not being a New Yorker and not living in New York

23. Being on Food Stamps while I was an Americorps volunteer

24. Leaving the Peace Corps so I could write again

25. My intensity (in the *Lost in Translation* sense of the word) when I teach

26. Picking a profession that doesn't pay shit

27. Being largely but not entirely vegan (sorry fishies!)

28. Not publishing a novel before 40

29. Being a gamer and a manga reader and a fanboy and an emo-romantic dreamer

30. Losing my 20-something body in my 30s

31. Being both a Midwesterner and a West Coaster (but not always in that order)

*Except the time that Zoe bit me so hard I threw her off of me by instinct and then felt like a human shit stain afterwards even though she was totally fine and I was bleeding, which makes me feel like an asshole and such a bad fucking Buddhist!

次に/Next:
1. Shoegaze, dream pop, fuzcoustics, or Lynchian atmospherics, what's the fucking difference? To (totally not) settle this pointless dispute, go to page 239.
2. To see Jackson playing Mozart in his grandmother's trailer, go to page 100.
3. Salty Jackson and His Moroccan Reimagining, only on page 189, which takes you to the exact same place as:
4. Turning the sweat-stained page and just getting physical, you beautiful Olivia Newton-John cosplayer!

47. Detective of the Lost World

The Moroccan sunlight was hot pudding on my hapa skin when we made it to the Palais de Badi in Marrakech. El Badi Palace was Ahmad al-Mansur's dream vision, the famous sultan of the Saadian Dynasty known as the Gold King, who wanted a replica of the Alhambra Palace in Granada before it was destroyed in the 17th century. In 2009, the Palais de Badi looked like the decimation of time and bloodshed, its palatial beauty becoming an act of willful reimagination ghosted by withered histories and colonial empires. LB and I waded through the debilitating heat, retreating to pockets of shade where I tried to picture the lost palace in my head: four reflective ponds, one in each corner of the courtyard where four shallow and desiccated rectangles were now. As I wiped my forehead, I pictured a fertile and lush grove of orange, lemon, pomegranate, and fig trees, a hammam gilded in beautiful blue and white tiles with gold fringe, clean, intersecting blue flower patterns, and endless rows of candles preaching to the skeptical darkness, their incandescent diamond heads reflecting (translating) haloes of swaying wet flame in every pool. Now, the palace was a degenerative paradise. With my fervid and sunstroked imagination, I felt the primal need to fill in the vacant historical space and reconnect curated rubble with embellished stories of faded dynasties and lost bodies, my daydreams stuck somewhere between the archive and the id.

次に/Next:

1. To see all the places Jackson has lived, go to page 38.
2. Best. Fucking. College. Anthems. Of. All. Time. On page 155.
3. Globetrotting, Jet-Setting/to avoid professional bed-wetting/carnival barkers of the American tribe/these cities of the world for my laid-back vibe/cuz every trip's a hajj and every hive's alive/you better come and kick it on page two-seven-five. Actually I lied. It's 217, but that didn't rhyme.
4. Wow, that rap was bad. In the '80s sense of the word, of course! Anyway, let's find out how the word "hapa" saved Jackson's soul on page 193.

48. Things I Daydream About Sometimes (or Used to)

1. LB calling me from work and telling me she's pregnant, my tears short-circuiting my phone

2. Editors beating the shit out of each other at the Frankfurt Book Fair as they argued about who was going to buy my next novel

3. Ex-girlfriends Googling me and then shaking their heads because they realize they married the wrong dude and/or that my shit got better with age or . . .

4. LB sleeping like a broken angel, her hair splayed on the pillow, the natural light creeping through the blinds and casting a halo on her face

5. Former classmates wiping their eyes (or shaking their heads) after reading one of my short stories in *The New Yorker* or . . .

6. Frenemies and long-term haters finding my website and then shouting at the screen: *He looks exactly the same! Does he even age?* Answer: Beige don't age

7. Readers masturbating to the sex scenes in my novels (they don't need to tell me, just knowing it makes me happy)

8. Q-tip, Kate Moss, and Leonardo DiCaprio inviting me to lunch at Little Pine* after reading this memoir, where we meet up with my good

friend and fellow hapa, Ivory, who arrives with a baby rabbit sleeping in the breast pocket of her blazer

9. Notre Dame and USC playing each other in the next college football championship

10. Pops calling me out of the blue ~~and telling me he loved my piece in the~~ ~~*Atlantic*~~

11. Carrying a thick wad of cash around like MJ and then buying strangers Christmas presents

12. Buying my mom a house in Santa Barbara

13. Living in Berlin, Tokyo, Paris, Vienna, Stockholm, Seoul, Shanghai, or Barcelona

14. Robbing the Beverly Hills G-Star in the middle of the night dressed in an all-black G-Star outfit

15. Living in the South Loop, Venice Beach, Harlem, or Jordaan

16. Living on Mars or traveling to another solar system

17. My ancestors smiling at me on the other side

18. The image of Morrissey playing Ping-Pong in his skivvies

19. A producer stopping me in the middle of the street in LA, handing me her business card, asking me if I speak any foreign languages, and then telling me I have the right look for a new indie dramedy that'll be filmed

in Silver Lake starring Q-tip, Kate Moss, and Leonardo DiCaprio (with food catered by Little Pine*)

20. Frank & Oak, G-star, Everlane, Gucci, and Burberry fighting each other to sponsor me if I'll agree to only wear their clothes exclusively

21. Common, Chance the Rapper, and Noname telling me they want to drop a track with me (Chicago love, baby!)

22. A functioning adult winning the 2020 general election who's not a white nationalist, nativist, business bro, or xenophobic misogynist, and who will read the daily Presidential Briefing once in a while

*Moby, feel free to send me that commission check whenever you get around to it, bro

次に/Next:

1. To eavesdrop on Jackson playing piano for his sobo (the humble version of "grandmother" in Japanese), go to page 100.
2. Is that Mendelssohn's "Wedding March?" No fucking idea. Best to go to page 182 and find out for yourself!
3. *The White Spies Who Loved Me in High School Because They Thought I Was White,* on page 165.
4. Next!

49. アメリカ人のお宅 (American Otaku) or When Words Make You Real

1.

When I was a boy, I felt disconnected from the kids in Traverse City. I played with Star Wars action figures and Japanese robots, creating intricate storylines inside my head about galactic invasion. I flipped through manga my fam brought back from Japan, even though I couldn't read kanji yet. I showed up to school dressed in a Miami Vice outfit where my classmates mocked me, a few threatened to beat me up, told me I looked "like a fag," which I didn't realize was a huge compliment (at least in LA) until I got older. I played ~~soccer~~ ~~futból~~ soccer and pretended I was a spy. On Saturdays, I went to my obāchan's trailer and played Mozart sonatas and *Sakura* on her piano. Sometimes, she sang along. One year, I dressed up as a samurai for Halloween. Another year, I was a ninja because come on! In junior high, I crushed on girls intensely when they smiled at me in the hallway. I always had a girlfriend, partially because they were open-minded, smart, affectionate, and understanding and partially because they always accepted me for who I was, someone who was part Japanese but never Asian. My Asianness wouldn't come until later.

2.

For most of my life, I daydreamed about living in Tokyo and having robot guardian angels. As a latchkey kid, I spent hours each day by myself at home after school and on weekends, playing Atari video games and old school RPGs on the family PC. I wrote three-chord pop songs on my synthesizer, played the piano in the dark, and biked through the neighborhood pretending I was competing in the Tour de France (the sportscaster's voice inside my head speaking with a fake French accent). I chanted itadakimasu before meals, which definitely raised eyebrows when the words slipped out of my mouth away from home. Once, I brought a Japanese medallion to class for show and tell after my parents returned from Japan. When I started to explain that my family was nikkeijin and that I had Japanese cousins, the teacher told me to sit down. More than anything, I wish someone had told me back then that there was a word to describe people like me who were illegibly Asian and mislegibly white, people like me who were culturally Asian in different ways but who read white (even if we didn't want to) to everyone except other mixed-race people who, like us, were also multilingual, bicultural, but not fluent in their diasporic tongue. I wanted, I needed people like me who would violate—almost religiously—the rules of phenotypic identity and racial community. I wish I'd known other hapa, mixed-race, and multiracial kids as a teenager who could have encouraged me to celebrate and not sublimate my own racial hyphenation. I wish that there had been bilingual Japanese schools in Northern Michigan when I lived there because I would have had a key to my own home now as an adult.

3.

Because I loved long baths as a kid, I didn't take my first shower until I was in sixth grade, which I found traumatic AF. One of my favorite meals growing up was Sapporo Ichiban ramen. My mom would add raw eggs, kamaboko, nori, shaved bonito, and scallions to the broth, transforming the meal of poor college students into a perfect Japanese dinner for four. Even the language we used to talk about our family was so different compared to our friends and neighbors. On my mom's side, my family had Japanese names that rolled off my tongue: Yukiyo, Eikichi, Chie, Shizuko, Hideo, Toshio. My obāchan had a thick Japanese accent when she spoke English. Sometimes, I had to translate for her when waiters got confused or snickered when she spoke. Sometimes, my hapa mom wore a Tina Turner wig and a miniskirt to work, just for kicks and my dad made Jackson Pollock t-shirts in the backyard with a toothbrush and acrylic paint, which he sold at Pick Wicker, the family store on Front Street, which was an endless source of gossip and adulation. In more ways than I understood at the time, my family was straight-up different, racially, professionally, and culturally. And though it took me twenty years to grasp, I eventually realized in college that I was more than just another Nisei after school special. For most of my life growing up, I wanted to understand which parts of me were based on how I looked to the rest of the world and which parts were based on who I was on the inside, including the Asian part no one could see (which, by the way, is the entire premise of my novel, *Ninjas of My Greater Self,* which New York publishers weren't interested in). As it turned out, confusion was the easiest part about being a nerd, a sensitive fashionista, a diehard romantic, a gestational artist, a hapa pretty boy, and a secret Asian trying to escape the beautiful but suffocating, anglonormative mid-city where he was born.

4.

I didn't understand until much later that like my hapa mom and my obāchan, I'd always been different than the white communities I'd lived in, at least until I'd lived in New York, Seattle, Djibasso, Chicago, Buenos Aires, and LA. I learned that my cultural divergence was a source of continuous pain and disidentification, but also one of the coolest and most crucial aspects of my metamorphic identity, slowly emancipating me from the fairytale of cultural normalcy or white performativity. Being both a (secret) nerd and a (secret) Asian gave me the space to negotiate my own cultural, racial, professional, and gender identities: I was equal parts Asian, American, and European, rebel, born-again child, and total smartass, klutz and athlete, sensualist and intellectual, metrosexual, composer, inconsistent vegan, gamer, permanent student, lover boy, and travel junkie. I was the very definition of cultural hybridity, even though it would take me years to see the importance and the necessity of identifying as mixed-race in a country where race was a tool of scientific racism for classifying and dividing people into castes, social hierarchies, and gradations of colorism in order to privilege and center whiteness above all else.

5.

As a nerd and a hapa (pretending to be neither), I learned that violence was not intrinsically masculine or American even though we still define masculinity by its proximity to physicality, violence, economic power, and exteriority. In America, masculinity is treated as a static category, synonymous with silence, stoicism, the accumulation of wealth, anglonormative standards of cowboy ruggedness, the idolatry of domination and aggression, and the excessive use of violence to resolve conflict. This (culturally relative) definition is destructive because it simplifies—and in fact, rejects—the inherent complexity of my own hapa masculinities, ignoring my interiority but also flattening my Asianness in a way I reject. In the '80s, the nerd was the anti-male archetype, the skinny, zit-faced white dweeb in thick glasses wearing ugly cardigans and pocket protectors. The nerd was that Asian dude getting thrown into a locker and slapped around by Paleolithic white jocks in the hallway in that racist '80s movie we all laughed at (even though some of us felt ashamed afterwards). But Asian and mixed-race standards of masculinity subvert these default gender roles, helping me defy and deconstruct cookie-cutter templates of identity while also expanding the repertoire of my own racial, gender, and cultural subjectivities.

6.

I may have suffered alienation, erasure, and illegibility as a teenager, not to mention linguistic isolation since the word hapa didn't even exist yet in the mainland, but I would one day grow to love my own hyphenation, I would learn see my life as the quintessential story of multicultural America in all of its permutations, narratives, self-inflicted violence, and self-bending contradictions. I may not have the face of this country's Asian immigrant past, but I certainly had the face, the story, and the phenotype of its demographic destiny. It took me my whole life to understand not only why I was so different from my classmates, but also so vital to America's cultural biography as a growing multiracial liberal democracy stuck in the miasma of white settler utopian nostalgia. As a hapa artist, I'm literally rewriting the plot structure of the American story every single day with my own life, with the stories of my cultural, racial, and sexual fluidity, with the reimagining of my own identity, and with the timbre of my voice, which is partially my own timbre and partially the vibrato of my ancestors. Of course, I do this with intense love and devotion now, but also with yearning too for all the years I was miserably and irrevocably lost, always fractional, always splintered, always fragmented by a country that couldn't see my wholeness and couldn't honor my hyphenation either. It wasn't until I discovered words like *hapa, multiracial, mixed-race,* and *nikkeijin* later on in my life that I felt real in an existential sense. Until there's a word for you reconfigured by people like you who understand you, it's like you don't exist in this world. In a very literal sense, you need language to reify your existence and sanctify your struggle so that you can be real to those who only see you as a derogation.

次に/Next:

1. To read about the things Jackson would like to forget (but won't), go to page 59.
2. Dear Natalie Portman, I was wondering whether you'd be interested in going on a double date with LB and me to M Café (the Melrose one). I guess you could bring the Frenchie (pourvu qu'il ne jacasse point ni prenne toute la salade de chou kale à la sauce d'arachide). I know you're not vegan anymore, which I blame partially on the French ballerina, motherhood, and also maybe the dermatological benefits of salmon. We could meet on page 198 for a glass of red wine first and then head over afterwards for dinner. Just think about it.

    Affectionately yours (but not too affectionately yours, if you know what I mean, porque LB me mataría),

    —ジャクソン
    Jackson Bliss, PhD (too much, right?).

3. To watch Jackson do a séance in a bowl of Miso soup, go to Tarot Parlor #126
4. Or just turn the page.

50. A Brief History of My Celebrity Crushes

1. When I was twelve, I crushed hard on **Whitney Houston** ("I wanna dance with somebody!").

2. Also in my early teens, I had the hots for **Alyssa Milano** (but who didn't?).

3. At Interlochen Arts Academy, I had a crush on a brilliant, slightly eccentric, but also completely gorgeous student named Ida. Eventually, this real-life crush morphed into a celebrity crush for **Mary-Louise Parker** in *Fried Green Tomatoes*, even though her character was obviously queer and she eventually got plastic surgery that erased the thing that once reminded me of Ida, who once lived in the same city I did.

4. I was completely enamored with **Uma Thurman** after watching *Dangerous Liaisons* on VHS. In related news, I wanted to be a French count.

5. I lost it when I saw **Mariah Carey's** *I Don't Wanna Cry*.

6. After watching *Trois Couleurs: Blanc*, I had dreams about **Julie Delpy** for like a week, which I never told my girlfriend at the time about. The best part of my dreams was that Julie Delpy and I did nothing but hang out at cafés on the Seine and argue about America.

7. After stumbling on a few episodes of *Ally McBeal*, I fell briefly but intensely for **Lucy Liu**.

8. In college, I crushed hard on **Natalie Portman** after seeing her in *Everyone Says I Love you*. That crush actually never went away, man. When I saw *Garden State* in Portland, I actually thought: *Fuck, forget about literary fiction. I need to write screenplays*, and when I saw her in that SNL gangster rap video, I swear to God, my crush multiplied by a hundred. Even to this day, every time LB sees an ad with Natalie Portman on it for French perfume or Hollywood flicks, she gets feisty real fast. In LA, I even sent Natalie Portman a short letter inviting her on a double date with LB and me for dinner to M Café, back when she was still vegan and I still believed in six degrees. That was the only letter I've ever written a celebrity. Immediately after sending it, I felt creepy, then defensive, and later sad.

9. After watching *Lost in Translation*, a movie that most of my APIA friends hate (except the Japanese ones), I had an intense crush on **Scarlett Johansson**, though it was impossible to separate Scarlett Johansson from her character, and her character from Sofia Coppola's screenplay, which I think says as much about Sofia Coppola's character development as it does about Scarlett Johansson's acting ability. This crush died a painful death, however, after *Ghost in the Shell*.

10. In college, I had an intermittent crush on **Lisa Lopes** (aka Left Eye) from TLC, especially after watching "Waterfalls" over and over again on MTV. It had something to do with her squeaky voice, her bangs, and her Latina pixie vibe.

11. After watching *Belle Époque, Abre Los Ojos*, and *Todo Sobre Mi Madre*, I became totally smitten with **Penélope Cruz**. The freckles on her nose used to kill me. Ditto with her madrileño accent. The day I learned that Tom Cruise and she broke up was the day I knew she was clearly too strong and too smart for Maverick.

12. **Queen Bey**, though none of us are worthy of anything except building sandcastles for her that wash away.

次に/Next:

1. To sip some maté with Jackson, go to Plaza Serrano on page 201. Be sure to bring a book of your guru on the cover.
2. To see Jackson and his brother eating Chinese food on Christmas Eve, go to page 86.
3. Literature curriculums have been colonized by dead white men for eternity, and our flawed narrative hero of this post-modern memoir is no exception to the rule as you'll find out on page 165.
4. ~~Or just turn the~~ paging reader, paging reader, there is a call for you on telephone #201.

51. Twelve Mate Sips

1. Cure the mate: if your mate is a gourd (and it better damn be), you have to cure it first. Think of Louis Pasteur and Jonas Salk. This will make you feel vaguely scientific. Fill the mate with yerba and hot water. Make sure the water isn't angry since boiling water makes the yerba taste bitter like people who cling to guns and religion. A half an hour later, dump out the water and fill the mate up again to the metal ring and leave it there for twenty-four hours. The next day, rinse the mate with hot water (no soap) and turn it upside down to dry. This is your countdown to a quintessential Argentine addiction.

2. Buy a stainless-steel thermos: armed with a good thermos, you can drink mate anytime and anywhere in Cap Fed. Mate will become your magic trick. Snap your fingers and you'll have the Holy Grail of stimulants. You refill your mate with hot water with the thermos you bought at a negocio near Catedral (even though you've never seen a church anywhere). After the woman on Florida Avenue charged you forty pesos, you said you'd take it for twenty-five. She swallowed her syllables. —My friend down the block charges *fifty* pesos, she stressed. You grumbled and forked over the cash, convinced you were getting conned. A week later you saw the same thermos inside a negocio window for a hundred pesos and suddenly realized the mate ritual hadn't softened your heart yet. Tomá tu tiempo, chico.

3. Be careful when you hold your mate in your hands: after you eat a white alfajor and split a juicy mandarin orange that explodes sunshine onto your t-shirt, a shirtless man walks up to you out of the blue with threatening facial stubble. He's holding a book of his guru in his hand and pointing at your tats. He talks for twenty minutes without

breathing. You don't get a word in, which never happens. As you wait for him to stop talking, you wait until he leaves before offering the mate to your girlfriend. She puts the metal straw to her lips and smiles like a crackhead.

4. Choose the right yerba: this is like choosing the right wine for dinner or the right friend for company. Sometimes, you want your yerba vigorous and strong like a gladiator. La Merced's *De Monte* yerba is powerful and bare-knuckled. Other times, you want your mate smooth and earthy like a mouthful of sweet grass. The red label of Jesper soothes you. And there really are twigs in the yerba, which makes you feel like a gerbil.

5. Carry it with you wherever you go: you don't know it yet, but drinking mate is a lifestyle, not a drink. You can buy drinks at any kiosco in Palermo SoHo, but a lifestyle is something you cultivate, assembling a series of habits that slowly define you. Mate makes you orally gifted (the bombilla is a steel straw after all) and patient (the water has to be the perfect temperature, otherwise you'll scorch the fuck out of your mouth and the yerba will taste like a fireplace). Drinking mate creates community since pulling out your gourd is always a potential invitation. Drinking mate also becomes a contemplative ritual. Inside your apartment in Palermo Viejo, you listen to boxes of produce being unloaded at the Coto loading dock across the street. You make your girlfriend promise you'll never stop taking time out of your life to drink mate together after you return to Chicago (which you don't honor back in the States). She nods and reaches for the mate. You wonder if she's heard a thing you've said.

6. Addiction: when you skip a day of mate, your head becomes a Seattle winter, but when you heat up water on the stove, your spirit rises up like smoke on a biblical altar. The sky in your brain always clears up after the first sip.

7. Drugged time: there are plenty of parks in Buenos Aires, but you don't visit most of them because you need the respite of shade when the sunlight eats its own. Because the two of you hate sweating and also sunlight (because you have gothy souls), you stick to Plaza de Serrano in Palermo SoHo, Parque de las Herras in Recoleta, and Plaza San Martin in Microcentro. These are the places where time slows down as if someone had slipped a roofie into the wine glass of mechanical time.

8. Swallow nature: as you drink mate, you inhale grass and leaves that come from the Argentine campo. Your yerba has twigs in it, actual pieces of wood that slowly expand each time you fill your mate with hot water from your underpriced thermos. The ritual of drinking mate connects you to the countryside. You tell yourself that you are closer to Argentina than your white expat friends who flush through Cap Fed like bleach poured on a bloody cutting board after another asado.

9. Ignite fellowships: the mate ritual is so simple. Always offer your friends mate first. It's rude to keep that pleasure to yourself, unless you're being harassed with a man with threatening facial stubble who carries a book of his guru and doesn't pause to breathe. Each person drinks mate from the bombilla, sucking until the gourd is dry. You'll meet your closest friends at Parque de las Herras and melt in the tenuous shade together, passing your mate around in a circle like a blunt. You'll walk to Parque Palermo with your girlfriend and drink mate on a bench, eating honey bars, chocolate slices, and Mandarin oranges in the shade while a porteña lies on the grass in a thong, which you'll pretend not to notice.

10. Redundant time war: one day, a shirtless man with menacing twelve o'clock shadow marches up to you and talks for twenty minutes about nothing because he recognizes your tranquility, sensing your emotional ergonomics with LB. As he grips a wrinkled book with his guru on the

cover like people who use guns and religion after every sip of bitter yerba (which always comes from the angriest water), you grip your perfectly cured mate tight in your hand. You know you're violating the sacred law of the mate fellowship, but you don't fucking care. You want your girlfriend to smile when she sips from the bombilla, not run away.

11. Mate as aphrodisiac: sometimes, mate makes you want to take your clothes off and liberate yourself like a porteña in a thong you pretended not to notice a couple weeks ago so you can melt on a park lawn where the sun is warm and gooey like a fresh medialuna (which complements mate nicely). You'll do anything to keep your pores radiant like a new hook-up when you sip. You'll do anything to make mate run down your throat like a long hot kiss.

12. Redemption: you almost believe that there is nothing that mate cannot save. You spend most the day inside your cramped and tiny apartment enjoying your vacaciones, far away from the IT professionals you teach English to who sexually harass each other and watch fútbol on their laptops as they pretend to work. You eat fried eggs on toast and check your email while days pass by like migrations of teal-winged swallows. With one thermos of hot (but never angry) water, a mate full of smooth yerba (and a little brown sugar), you and LB salvage a day blunted by lassitude. You walk together to your favorite park in Palermo and share cookies, brownie bites, and a granola bar drenched in honey that rots your teeth. Sometimes, the rules of mate are the rules of happiness: you need patience (like waiting for the water to cool down), connectivity (your love for LB, for Cap Fed, for the smell of the campo in your yerba), and serendipity (like a stubbly acolyte prattling about his guru or finding LB on My Space out of the blue or learning how to drink mate correctly from one of your students who brought his own gourd during an English conversation lesson to give you a taste of his country). LB and you stay cool in the respite of shade. There were days when it felt mandatory to sip your mate in a park full of chatty, unshaven, and half-dressed people on a scorching winter day. After all, happiness

should always involve the testimony of strangers and the soft declaration of tea. It should always come with a long metal straw. It should always have an undocumented power to compress time into a smooth object of desire and flush our skin with every refill, erasing the rules of our American life with every first sip.

次に/Next:

1. When times ceases to exist in an African village in Burkina Faso (or on page 168).
2. To learn about Jackson's favorite songs in junior high, go to page 73.
3. If you're feeling kinda mean, clap your hands/if you're into bawling grad students, clap your hands/if you wanna see the damage in the land of purgatory, then you gotta flip to two-O-seven [clap clap].
4. I don't know what the hell is going on with my upstairs neighbor in apartment #3, so what do you say we just turn the fucking page, bro, because I can't deal . . .

52. North American Cities I'd Visit Every Year If My Future Agent Sold My Next Novel for a Million Dollars

1. LA (now that I moved back here, it doesn't hurt to write this anymore)
2. Vancouver
3. New York
4. Montréal
5. Both Portlandias
6. Phillie
7. Toronto
8. New Orleans
9. Ciudad de México
10. Québec City
11. Traverse City (but just to visit)
12. San Francisco
13. Honolulu
14. Pittsburgh
15. Austin
16. Seattle
17. Chitown (represent!)

次に/Next:

1. To read about the first time an Argentine boy stole his cell phone, go to page 45.
2. To see Jackson praying for rain in West Africa, go to page 105.
3. Jackson's first TPE (Twitter Personal Essay) available on page 219 for the first time!
4. To watch Jackson "experimenting" with his life in ways that would make a stoic Buddhist warrior blush←Total exaggeration, for the record, go to page 230.
5. To turn the page, just . . . turn the page.

53. Null and Void

1.

I was about to step inside New Haven's Union Station when an old Black guy with fuzzy grey hair and glasses stopped me on the sidewalk and asked me if I had a light. Though technically I'd stopped smoking once I'd started grad school, my bad habit resurfaced at the end of every semester like a repressed multiple personality. Mostly, it was the stress. I was almost done with my first semester at Yale, the reading period in full swing, when I pulled out my lighter with a little guilt and tried lighting his cigarette. It was a cold and blustery day, the wind extinguishing the flame every time I rolled the flint for him. As I became impatient, I grabbed his soft, wilted old hand and cupped it with mine, lighting his cigarette undisturbed. He took a big puff and exhaled. Then he nodded his head, smiled at me, and said, *Thank you, son.* By the time I was inside the train station, I was bawling my eyes out. If you've read a decent amount of this memoir, this probably won't surprise you, but it shocked me at the time because I was an author without a memoir.

2.

After I found a seat on the train, I tried to understand what was going on, but I didn't get where my tears were coming from. Maybe, I thought, it was the anxiety of having to write three 30-page essays in the next ten days. Maybe, it was my dread of seeing my on-again-off-again girlfriend in New York (mentioned in chapter 15) who I fought with every weekend like a professional scrapper, always anticipating the first blow that I knew was coming. Maybe, it was the dreary Connecticut weather finally getting inside my head at last, weather exactly like Dante's description of purgatory that I'd been reading about in my Divine Comedy seminar at the Divinity School. Maybe, I was just sad because I was a poor grad student from

Chicago who sometimes felt lost and out of place in New England where history was a thing to understand, celebrate, and revere instead of question, critique, and subvert. And maybe, I was just emotionally vulnerable that day for reasons I wasn't aware of. Whatever the reason, the tears poured out of me inside the station, on the escalator, and on the train where I looked out the window to avoid the confused and dismissive looks of commuters who wanted nothing to do with me.

3.

My dad is old school, which means he's horrendous at expressing his affection, unimpressed by my academic trajectory, and self-forgiving for his continuous absence in my life. While he's slowly learned to respect me as a man (I think?), we've never been close. When we hung out in Chicago, for example, I almost always initiated it. Because we're different politically, socially, racially, and professionally, we've also had to strain at times to understand each other. One feeling I've never been able to kick, however, even in adulthood, is that my dad doesn't appreciate my mind even though I'm better educated, better read, better traveled, more objective, more creative, and more empathetic than he is. Some parents can appreciate their kids, even if they turned out differently than they planned, but not mine. My intelligence isn't something they know how to respect, at least openly, maybe because they don't see its value or because it's just a massive irritant for them that makes their lives more complicated. Even now, I'm astounded by how often I feel dismissed, ignored, talked over, underestimated, and muted in their company, even when my knowledge and personal experience far exceeds theirs on a given topic. Part of the problem, I think, is simply one of framing.

I was a latchkey kid, so I only saw my parents for a couple hours a day during the week, most of our time spent in the kitchen and the TV room. I honestly don't remember my parents hugging me as kid, though I'm sure it happened rarely. I just don't remember their affection. I've never felt my dad was proud of me, except when I graduated from high school, but even then, I dyed my hair a deep burgundy in a gesture of grunge rebellion, which he hated but also caused in more than one way. Even when I gave my MFA reading at Notre Dame, I remember not being surprised that he didn't show up even though I asked him to. Little by little, I've learned to overcome most of my issues with him by not expecting anything, which no one should have to do with their dad, even an absent one, and this is why male approval has remained a backdoor vulnerability of mine to this day. It's sad, I know, but even now, I still seek the love, the respect, and the acknowledgement of older men, even complete strangers, who might see my worth and remind me that I'm lovable, smart, and talented, if only for a split second. I hate myself for it, but I still text my dad on Father's Day and I still send him Christmas cards and his silence tells me everything I need to know about the relationship we never had. At least now, I have my words. I use them to build snowmen and igloo in the winter storm to keep watch and protect me from the slow rumble of the avalanche.

次に/Next:

1. Your game shelf, just like your book self, tells us so much about you. So, what do we learn about Jackson on page 108?
2. Grab some Kleenex and cry a little with Jackson on page 243.
3. To take a break, dream a little, and make some origami, go to page 57.
4. To figure out what a Gen X college student listened to, skedaddle your ass to page 155.
5. Or just turn the page.

54. Languages I'd Like to Study Someday (Because Polyglots Gonna Polyglot)

1. Portuguese
2. Catalan
3. Russian
4. Arabic
5. Turkish
6. Sanskrit
7. Aramaic
8. Ancient Greek
9. Swahili
10. Cajun French
11. Chiac
12. Italian
13. German
14. ASL

次に/Next:

1. WTF does "hapa" mean anyway? I dunno, but page 296 seems like a good place to start.
2. To see Jackson and his brother eating Chinese food for Christmas Eve, go to page 86.
3. To hear Jackson's advice for his 13-year-old self, dial 867-5309 and ask for Jenny.
4. Le voici, mesdames et messieurs ! Ça va faire mal, mais hélas, la vie est dure comme ça. Pour ceux qui s'intéressent à assister à la décapitation publique de Jackson (c'est-à-dire, tous les masochistes, hein ?), s'il vous plaît, allez à la page 159. Sinon, restez là et bouder tant qu'il vous plaira.
5. Or just turn the bloody page, Mr. Frogger!

55. The Lost Distance

1.

My friend Sevda said that Azeris aren't religious. Some were rediscovering Islam, she'd explained, but the concept of God was still an anomaly in the former Soviet Republic. Sevda, on the other hand, was a quiet iconoclast in Azerbaijan, which is why I liked her so much. She was always standing at the cultural periphery, it seemed, self-examining herself and her country in the full-length mirror of its own history. When we talked, her thoughts eventually left Zarat and circled the polluted Caspian Sea before heading towards the Iranian border to the south, beyond the Armenian-occupied region of Nagorno-Karabakh infested with landmines and military bunkers, gliding northwest over the scenic mountain villages of Armenia and past the Christian churches of Tbilisi, and then finally heading southwest to Turkey, the idealized motherland for many Azeris, the country where I became an adult (cf. Chapter 35).

2.

On most afternoons, Sevda and I drank chai and talked about Rumi, Turkic grammar, and the history of Azerbaijan, a revolutionary thing to do for a man and woman not courting each other, even in 2003. Other times, we talked about the people we loved (or failed to love enough), the countries we'd visited, and the cities we would never see. Sevda became one of my closest confidantes in Zarat. As a young Muslim woman following the five pillars of Islam sincerely and reading the Koran with an open heart, her religiosity made her unique in Azerbaijan where lingering Soviet atheism blurred effortlessly with Turkish secularism, south Caucasian superstition, and hardline Shi'a Islam. One of the reasons we got along so well is because neither of us fit perfectly in the countries we were born. We both inhabited the cultural margins. Our friendship was a delicate bond of mutual respect,

211

cross-cultural exchange, and authentic rapport. We also shared a fascination with the other side of the world and a personal history of alienation in our own countries.

3.

The closest we ever became was after I told Sevda about my religious experience flying to Istanbul. —It was the first time in my adult life I was traveling, I said, sure, I'd driven to Montréal, Québec City, and Toronto with friends in college. I had a vague memory of visiting Jamaica, the Cayman Islands, and México as a boy. But I'd never been to Europe or Asia. It was the first time I was traveling as an *adult* and by myself.

—And so? she asked, her trademark follow-up question to almost any statement.

—I was so ecstatic I got scared.

—Why?

I hesitated. —I guess I was afraid that something bad was gonna happen, like the plane was gonna crash or I'd have a heart attack or PKK terrorists were gonna hijack the plane. I was going on one hour of sleep at the time, so I wasn't thinking straight.

—But why did you fear those specific things? she asked.

—I was *so* close to something amazing, something life-changing, and I felt like I didn't deserve it.

—Wow, she said, raising her eyebrows.

—But just then, something amazing happened on that flight. As I was freaking out, my chest heaving dramatically, suddenly out of nowhere, tears streamed down my cheeks. I felt this indescribable, almost numinous state of peace and then the next thing I knew, my lips were muttering these words:

God is love. Love is God. There is no difference between the two.

God is love. Love is God. There is no difference between the two.

A few things I should mention about this story: for one, I didn't read *The Story of My Experiments with Truth,* Gandhi's autobiography, until

2004 when I was an Americorps volunteer, so I wasn't ripping off the Mahatma. For another, I was (am) a huge fucking cynic when it comes to organized religion, so breaking out into a mantra was completely out of character for me. Almost absurd, really. But those words found me, not the other way around, and my last year of college changed radically because of my intercontinental epiphany.

Sevda and I had tears welling up now. We cried, our tears scattering like buckshot.

She wiped her eyes and swallowed. —I could feel your emotion as you told me your story. I could feel what you felt.

We who were always hiding in the cultural periphery like outlaws, always squatting in the limbo of hope and seclusion, self-discovery and self-alienation, always trying to work out the mystery of the fragmented world inside us that always got so distorted when we reflected those images of ourselves back into the shimmering surfaces of the material world.

We hugged each other and sniffled a little bit, our friendship violating every rule of decorum in that tiny Azeri village just a few steps from the Caspian Sea.

4.

A month later, Sevda was shouting at me in exasperation. —Jackson, it's going to take an *hour* to get there. We can't drive back in the dark!

—Coming, I said, throwing on an oversized jacket that was an artifact from my hip-hop days. I said goodbye to Maribaum and Shahbaba, my host parents, who I'd been living with for the past two months. I told them in my primitive Azeri that we'd return before nightfall. Sevda, Kristin, Gene, and I hopped in our rented car. Sevda gave directions to the driver. Seconds later, we cruised down the highway. This was my first and only road trip in Azerbaijan with friends I would never see again once I returned to Portland. I haven't heard from Sevda since the day I left. Supposedly, she got married to a hyper-religious guy and cut herself off from her foreign friends, which is the downside of religious orthodoxy, sadly.

5.

Our driver parked and we walked towards the mountain trail. Besh Barmag was known as the five-finger mountain because of its resemblance to a closed fist. The peaks looked uncannily similar to untrimmed fingernails. Besh Barmag was also a holy site that practicing Muslims traveled to for the hajj. I carried a plastic bag of traditional treats Kristin's host mom had given her that honestly tasted like sugar cookies made from dirt. No one was hungry, so I carried the bag like an obsessive environmentalist looking for a trashcan that never came.

6.

We walked until we came to a crude stone staircase that wound up one side of the mountain, going on forever like a verbose dream sequence. It was like standing at the Stairway to Heaven, the steps leading up to the sky before vanishing in the clouds. We climbed up the uneven and misshaped stone staircase, sometimes scaling awkward ladders with rungs spaced so far apart, you wondered if a different race of Azeris had once lived here. We stopped several times to catch our breath or to pay our respects to pilgrims who'd died during their hajj here. During one break, an old Azeri woman told Sevda the story of an 18-year-old girl who had died suddenly climbing up Besh Barmag, her face now immortalized in a haunting monochromatic portrait carved into a marble memorial.

7.

We slogged our way up the staircases, one step at a time, Roma women greeting us at every stage and altitude. They would rush towards us like shriveled orphans, their discolored and prune-dry hands opening up in gestures of alms. They mumbled indecipherable prayers to us in makeshift Arabic and singsong Azeri. We handed out Manats generously in the beginning. Later on, as we passed more and more Roma women, each sitting in her individual station, each requesting donations for blessings, tiny cosmologies, and pilgrimage history lessons, we ran out of money and then patience. Still, their stories entranced us, keeping us hostage in a tower of mythology. I don't remember her exact words, but they went something like this: *Here, an angel sliced the mountain with his sword*, Sevda translated, *and this small valley produces the miracle of tears, crying once a week and here Jackson, you must walk around the boulder three times with your back facing north and after the third time you must take a pebble from on top of the boulder, donate a few Manats, make a wish, and walk around once more.* I grabbed a pebble, asking god to deliver me home safely to Portland so I could be reunited with a girlfriend who'd invited three guys to live in our house in my absence: one guy she'd fucked years ago before we met, another who used to be her drinking buddy and make-out partner (in that order), and still another she'd been lusting after since college. To say that our relationship felt precarious to me all the way in Azerbaijan was a fucking understatement. But I loved her and didn't want to give up on our relationship without a fight. Two weeks, I left Azerbaijan for good with intermittent heart palpitations and a wad of Manats I couldn't exchange at the Baku airport, a perfect collective metaphor of my time there and my relationship in PDX.

8.

At Besh Barmag, I put the nondescript stone in my pocket underneath my I.D. and a small wad of Soviet-style hard candy that dragged my pants down like a homie. We crossed a plank to the apex of the mountain and looked all the way down. From our aerial view, the countryside was split into villages and industrial zones, paved and dirt roads, salinized beach and polluted water, everything organized perfectly like a high-contrast train set for a family of giants. To the north, I saw my beat-up elementary school in Zarat where I taught English. Farther in the distance was Siyazan, a town with boutiques and stores that villagers traveled to via marshutka to buy groceries and supplies. Farther in the distance to the South was Sumqayit, one of Azerbaijan's biggest and most polluted cities, which left an odd, slightly burnt smell in your clothes when you visited. Surrounding us on all sides was the glorious, but dead Caspian Sea. The water was a deceptive and impossible cobalt blue, hiding the petrochemical damage of a million oil tankers heading to and from Turkmenistan and Kazakhstan and decades of toxic sludge that obsolete Soviet chemical factories had excreted into the salt lake. High above the expansive countryside, standing on the fingers of Azerbaijan's holy fist that disappeared into the clouds, we'd finally gained access to a god view of Eurasia, everything so lovingly divided and organized into separate puzzle pieces and geographical biographies down below. The view on top of Besh Barmag would turn out to be a microcosm of my American life: intelligible and beautiful only from a distance, a broken mountain top inflated by spiritual longing and latent acrophobia, and a country haunted by a history of suppressed violence and cultural eradication, every resurfacing memory covered in the stage makeup of creation myths, poverty, and martyrdom.

次に/Next:

1. Che, para echar un vistazo en la vida porteña de Jackson en cap fed (de Buenos Aires) durante la estación lluviosa, andá a la página 121.
2. Take a Virtual Tour of Morocco on "North Africa Travels" at ten here on Channel 189.
3. To see Jackson living in parallel worlds, go to page 75.
4. Or just turn the page, Betty!

56. Cities Outside of North America I'd Visit Every Year If My Future Agent Sold This Memoir for a Million Dollars (because a Boy Can Dream)

1. Tokyo
2. Paris
3. Barcelona
4. Berlin
5. Istanbul/Baku
6. Ōsaka
7. Vienna
8. Buenos Aires
9. Prague
10. Sapporo
11. Copenhagen
12. Rome
13. Seoul
14. Lhasa
15. Budapest
16. Kyoto
17. Dubrovnik
18. Hong Kong
19. Papeete
20. Stockholm
21. Amsterdam
22. Aix
23. Dubai
24. London
25. Shanghai
26. Moscow

次に/Next:

1. To read the things Jackson used to pretend as a kid, go to page 30.
2. *The Hapa Spy Who Loved Me*, on page 201.
3. Some of Jackson's Favorite High School Anthems, tonight on Channel 138.
4. Are you a mixed-race person looking for happiness, marriage, & genealogy? Then come on down to Ōsaka and find that missing link. The 224 train is your key to unlocking yourself.
5. Orj us ttu rnt hep ag e.

57. Cloud in Trousers: A (Revised) Twitter Thread

1. My mom texted this picture today & I suddenly saw my old life as a Gen X college student: here was one of my mixtapes, crammed with songs by The Smiths, James, Cocteau Twins, A Tribe Called Quest, Dead Can Dance, Wynton Marsalis, Billie, The Sundays, Deep Forest, & Montell Jordan.

```
              What $80.00 could buy for a young child

     I.   Some exceptional C.D.'s
          A.  Beethoven
              1.Symphony no. 6 in F major (Pastorale)
              2.Any of his piano sonatas
          B.  Bach
              1.Any organ works
                 a. Pasagalia in C minor
              2.Any Cantatas or Motets
              3.Any preludes or fugues
          C. Mauhler
              1.Symphony no. 1 in D minor
              2.Symphony no. 5 in C# minor
              3.Symphony no. 9 in G minor
          D. Any Prokofiev pieces
          E. Any Rachmanioff pieces
     II. Clothing
          A.Gap
              1. Pants
              2. Sweaters
              3. socks
              4. sportjackets
              5. oxfords
     III. Books
          A. Joanna's The Idiot
          B.Other intellectual books
          C. other Dostoevskey books
              1. Crime and Punishment
              2. The Karsokov Brothers
```

2. This note/list was typed on a Brother word processor with a screen that was barely two inches, had no spell check (hence, the horrendous misspellings I was too lazy to correct even though they grated on my nerves), & was enumerated like a debate brief, because I was once a HS policy debater, even went to Nationals for the Southern California district.

3. I became obsessed w/ classical music after I started taking piano lessons in 6th grade, played the third movement of Mozart's A major sonata for my recital, played Bach for my おばあちゃん. In college, I became obsessed with Russian culture, I read Dostoevsky, Tolstoy, Pushkin, Chekhov, Nabokov, Pasternak, Mayakovski, Beli, Gogol, Lermontov, & Turgenev.

4. My Slavophilia extended through college with Rachmaninov preludes and "Rhapsody on a Theme by Paganini," Prokofiev's piano concerti, the "Romeo & Juliet" overture & symphonies by Tchaikovsky, & Scriabin études, especially the D# minor one. Eventually, I became obsessed with Soviet propaganda art, chess, & Mayakovski's double consciousness as a poet & propaganda writer.

5. I told my neighbors at French House (at Oberlin College) that I was a socialist just to fuck with them, I even taped a pic of Mao on the outside of my dorm door and superglued a cigarette coming from his mouth, but this was my standing joke. After I studied Marxist theory with the engaging AF Professor Blecher, my intrigue blossomed, but I never became a revolutionary leftist for the simple reason that I'm too urban and bougie, and also I knew that artists, intellectuals, writers, college students, and professors would be the first people arrested in any proletarian dictatorship because history.

6. Reading this note, I have so many questions now: what intellectual books did I have in mind and how deeply entrenched in the Western Canon were they? Who the hell was Joanna? Was this the Joanna I knew from the Speech & Debate team at San Dieguito? Had she lent me her copy of *The Idiot*? Who was this list for, my mom? For me? And why did I self-infantilize myself?

7. Was this note just the world's most pretentious birthday list? Had I written this for myself in high school to give myself goals for my first summer in Chicago and beyond into college? Who was I trying to be? My best guess is that I wrote this note after moving to Chicago from SoCal and experiencing my first withdrawal symptoms from the Golden State.

8. At the time, I felt like I was behind everyone else: my vocab wasn't great, there were so many books I hadn't read, all my Speech & Debate friends were better read than I was even if I was more eloquent, they had more stable lives, all of them had a personal literary engagement I'd lacked but wanted to correct, so this list could have been part of my

attempt as a 17-year-old to evolve quietly on my own before I started classes at Loyola Academy.

9. In a family where no one read books, where I was compulsively alone that first summer in Chicago, my dad leaving me in the scorching apartment all day & night as he worked & then went out eating & drinking with coworkers, coming home between 9 pm and 1 am with Styrofoam containers of to-go food that I devoured, hurt at being ignored, I taught myself to read for knowledge, pleasure, time-travel, and inspiration.

10. My dad often got ready for bed as I scarfed down wedge fries. It became obvious that he didn't want me, had wanted to send me back to live with my mom who had moved from CA to FL with Mike, her partner, my teenage life completely in flux now, estranged, irredeemably broken by the broken promises of the adult world.

11. And so the books in this list, my obsession with classical music, my wish-list of gap clothes as a way of visually re-entering a society I felt totally excluded from & couldn't control, the refuge I found in playing piano, was all an imperfect attempt at creating order and art and beauty for myself precisely because my life was in shambles.

12. I was sad, poor, & confused back then. I didn't know Chicago yet, I didn't know we had an AC unit as I sweat my ass off every day, I didn't understand how much of my world I controlled, and I didn't understand why my fam was split between MI, IL, & FL.

13. I didn't understand why CA still lingered in my soul as the last place I felt understood in, where I'd fallen in love & lost my virginity to J, gone to nationals in debate, & skipped class w/ friends to drive up the coast listening to Chris Isaak's "Wicked Game."

14. This list from HS & this mixtape from college that my mom had sent me a pic of, was my adolescent prayer of becoming, my transformation from a hapa pretty boy into a global citizen who knew he was three steps behind everyone else. I had so much to learn.

15. This list was a source of consolation that would ironically stay with me for the rest of my life like a drunken Tijuana tattoo I almost got before moving to Chicago. This list was my superficial ars poetica, my aspiration & my vocation in microcosm, a way of plotting out my life.

16. My life was constantly falling apart after four high schools in four years, after being the new kid each & every year, after longing to sit still & become a whole human being who was safe, loved, understood, appreciated, and protected after passing through time zones and alternate destinies as my parents' unwilling sidekick.

17. This list was the only thing I could control back then, my first honest attempt at finding consolation in my own words, by controlling my own moral education, by finding consolation in storytelling, austerity, discipline, & aspiration, by finding consolation in the power of my own narrative and voice, in sadness & in song.

次に/Next:

1. To read about the things Jackson would like to forget (but won't), go to page 59.
2. After watching *Mozart in the Jungle*, you suddenly realize that you want mate again. You're not Argentine, of course, so you feel a bit strange about this, but then again, neither is Gael García Bernal, so what do you have to lose, except 201 friends?
3. Learn how to live on just salad and bread in West Africa on page 168.
4. Or just turn the page.

58. Midwestern Nomenclature I Used to be Embarrassed About but Now Fully Embrace

1. *Pop* to describe soda

2. *Gym shoes* for sneakers (though kicks will always be kicks regardless)

3. *Brats* as an umbrella term for all hot dogs

4. *Aquaduct* to describe an overpass

5. *Breezeway* for outdoor corridor

6. *Hang the W* as a way of saying "Go Cubbies!"

7. *Finna go* for "gonna go," though only when code-switching

8. *Guyz* for *y'all* since I can't say *y'all* without feeling like a fake asshole, even though it's gender neutral in a way I really appreciate, so I'm left with *guyz,* which of course, sounds like *guys,* but in my heart, I know the truth

次に/Next:

1. Things Jackson used to pretend as a kid on page 30.
2. The day that Jackson said goodbye to his freedom forever (←Not actually true at all) on page 182.
3. Hurry boys, she's waiting there for you, an obvious '80s reference to one of the greatest songs with some of the most ridiculous and problematic lyrics of all time, available on page 99.
4. oR JuSt tUrN tHe pAgE.

59. Dense Mysterious Object

1.

I dug up my roots at the overripe age of thirty-seven because the struggle to find my Japanese family was a chronic sickness I couldn't cure and couldn't ignore. After my obāchan passed away in 2003, I sent my Japanese family emails in botchy ローマ字(romaji). I never heard back, so I never knew whether my Japanese family had never received my emails or whether my questionable Japanese language skills confused the hell out of them. Ten years later out of curiosity and confusion, I sent my aunt Shizuko and my cousin Eikichi two letters written in improved-but-still-ten-year-old Japanese to the addresses my obāchan had written down on a piece of wrinkled school paper years ago. They were returned a couple weeks later. Their reentry into my life felt like the final rejection of my Japanese heritage. My obāchan's list of family addresses was now completely obsolete. As a last resort, I looked my cousin up on Facebook and found him in exactly three seconds, posing in front of a car the way that Asian men like to do as a visual performance of class mobility. Social media helped me find my Japanese fam in a way that the USPS couldn't. For a brief moment, the ruptured 円相(ensō circle) inside my hapa soul (signifying emptiness, strength, and enlightenment) was healed, sutured by a tangible genealogy that had split at the seams after obāchan passed to the spirit world. I suddenly found a way to reconnect to the Japanese side of my family, the only side I could directly trace, connect to, and understand, if just barely with my humbled Japanese skills.

2.

Like most white people I knew, the French, Irish, and English sides of my family were abstract bedtime stories of lost nobility and blurry family crests because white people love discovering ancestral links to forgotten royalty, it

224

makes them feel more important by association. Rediscovering a family coat of arms always make white people feel less mundane and less economically exploited by the economic system their ancestors helped build in America. The stories of the European side of my family are both romantic and conflicting: supposedly, there was a tiny village in Normandy called Blay (spelled Bleis in the 11th Century), which became a toponymic surname for its villagers. I guess our ancestors in Worcestershire were called de Blez. I guess there was the medieval English word, Blisse, which fits my own temperament perfectly except during pandemics, white nationalist rallies, and economic crises. I guess English immigrants with my last name sailed to Massachusetts, Rhode Island, Connecticut, and New York as pioneers, adventurers, and colonizers. The problem with these stories is that they have always felt apocryphal even though they're historically accurate to the best of my knowledge. The problem with these stories is that they feel like tales invented for the white imagination as a consolation for an unexceptional life. The literature scholar in me wanted to historicize, situate, and deconstruct them the instant I'd finished reading them. It's not that I doubted the Bliss family genealogy per se, it's just that being 日系人 (nikkeijin) and 二世 (Nisei) required no historical research, no archival excavation, and no narrative reimagining beyond a simple phone call. My mom and obāchan were the artifacts of my Japanese ancestry, not a website built in the '90s or a zoomed-in microfiche entry from ancestry.com. Being Nisei had (still has) immediate benefits of tangibility, credibility, and traceability I find both reassuring and heartbreaking, and therefore more credible because it's easier to believe in a genealogy of pain over one of prestige. As the son of Japanese immigrants on my mom's side, the paint is still very wet, so the fingerprints of my Japanese ancestors are all over me, so to speak.

3.

LB and I took a JR train with Eikichi and Megumi (his wife), to feed the royal deer in Nara Park. Pesky little fuckers. We stopped by a local café, ate ぜんざいお汁粉 (sweet red bean soup), and sipped 玄米茶 (genmaicha) to stay warm. A few days later, I met my aunt Shizuko, my grandmama's closest sister, and her daughter Chie for the first time in the lobby of our little boutique hotel (thank god the interior was relatively cute, the shame of meeting in an ugly hotel lobby would have been too much). Seeing them for the first time changed my life. Until that moment, my Japanese family had always been more graphic memoir than autobiographical anime, a monochromatic storyline told in tiny chapters after every phone call and trip to Tokyo. We drank ocha and split a piece of Strawberry tooth-rot cake in the hotel café, talking and laughing in Nihongo and English. Afterwards, Eikichi and Megumi took us around 心斎橋 (Shinsaibashi) where I lost count of stylish Ōsaka girls dressed in elaborately matching outfits and corresponding purses, each one holding a phone in her hands, each one with a designer bag and/or a kawaii ぬいぐるみ (plush stuffed animal) keychain. The four of us walked to a shopping mall where we ate お好み焼き (okonomiyaki), quintessential Kansai food. The thick omelet crammed with enough shrimp, octopus, and fish to feed a family of six, sizzled before our eyes on the table griddle, drenched in okonomiyaki sauce and Japanese mayo, which the waiter had squirted from a distance like a sharpshooter. The food was so hot and so delicious it almost made me cry. After lunch, we took the subway to 大阪城 (Ōsaka Castle), pushing our way through gaggles of stylish Japanese girls texting distant friends: どこいるの？ I imagined them saying. We climbed up the stairs inside the castle and roamed around the museum. Halfway to the top, we drank amazake, a sweet, non-alcoholic sake, and inhaled the panoramic view of Ōsaka from the gated balcony. The wind blew our scarves into our faces, penetrating every layer of clothing and removing the LA sunshine from our bones.

4.

Later as we posed for pictures in front of the Ōsaka Castle from different angles and positions, we took a taxi to the space-age 梅田スカイビル (Umeda Sky Building), which looked like a Jetsons theme park (and later, the album cover of my first LP). We took the escalators up long and winding tubes to the sky. Outside on the rooftop, Ōsaka was a blustery and bone-chilling dream again, flushed with blurry violet and red skyscraper lights, a panoramic pachinko board of electric color droplets bleeding into a smeared cityscape. We retreated inside and ordered more ocha before taking the subway to my Japanese family's apartment, my first time meeting my entire Japanese family, at least the side closest to my obāchan. I sat inside their apartment after twenty years of listening to her story-talk about them like they were characters in an epic Japanese radio opera, reminding myself that I was really in Ōsaka chatting with aunt Shizuko, uncle Toshio, and my cousins Chie and Eikichi in my ten-year-old Japanese, playing with their chocolate brown puppy Lin-chan, eating Makizushi, and sipping sake. I drank ocha and laughed with my Japanese family. I lit incense and bowed my head at the family altar with Aunt Shizuko's guidance before learning the tea ceremony in the tatami room. I played cheesy John Lennon duets on the piano with Chie. For the first time in my adult life, I was linked directly to my Japanese heritage, rekindling my racial and cultural identity in the motherland, sharing my reunion with LB, the love of my life, our love witnessed by the only family I had ever known or understood, albeit distantly in this broken world of ours that had always been separated by an obese ocean, different languages, and multiple generations and time zones.

5.

In a small but permanent way, my time with my Japanese family helped me understand who I was and where I came from, at least the part that mattered the most to me. Seeing Kansai for the first time, the province of my ancestors, not to mention the streets of Ōsaka, where my obāchan lived for much of her life before America turned 日本人 (Japanese people) into laboratory rats for the Manhattan Project, changed my life forever. So did watching Japanese teenagers in hip-hop outfits posturing in アメ村 (AmeMura), filling our grocery bags with freshly sliced sushi, juice, snacks, and mochi at the local スーパー on New Year's Day, watching Japanese singing game shows, seeing my Japanese family in their own home (once just a collection of crude '80s snapshots), witnessing the language of their faces as they talked, and memorizing their distinct voices and speaking styles, their soft but expressive gestures. The autobiographical manga of my life story turned to anime and then live-action drama, a transformation which helped me understand my racial hyphenation better and simultaneously put in context obāchan's sexual assault, her cultural separation, and her feuding memory during the last weeks of her life, all metaphors for each other. This was the day my Japanese family became three-dimensional, my origami body shifting into new designs and new creatures of fragmentation before my eyes. Our shared experiences in Ōsaka had rejoined and interconnected us together for the first time in our culturally fragmented lives. It was as if the weightless story of my hapa life in America that I'd worn around my neck like a rusty amulet, that I'd raised above my head like a tiny galactic shield, had suddenly become infinitesimally real. The musty photo albums of my childhood, Mom's pictures of this same apartment, obāchan's color-blunt Polaroids of the family in Ōsaka, the multimodal daydreams of my adolescence, the chapters of my racial bildungsroman I'd written for my dissertation, my daydreams of moving to Japan as a boy, and the narrative morphology of my Japanese family throughout the years, they all smashed into each other. This trip was my inflection point. My Asianness (that illusive and narrative cosmology of the self I was always ignoring, misreading, and denying) was no longer an existential fairytale of self-invention anymore, but a tactile object of loss, denial, and reification in Kansai. My mixed-race identity became a hard, perfectly polished and mysterious Petoskey stone that I found in my back pocket of my skinny jeans after a long stroll through the Japanese city, a dense and smooth artifact I caressed with my thumb and then skipped across the Yodo River as the sun was crowning the industrial horizon, spreading its gospel in the wrapping paper sky that would soon rip apart once the stars poked peepholes into the lewd universe.

次に/Next:

1. To learn where Jackson went to feel safe as a kid, go to page 22.
2. To see how words could be shivs for Jackson's heart (what a goddamn sadist, what is WRONG with you?), go to page 103.
3. To see Jackson on a Beach in Southern California for Christmas, go to page 17.

4.   To take a break, dream a little, and make some origami, go to page 57.
5.   ページをめくって下さい。

60. My Experiments with Reality

1. Taking a vow of silence for one week (and breaking it only once to talk to a lonely girl on a beach in Encinitas who asked me to walk her home to her apartment in Leucadia)

2. Going on a 7-day juice fast that became a 6-day juice fast and eventually a 3-day juice fast (that ended with me slurping strawberries frantically like a crackhead)

3. Walking around Pioneer Square in Portland at 1/100 the natural speed for a full hour (and a million confused looks)

4. Making out with a handful of boys to see how it felt, for self-understanding, curiosity, greater self-awareness, exploration of desire, etc., etc.

5. Living in West Africa without electricity or running water (and not hearing English for weeks, except on BBC Radio)

6. Working in Buenos Aires and being paid in pesos

7. Living on the East Coast, West Coast, in the North, and the Midwest

8. Living without a TV for eleven years

9. Doing a Vipassana retreat and then bailing after three days to buy sandals (Oh, sue me and my metrosexual heart!)

10. Wearing my girlfriend's pink Laura Ashley dress as I mopped the kitchen floor to protest domestic labor (and also piss off/scare/confuse my dad, who had it coming)

11. Taking a road trip to New Orleans where I learned to drive stick shift

12. Getting high and walking around DTLA at night

13. Being on Food Stamps as an Americorps volunteer

次に/Next:

1.   To read a hilarious note that Jackson wrote to himself in high school, go to page 219.
2.   To read the things Jackson used to pretend as a kid, go to page 30.
3.   The hottest and raunchiest Moroccan daydreams, all available in HD on page 189.
4.   To see Jackson turn into a 30-something sitcom, go to page 63.
5.   Or just turn the page.

61. Lyrics Without Songs

It was an idyllic spring afternoon when my mom beat the shit out of me, the zeppelin inside my heart bursting into flames. Before I stepped inside the house, the treetops were drenched in untranslatable komorebi amid the rolling green hills of yesterday. Dandelion clocks disintegrated in a puff. Posters of paint-smudged fishing towns hung from living room walls of houses I passed on my bike. The fuzzy navel sunset spilled onto the parchment horizon. When my mom wailed on my body like a disobedient dog in the kitchen, I lost faith in the entire world. My adolescence became scented in its own fragility. The ground around me slowly disintegrated. I lay in a daze that night, daydreaming on my bed about the butterflies that had hovered over my bike like protective spirits. I craved a magic eraser for every mistake I'd made and every rule I didn't understand. I cried until the darkness shushed me to sleep.

My mom had told me not to play with Blain because he was *weird,* an argument that felt sophistical. As a hapa family, we were always treated as racial spies collecting intelligence for both sides of our racial identity unless we played white. I was biking around Traverse City, a small hamlet in Northern Michigan where sakura groves exploded with pink hues like touched-up impressionistic stills, tart cherries and morel mushrooms were sold in cardboard crates on the corner, and the sunlight dripped down the foliage like exquisite nectar. I remember pedaling through a cloud of pulsating monarchs. They flexed their wings on my handlebars like Icarian parables. That's when I noticed Blain standing in front of his house like an inscrutable omen. We played until the galvanized scent of sautéed ground beef and broiled cheese stuck to the air like sensory ornamentation. I biked home, cloaked in the fading mango sunshine, my face baptized in flower pollen and birdsong.

When I walked into the kitchen, my mom scrutinized me. —Where you been?

—Nowhere, I said.

—Did you play with him after I told you not to?

—No, I said, confused.

—Tell me the truth! she yelled.

—I didn't, I pleaded.

—You little liar, she screamed.

My mom grabbed a yardstick from the kitchen closet and struck me on the backside with all her force. The house was hauntingly empty except for this sound: *wack, wack, wack.* Tears streamed down my cheeks. I hurled apologies at the air with a quivering voice, but she hit me again and again with incanted strength until the yardstick splintered into two pieces. In my mind, the broken weapon was clemency. The clumsy providence of a lazy god. But then she grabbed a three-foot clothespin from the closet and started wailing on me again. In syncopated sobs, I begged her to stop. I pleaded. I whimpered in contrition. I apologized for my existence. I promised never to play with Blain again. I promised not to be myself if it would protect me from myself. Nothing got through.

The trauma of that day lingered in my mind for years afterwards. After all, trauma isn't just cellular pain. The indefatigable memory of trauma is itself a survival strategy. By not allowing me to forget the things that destroyed me, my trauma tried to protect what it refused to erase. I have never located the boundary separating pain from trauma. I don't know if we overcome trauma, or merely coexist with it. I just know that kids used to point and laugh at my Miami Vice sports coat in 6th grade and tell me I looked gay. I just know the random violence of neighborhood boys punching my pretty hapa face for made-up reasons, coming home to a dark and silent house on the hill that signified I was alone, and the abuse of gravity breaking apart my daydreams with every bike wipeout and playground felony. The psychological arithmetic of childhood pain never disappeared because my survival depended on not forgetting the numbers.

Like all perpetrators of violence, my mom was intransigently unmoved by my suffering as she beat me into submission. The only sound inside the vacant house was this: *wack, wack, wack.* The next day there were indigo bruises covering my ass and thighs like divots in a ravaged lawn. When I looked at myself in the mirror, my relationship with my family that had failed to protect me or notice my temporary limp, had changed radically. I was the only one who knew about my secret secession, the only person in my house who dreamt of running away to Tokyo or Paris or Interlochen to find safety and community. What my mom did that day she never did again, but I've remembered it for the rest of my life because of the way that pain became the dominatrix of my memory: restraints to my rage, paddle to my oblivion, my boyhood in handcuffs, my hope tickled by the popper, my safety words smacked hard by the whip.

When my parents got divorced, I had to choose a parent. I picked my dad, not because we were close or because he was affectionate with me or because he showed any interest in me, but for the simple reason that he'd never hurt me. He'd never left his signature on my body. Pain requires intervention and he lived on the sidelines of every conflict. I picked my dad because pain is always an overdeveloped photograph of the psyche. I was just a twelve-year-old kid trying to survive in a world that kept changing its rules and then falling apart on me like a window display of Styrofoam. Our dad may never have consoled us, asked us how we were doing, expressed explicit affection, or displayed solicitude or empathy for us during the divorce, but at least he'd never written us letters saying we'd killed him because we were selfish sons as our mom had done the day we'd stopped by her apartment on Center Road to take her out to dinner for Mother's Day. We picked our dad because the atomic weight of our pain was enormous and invisible and neither parent acknowledged it but only one parent intentionally caused it whenever she felt betrayed or ignored. Neither parent acknowledged how much the divorce blew up our lives in the house on the hill, but only one parent tried to perform normalcy, even in the face of bankruptcy and familial detonation, an illusion I craved during every catastrophe. Shock prevents victims from grieving for themselves in the beginning. I think it also freezes their hearts to other people's suffering. This is how my mom ignored the trauma she'd caused me in the kitchen, convinced that her own trauma was an alibi for the damage she caused me. But pain is a morphology of the self and no one knew this better than my mom. Her pain changed her and her pain changed me.

I was broken for a very long time after she beat me and I broke at inexplicable moments afterwards as a teenager. Sometimes, I wished someone in my family would have cared, or at least acknowledged how fucked up it was to make me attend four high schools in four years. Sometimes, I wish my dad or anyone in our extended family had asked Wick and me if we were okay, if we needed anything, if someone was abusing us.

Because I was broken, I learned to glue myself back together through trial and error like a stepped-on, torn-up, crinkled origami swan. This is how I survived:

1. I found refuge in obāchan: she took me to piano lessons, baked TV dinners for me, sang along me when I played *"Sakura"* on her piano, watched me play video games in the arcade, and played Gin Rummy with me at the kitchen table before I took a nap on her couch.
2. I found refuge in my body: I biked around town and pretended I was in the Tour de France. I took baths religiously. I ran through thunderstorms in the summer. I went sledding in our backyard during sunsets and winter blizzards. I played Chopin nocturnes in the dark. I discovered pleasure in puberty, the thrill and the charge of every movie-theater kiss.
3. I found refuge in performance: I listened to Pet Shop Boys and the *Breakin'* soundtrack on the stereo and pretended I was a dancer in '80s music videos. I pretended I was a French exchange student visiting America for the first time. I made up stories about robot guardian angels from the manga my parents brought back from Japan.
4. I found refuge in desire: I crushed on flirty girls in the hallways, at pop-and-potato-chip parties, under the shimmering disco strobes of the

roller-skating rink, strutting down *Front Street* in a new outfit of denim and plaid, and sitting on the beach all alone. I freestyled fake Shakespearean sonnets at parties before I kissed girls.

5. I found refuge in storytelling: I was a cultural spy, a double agent, and a secret ninja. These hidden identities helped me feel like I controlled my own alienation and belonged to an underground society of badass revolutionaries who sought their own marginalization as a means of maintaining their secrecy.

6. I wrote unfinished handbooks about a society of ninjas that was supposed to protect mixed-race, hapa, and Japanese American kids like me from bullies.

7. I created talk shows with a tape recorder where I interviewed mushy apples.

8. I survived the way only a kid could, through unbridled imagination and unjustified hope. I frequently invented alternate destinies inside my head as an emotional counterbalance to the real world.

Victimology has no first cause, no first victim. It's a tragic part of the human discourse. To be human is ultimately to participate in the discourse and the dynamic of trauma. My mom victimized her sons because she was a victim herself. When my white grandfather came home drunk, his pores gushing with stale whisky, he molested my mom, hit my obāchan, and sometimes raped her. He forbade his Japanese wife and his hapa daughter from speaking Japanese in their own home even though Japanese was their first language and they lived in Yokohama. He shipped my mom off to Buckley, Michigan, where she lived with her xenophobic aunt who locked her in a basement and forced her to clean the house like a contemporary hapa fairytale. My mom washed dishes, cleaned the house, and cried herself to sleep while her white cousins stared at her and made fun of her beautiful hapa face and called her a Jap. My obāchan sewed clothes for my mom and sent her care packages from Japan along with money and letters, which my aunt promptly gave away to her own daughters. She pocketed the money. This is a circuitous way of saying that victims replicate their victimization in others because at first they don't see themselves as victims and then later because they see only themselves as victims. I make no excuses for my mom's intermittent abuse. I only place her trauma in context, situating it within a continuum of violence, assault, and dehumanization that will outlive all of us. We cannot erase it. We can only leave bite marks with our crooked teeth.

The cyclicity of pain is often a cold and plummeting fall that girls cushion with their braids and warm with smoldering hearts, a broken place that men rebuild over and over again with giant cranes, that women prop onto their shoulders and throw back into the sky, that boys hurl rocks at ever since the days of Goliath and the age of fox spirits. In my best moments, I know how to help others with their pain by simply listening, entering into their emotional space, holding their hands, itemizing everything that pain steals from them, loving them for their vulnerability and leakage, and forgiving them for their brokenness and shedding, but I have no solutions to my own pain and trauma. I only know how to stab the monster with the sharp edge of my sentences and hurl words at its jugular like shuriken. When everything is said and done, I only know how to hold hands with the blade.

Despite the insight I have about my own pain, at heart I'm just a punch-drunk karaoke singer who knows the lyrics to every love song, but can't sing them out loud when the mic is live on stage. The truth is that I don't want other people to know how deep the pain goes inside me, how much I crave the balm of the melody, or how afraid I am of being seen and dismissed. If they see me, then they will see right through my gossamer heart. They will know that I'm still in love with this disastrous world, even after all this time.

次に！/Next!

1. Feeling nostalgic? Fuck nostalgia and go to page 92!
2. Looking for a 夢 dope playlist? Here's one of Jackson's from High School on page 138!
3. Have a good one. Do you guys have any pop? Go Cubbies! Want a Brat? All on page 223!
4. Jackson is *always* daydreaming. Don't believe me? Go to page 190 & see for yourself!

5. Don't just turn the page, FLIP that shit!

62. Best Damn Dream Pop Albums for Writing This Memoir (Come at Me, Bros!)

1. *Moon Safari* and *Talkie Walkie* by Air
2. *Cigarettes After Sex* by Cigarettes After Sex
3. *Always, Sometimes, Seldom, Never* by Tears Run Rings
4. *Saturdays = Youth* by M83
5. *Clinging to a Scheme* by The Radio Dept
6. *So Tonight That I Might See* and *Among My Swan* by Mazzy Star
7. *Slowdive* by Slowdive by Slowdive
8. *Kill for Love* by Chromatics
9. *The Year of Hibernation* by Youth Lagoon
10. *Split* by Lush
11. *The Bird of Music* by Au Revoir Simone
12. *Dots and Loops* by Stereolab
13. *Treasure, Head Over Heels,* and *Blue Bell Knoll* by Cocteau Twins
14. *Romantica* by Luna
15. *Agaetis Byrjun* by Sigur Rós
16. *Things We Lost in the Fire* by Low
17. *And Then Nothing Turned Itself Inside-Out* by Yo La Tengo
18. *Disintegration* by The Cure
19. *Hardcore Will Never Die, But You Will* by Mogwai
20. *23* by Blonde Redhead
21. *Gemini* by Wild Nothing
22. *Loveless* by My Bloody Valentine
23. *Asobi Seksu* by Asobi Seksu by Asobi Seksu
24. *Depression Cherry, Thank Your Lucky Stars,* and *Bloom* by Beach House
25. *The Best of the Velvet Underground* by the Andy Warhol Crew
26. *xx* by the xx by the xx
27. *Born to Die, Lust for Life,* and *Honeymoon* by Lana Del Rey

28. *Blind* by The Sundays

次に/Next:

1. To see Jackson's list of favorite foods sung like a Blink-182 song, go to page 180.
2. People feel strange/when you're in Paris/Frenchies look ugly on/ page 94.
3. To see Jackson bawl his little eyes out at the New Haven Union Station, go to page 207.
4. Or just turn the page.

63. Quantum Nostalgia

LB and I went to a ridiculously named coffee shop in Amsterdam called ~~We Be the Fattest Blunts in Candyland, Motherfucker~~ Smokey's. Since this was the first time LB had smoked weed, I bought a pre-rolled j mixed with organic herbs that tasted light, smooth, and minty, which she smoked like a fucking pro, taking these massive puffs like some '90s OG about to spit a dirty rap video or do a mid-afternoon drive-by on a Hollywood set. She never coughed, not once. As we smoked, we sipped our too-sweet and too-cold smoothies and laughed. We walked back to our hotel, made love to the cushioning smell of freesia from a nearby apartment, and ate paprika potato chips, organic dark chocolate, and sipped juice boxes of fruit cocktail from Biomarkt, a Danish health food chain. Later, we walked around the canals, just as the sun was fading into the gelatinous skyline like an infused blood orange. We danced with Hare Krishnas at Rembrandtplein and inhaled the smell of dirt and fertilizer, Gardenia, Lilac, and Peonies at the Flower Market. We crossed a million bridges, the water beneath the canals gurgling under our feet, until we'd arrived at Jordaanplein.

At a quiet and spacious Thai restaurant, we devoured Pad Thai and chatted with the waitress. When LB and I told her we were from Chicago, she said: *I love Chicago! I lived there for one year. Kuwait and Amsterdam, I knew well, but Chicago, I loved.* We told her we were crushing diametrically on Amsterdam, a crush based on deficient knowledge (as love so often was). As the waitress made her rounds, LB and I wondered how much rent was for a two-bedroom apartment in Jordaanplein. We wondered whether LB could find a job as a pediatric nurse and whether I could postpone grad school and spend another year as an expat writing the great hapa/mixed-race novel. We wondered whether we'd ever live in Europe, whether Dutch grammar was unapproachable, whether Dutch people got sick of sleezy sex tourists and American teenagers clogging up the bike lanes. We wondered how our life might have been different if we'd lived in the Netherlands instead of Argentina for the past year, we created a counterfactual autobiography in Amsterdam together, telling each other a series of alternative realities out loud we would only imagine and envision through storytelling. The stories we told ourselves at the Thai restaurant, the stories we'd invented, felt detailed enough to be real to us.

Sometimes, the right chronotope gives you feelings of contemporaneous pain, joy, longing, hope, desire, and regret for a parallel world you instantiate and then resuscitate through longing, imagination, and desire alone. Sometimes, the rearview world you sketch with the pastels of your nostalgia, the alternative world you've created for yourself with the bold acrylics of the imagination, and the shattered pieces of culture you've collected carefully for years like the rubble of demolished buildings, all tell the same story of longing and displacement, counterpoint and fugue states. You become haunted by all the lives you've already lived in your mind, by all the choices you left unexplored and undiscovered in the cultural fractal of the city, by every street you didn't see as an inflamed tourist of culture with a dog-eared travel guide and a quantum appetite for counterfactual plot lines. Amsterdam was the first city where I missed a life I had never lived.

次に/Next:
1. WESTERN CHAUVINISM BRAINWASHED JACKSON and other deep thoughts about the heteronationalist canon as seen from the School of Page One Twenty Four.
2. The Maudlin Show, hosted by Jackson Bliss, here on Channel 243.
3. À la recherche de la musique perdue (searching for lost music) à la page 94.
4. Or just turn the page. Or don't.

64. Shit That Makes Me Cry

1. The way LB looks at me sometimes when she leaves for work

2. The thought of losing her to sickness, old-age, accident, and the slobbering jaws of time

3. Watching *What Would You Do?* episodes on YouTube

4. That goddamn Apple Christmas commercial (December 2013)

5. Seeing animals abused, hurt, or neglected. In other words, *Earthlings*

6. The normative anxiety, fear, disbelief, and rage that is all part of watching a pandemic explode in a country that could have prevented tens of thousands of deaths if we'd simply been less selfish, respected science, had more federal leadership, and valued the lives of (brown, Black, Native, and Asian) people living in cities as much as we worshipped the market, freedom, and gun ownership

7. Macklemore and Ryan Lewis's *Same Love* video (Nas and Jay-Z deserved the Grammies though)

8. Old dudes calling me son

9. Little kids touching my face or grabbing my hand out of the blue

10. Seeing people coming together for humanitarian reasons (like when Greek volunteers helped Turks after a massive earthquake in response to Turkish volunteers doing the same for Greeks earlier)

11. Watching kids stand up to, and band together against, the school bully (or gun violence or institutional racism or police brutality)

12. Genuine kindness from strangers

13. The day my mom called me and told me that obāchan had stage-4 lung cancer

14. LB grabbing my hand in her sleep

15. Pictures of Nagasaki and Hiroshima survivors

16. Getting into my PhD program

17. Saying goodbye to Wick when he left Chicago in the Grunge Era

18. Anything having to do with 9/11 (since I wasn't here when it happened and I feel really guilty about having avoided such a quintessential American tragedy)

19. My first encounter with god (the divine, the cosmos, the universe, cosmic energy, whatever concept works for you) as I was flying to Turkey. Just as cheesy as it sounds!

20. Spending my first summer alone in our Chicago apartment, sweating my ass off, flat broke, and lost in the Second City

21. People showing vulnerability

22. Mazzy Star's "Flowers in December" and Beyoncé's "Sandcastles"

23. The good kinds of flash mobs

24. Creative, non-gimmicky marriage proposals, especially with gay couples (once a romantic always a romantic)

25. Seeing tough dudes cry

26. Expressions of genuine gratitude

27. The day I sold this book (21 February 2020, to be exact. Thanks, Esme!)

28. Seeing people in love

29. Bold declarations of love (paternal, romantic, Glee song and dance, Bollywood video, doesn't matter. We need more of that shit)

30. Listening to dream pop at night and feeling kinda melancholy cuz, you know, emotion is a terrible thing to waste

31. Not having something for #31

次に/Next:

1. Introductory Midwestern English, available for a short time on page 223.
2. To read about the things Jackson's parents used to do that embarrassed him growing up, go to page 80.
3. If you want to see Jackson sample religions like tapas appetizers—olé, olé olé olé Jackson, Jack-son! Random sidenote: Jackson and LB once had to listen to this song over and over again while taking a train from Barcelona to Paris in 2009 after Barça defeated Manchester United in the Champions League, which a Spanish teenager announced at two in the morning as groggy passengers tried to sleep and cursed at her under their breath, before she moved on to the next car and made the same announcement—go to page 257. Wait, what was the antecedent again?
4. O, ¡pasá la puta página!

65. Love Song for a Parallel World (or Her Name is Chlöe Addison Bliss)

In 2012, my wife and I returned to our hometown of Chicago to start a family. We'd already decided that our daughter, if we had one, would be named Chlöe Addison Bliss. Addison was a Chicago landmark, Chlöe was the first female protagonist I'd ever created, and also the name LB has chosen for her daughter years before we met. Such kismet felt too pure to ignore because love is always a type of emotional dreaming. Chlöe's name comes from χλόη (khlóē), the summer epithet of Demeter, the goddess of harvest and fertility. The excavation of her name still stings me every time. Let me explain before you erase this like they erased her story.

After a series of tests at Northwestern Prentice, we learned that LB's depleted ovarian reserve and history of endometriosis made our chances of conceiving extremely low, so we chose I.V.F. to improve our odds. Our fertility specialist said he was cautiously optimistic. Before I fell in love with my wife, I didn't want to be a dad, but love changed the way I saw our relationship. It changed the way I saw myself as a man, a Buddhist, and a writer. Slowly, we became unsatisfied with the integer of love, craving tiny sweaters folded in a pile on the dryer.

During one night shift at Lurie Children's where LB worked as a pediatric nurse, a nosey mom asked her if she had children. My wife replied that she was the proud mother of two fur babies. The woman shook her head and gave a disgusted look. She said LB would never understand true love until she had her own kids. I believe that we are all creating family using different definitions, but some people want to be eternal through genealogy, some can't acknowledge their own speciesism and biological narcissism, and some simply need the existential shortcut. The clarity of caretaking and the redistribution of energy. Some people see relationships as the landscaping for their family trees. For us, our relationship is the flesh of the fruit of the tree.

¤

After giving LB Gonal-F, Menopur, and HCG injections to induce egg maturation, my wife's body resembled a pincushion. Our one successful egg retrieval was later fertilized by an embryologist, but it wasn't maturing correctly. Inside our Rogers Park apartment, we would think about little baby embryo, trapped inside the embryologist lab, so tiny and so alone in that sterile environment and we'd cheer her on to maturation. —Go, go, go, baby embryo! Fight, fight, fight! we'd shout with obscene hope and longing, some of it inspired from my years as a M.F.A. student at the University of Notre Dame. After two days, the embryologist called to tell us that the egg had matured. LB and I hugged each other and cried. We walked around the neighborhood and held hands, talking about baby shoes and trilingual preschool. After the successful embryo transfer, I gave my wife progesterone shots as we waited for a positive pregnancy test. Suddenly, the promise land of parenthood became a tangible geography of desire. I felt ashamed of my fear and embarrassed by my apprehension.

A few weeks later, LB experienced excruciating pelvic pain. A series of flares detonating inside her body. She couldn't sit down. She felt light-headed. She swayed in my arms. When she passed out on the sidewalk in in Wrigleyville, I carried her to her parents' apartment. At urgent care, the doctor encouraged LB to visit the emergency room. Just to play it safe. She didn't want to go, but we went anyway. After sitting in the wrong emergency room for ten hours, she was finally admitted. Inside the exam room, the on-call gynecologist thrust the ultrasound probe inside LB like a smoothie stick. My wife started crying, gripping my fingers tight, her pain treated as an uncontroversial premise that was both expected and unavoidable. I squeezed back, incredulous, exhausted by the street fight of my anger and fear.

LB spent the next ten days in the hospital with a high fever. Her blood pressure was dangerously low. Her kidneys showed signs of toxicity after countless rounds of I.V. antibiotics pumped into her body. For the first time in my life, I was afraid that she might die. Of course, if we hadn't gone to the E.R., she would have gone septic, but the idea that the love of my life might die simply trying to have a child through I.V.F. struck me as cosmically unjust. I confessed to her by her side: *I can live without kids, baby, but I can't live without you.* She smiled faintly and held my hand and tried not to cry. I squeezed her hands and kissed her fingers as her tears splat her hospital gown. We were destroyed with grief. Our devastation went so deep inside us it felt skeletal, practically carved into our bones. For months afterwards, our love was all ricochet, hitting everything except its intended target.

When I returned to her hospital room every evening with bags full of udon or vegan sandwiches, her fever spiked like the motif in Thomas Mann's *The Magic Mountain* all over again. LB had always been my center of gravity, the centripetal force in the daydream haze of my life since the day we crushed on each other in a hipster café in Wicker Park that eventually became a non-descript bank (capitalism 1, culture 0). I told her that if I had to choose between being a father and being a husband (and why did I have to choose?), I'd choose her every time. Nothing mattered if she wasn't in my life. My exclusive focus on love and its infinite potentiality of loss and vertigo helped me avoid thinking about worst things, like the academic labor market that had shunned me since I began applying for tenure track jobs without a book from a Big-5 press. By centering my love, a decision that has always clarified my existence for me, I didn't have to think about the numerous literary agents ignoring my query letters as they searched for the next viral short story or consider the hospital bill we would receive a month later for one hundred thousand dollars.

When my wife returned home after ten long days, Zoë and Gogo (our diva shiapoo and dainty pomchi) whimpered with joy. They slept on her lap and curled up on her belly. LB took antibiotics for the next month, so she couldn't eat solid food until the middle of January. Grief voided the holidays. Again and again, we fell down the rabbit hole of depression because there was no way to identify its camouflaged trapdoor until we were already freefalling into a shadow world. Not even our little dogs could heal the obstreperous void in our hearts, though they tried. Maybe, this essay is part confession, but it's also part exorcism for the ghosts of our imagined parenthood that haunt us every time strangers ask us if we have kids and every time we walk through Little Tokyo and every time we pass a Montessori elementary school during recess. Now, when the couple across the street appears in the window with their newborn baby swathed in the natural light of Southern California, I'm reminded of a particular wound that won't completely heal. Even after all this time.

In this particular case, I hate the summary as much as the story, but this is what happened: during the embryo transfer, the doctor nicked one of her ovarian cysts, causing a massive pelvic infection that slowly killed baby embryo. Though we didn't know it at the time, LB had tested positive on her pregnancy test the day she'd been admitted to the ER. It would be the one and only time in her life she was pregnant. During that brief window of time, we were parents, speaking the language of dreaming, becoming, and biology. We were messengers of the sublime. We were trapeze artists of the void. We saw our future together so clearly before the snow globe was shaken. But our parenthood was only discovered after its erasure. We were never allowed to celebrate our joy while baby embryo was alive. We were only allowed to love her once she was gone, all shadow and hum.

Several months later, we attempted one final egg retrieval. As I waited in the lobby to be called back for my sample, dreading the wrinkled porn magazines and half-erased pornos scattered in the fertility rooms for no one, I watched anxious couples exchanging broken glances, slowly disappearing as their names were called one by one. I felt sick to my stomach. My heart clenched when I thought about LB all alone in the procedure room. After an hour, they called me into the operating room. When I entered, she was sobbing. The nurses spoke in apologetic whisper. The doctor, the same doctor who had nicked my wife's cyst months ago, gave me a sad look that was devoid of self-incrimination. The retrieval had failed. I hated him for not looking guiltier. I hated him for stealing our family from us twice, once by accident, once by silence.

As I wrapped my arms around her, I kissed LB's head and held her hand tight. I walked her to the hospital bathroom, cleaned her up, helped her pee, and dressed her as gently as I could, her body limp like a wilted celery stalk. I felt her sadness in her every movement, which would linger in her cells for years. In the coming weeks, after falling into debt, becoming incurably hopeless, and crying in our sleep, we realized that we would never conceive a child of our own. We felt beat up by Chicago, the city that had brought us together and then hurled our bodies into the ground. We felt stung by the city's negative space, engorged by its culture of tragedy, family, and (self-)violence. We vowed to leave before we disappeared too.

Soon afterwards, Sophia, my 22-year-old sister-in-law, got pregnant after messing up her birth control. When my wife heard the news on the phone, she bawled in my arms, a totalizing figure of grief. Soon afterwards, Sophia asked LB to go with her to her ultrasounds, which seemed incredibly tone-deaf, insensitive, and selfish to me. How could she ask LB to see a fetal heartbeat after what she'd lost and why did Sophia's needs always supersede her sister's? Though unintentional and inadvertent, Sophia's pregnancy denied LB the space to grieve out loud and say goodbye to her dreams of motherhood. Instead of giving her the time to come to terms with the throbbing void in her soul, her family was now busy preparing for its first grandchild, so it failed (or pretended not) to notice her invisible black clothes that she wore to every family function for months and then years. LB made me watch videos of baby elephants. We listened to The Smiths and cried. We held hands on the El. We played with the dogs on the bed. We had picnics in Edgewater. We were still in love, but we were shattered mirrors now, dangerous to touch, faces broken but reflecting brokenness. Our love shifted into a thing we couldn't glue back together for years. Of course, without our altered love, we would never have survived, but still I wondered: why had our families refused to acknowledge her trauma? Why hadn't they given her the space to grieve? Why wasn't her suffering centered at all? Why didn't they swallow her pain as she had swallowed theirs her whole life?

Our families denied LB the right to mourn. They unconsciously rationalized her suffering by weaponizing their optimism for a future that never happened. My wife learned once again that her own needs didn't matter as much as her younger sister's, even after her life was in danger, which felt like the price she paid for being the grounded and sweet daughter instead of the outspoken one lost in her dreams. There aren't enough exclamation points in my spleen to underscore my rage for the way this world takes human kindness for granted, but this essay is not about rage, it's about the pulsating emptiness inside my heart when love is carved out, tossed aside, and then left to fend for itself in the rabid light of day. And I get it: it was easy to take our relationship for granted because for the longest time, we were stable, delirious, and deeply in love in a demonstrative and Instagrammable way. But refusing to concede defeat for our sake also meant rejecting our trauma and rejecting our suffering. It meant rejecting our devastation religiously, which hurt so much more. Sometimes, love must be inconvenient for it to mean anything. When you love someone, you accompany her up the staircase of desolation as often as she needs to take that journey, wherever it takes the two of you, even if the sky catches on fire as you hold hands and tremble into flames together. When you love someone, you give her space to grieve according to her timeline, not yours. You give her time to say goodbye to the closing door of alternate worlds. You center her subjectivity before your own, before anyone. Otherwise, you love conveniently, which is not love at all. But we were not convenient lovers. We were not convenient mourners. And the world should have made space for our inconvenience.

LB is a pediatric nurse. She heals children every day, but none of them are her own. If anyone deserves to be a mom, it's her, but merit has nothing to do with motherhood. LB had a depleted ovarian reserve, a history of early menopause on her mami's side, and a mysterious lack of nieces on her papi's side. That's it. Pregnancy is just the biological short story that some bodies write and others don't. The storytelling itself has nothing to do with who deserves to be the storyteller.

When we returned to LA in 2014, we vowed to restitch our broken souls with Californian sunshine. Now, every time I check the mail, I make sure to intercept catalogs sent to us for Scandinavian baby furniture, gendered kids' clothes, overpriced infant shoes, and plastic toys. Each catalog is a hidden wormhole to the beginning of grief again, another stumble into a parallel world where we're parents of a mixed-race girl who speaks with a lisp and falls asleep in my old kimono, reading manga by flashlight, her hair in colitas.

We have a single picture of baby embryo. It's a reproductive blur on a low-grade photograph that we've kept to ourselves out of sadness and shame because it's all we have of Chlöe now. We know that she is just a beautiful idea conjugated into a thousand different versions of our reality. She is just a love song for a parallel world. Because of her, though, we were allowed to believe in the unlimited possibilities of our love, to peer into the snow globe of our imagined family and fall asleep knowing we had already welcomed her into our hearts. We think about her all the time from our distant and inhospitable world. We don't love her less just because she wasn't born and neither should you.

次に/Next:

1. Extra! Extra! Read all about it. Jackson meets his Japanese family for the first time on page 224.
2. To learn how Jackson stopped the cycle of abuse, go to page 232.
3. To take a break, dream a little, and make some origami, go to page 57.
4. Or just turn the page→pame→name→nome→nomi. Turn the nomi, homie.

66. Words I Always Misspell (Without the Invisible Hand of Autocorrect)

1. Misspell (the irony is absurd and probably seems self-conscious, I know, but it's true)

2. Occurring (why the double C?)

3. Occasionally (why the single S? Just why?)

4. Pomegranate (this spelling looks like it should be pronounced "poem-granite")

5. Annihilation (silent Hs are so rare these days)

6. Photo (I like *foto*)

7. Accommodate (yes, *please*)

8. Ecstatic (how is there not an X here?)

9. Embarrassing (again, I'm aware of the self-irony here, but it's not less true just because it's ironic)

10. Mischievous (so fucking autological it's criminal!)

次に/Next:

1. There was that one time that Jackson translated for a West African refugee seeking political asylum in America on page 110.
2. To read about Jackson's favorite dream pop albums, go to page 239.
3. To learn about the things Jackson wanted to be growing up, go to page 47.
4. Or just turn the page.

67. Radical Nomenclature

It was a hot and humid summer day in the East Village when I retreated into the Tower Records on 4th and Broadway (RIP, old friend) and wandered around CD racks and listening stations (RIP, old friends) in a sticky daze, trying to lose the persistent August heat that had burrowed itself into my core. As I wandered into the book section where New Yorkers were flipping through wrinkled copies of rock star memoirs and edgy, celebrity softcore photo books, I stumbled on Kip Fulbeck's *Part Asian, 100% Hapa*. I assumed the position and started flipping pages until I came to a picture of a mixed-race boy who looked just like me and then I started crying because his picture made me stop feeling alone, because there was suddenly a word now to describe people like me whose cultural and racial identities were mostly Asian, but whose phenotypic markers were mostly white. It was in that book that I learned how the visual language of photography could help reconnect the fragments of your racial hyphenation by establishing a radical new nomenclature for your own existence. I learned the unique and healing role that the word hapa played in filling in my own existential potholes, even if it wasn't a perfect word with a perfect history. I learned after reading that book how to reconstruct myself as a complete human being in this country with its long and torturous history of racialization, colonization of native people and native lands, military violence against developing nations, police violence and voter disfranchisement against Black people, racial and class segregation, and the institutional racism against Japanese Americans, Asian Pacific Islander Americans, and other people of color of all gradations, percentages, and racial mixes, each group with different timeframes and specialized traumas. When the state hacks you apart into a thousand pieces, you either cease to exist or you spend the rest of your life putting yourself together like a patchwork monster narrative.

Eurasian hapas have a unique vantage point in understanding the complexities and also the weight of inter-racial identification since they inhabit both hegemonic and subaltern spaces concurrently. They know what it's like to have the mic thrown in their hand when they didn't ask for it and also what it's like to be muted and spoken for when they have something to say. Like all mixed-race people, hapas can be cultural, racial, and historical bridges between diverse communities, countries, and histories but they can also be treated as racial and cultural spies. Hapas can be racially ambiguous and/or racially illegible, which frustrates the categorical imagination and racial assumptions in an important way. For example, most white people think I'm white, but when I explain that I'm hapa, they either looked confused because they don't know that word, they become shocked as if the idea had never occurred to them that I might have incongruous racial markers and identities, they look at me in disbelief as if I'm playing a joke on them to test their open-mindedness, or they become hostile as if I'm trying to disqualify myself from their own white privilege. Most mixed-race people I've met, however, are preternaturally comfortable with my hyphenated cultural identity and will happily admit having mixed-race identities themselves once we've exchanged our respective race cards.

Being hapa means being racially mislabeled, whitewashed, dismissed, fragmented, and erased my entire life. It is the experience of having a secret identity I wish more than anything was conspicuous and easy to register. Being hapa also means being forced into the straitjacket of binary identification, which is categorical violence against racial and cultural hybridity. Being hapa is the quintessential experience of being both the outcast and the iconoclast, my racial hyphenation connecting, intersecting, uniting, and violating cultures, histories, and races every day in a way that is both unheroic, controversial, and inflammatory. Political systems, academic discourse, delusional post-racial rhetoric, and social engineering have all failed to understand and stick up for the multiracial demographic destiny of America, so hapas will have roll up their sleeves and work harder to be less exceptional. The simultaneous existence of being granted the various privileges of legible (or honorary) whiteness in one space and then suddenly being marginalized in both a marginalized and a hegemonic space is a typical but confusing hapa experience. The experience of identifying largely with an invisible part of your ancestry and/or disidentifying largely with the visible white part, the experience of not being white enough or not being Japanese enough (especially when you speak ten-year-old Japanese like I do), is the rule of multidirectional alienation, the unspoken law of multiracial identity in every family tree. But maybe, the problem isn't me. Maybe, the problem is that Americans are too impatient with ambiguity. Maybe, the issue is that many hapas are the children of recent immigrants, so our lives are always a collection of linked short stories that no one wants to read except other mixed-race people. We live in a country where people still listen to AM radio, where even educated Americans stop reading once they graduate from college. Four years is not enough time to understand the world. It definitely isn't enough time to understand yourself.

次に/Next:

1. To spend time in Amsterdam like the giant tourist cliché that you are, go to page 241.
2. To read about Jackson's trip to Prague to escape his heartache, go to page 99.
3. Because there's nothing quite like being humiliated in French class on page 159 . . .
4. Or just turn the danky page.

68. The Different Religious Stages of My Life

1. Default (forced, part-time) **Methodist** (elementary school): basically, whatever the hell you were when your parents dragged your ass to the local Methodist church for Christmas and Easter. I'm grateful that was it.

2. Self-proclaimed, but slightly bellicose **atheist** (high school): which could only happen at a Jesuit prep school that both encouraged and demanded academic rigor, caritas, cross-cultural dialogue, empathy, and intellectual inquiry. I'll never forget the day I told my dad I was an atheist, thereby rejecting his forced, part-time default Methodism. His response: "You're not an atheist, you just don't know WHAT you are." To this day, I still have mostly atheistic beliefs, which is why Buddhism became such an organic fit for me. Shockingly, I knew myself better than my parents, even in high school.

3. Silent **agnostic** (early college): because Nietzsche and Bertrand Russell killed my goddess.

4. Two-month **Taoist** (mid-college): a by-product of studying Chinese religion and searching for an alternative, non-theistic belief system, which I found in the Seven Sages of the Bamboo Grove, who paved the way for my eventual interest in Buddhism my senior year (with guidance from Professor DiCenzo, my Japanese history and literature professor and mentor, who I loved and adored for his intelligence, wisdom, guidance, and hands-off approach to enlightenment, RIP dear friend).

5. Silent **Buddhist** (late college and grad school, the first time): partially as a coping mechanism, partially as a spiritual amulet, and partially as academic study. My Buddhism and Modernism class at Yale, for example, was life-changing, as was my endless poverty and my inability to pay my graduate tuition.

6. Failed **Buddhist** (Seattle): Once you've read "Mortality Love Song" (p. 63), you'll get it.

7. **Atheist** (West Africa): after you've killed four hundred flies out of anger, boredom, vulnerability, and frustration, it's hard to believe in a higher power, or anything, really, except that Sartre was fucking right and that cold Fanta can be a more profound religious experience than the Gospel.

8. Silent **Buddhist** (Portland): because there were SO MANY PREACHY BUDDHISTS there, some of them COMPETING with each other to prove who was more mindful of their mindfulness, which made me say, "Nah, I'm not telling anyone SHIT about my spiritual beliefs!"

9. Wavering **Buddhist** (Chicago): another shitty relationship that lasted twice as long as it should have, another spiritual implosion that made me question my entire belief system and my egotistical reasons for choosing a spiritual belief system in the first place.

10. Firm **Buddhist** (grad school for my MFA): probably related to doing exactly what I wanted to for the first time since college. I was just a short train ride away from Chicago, writing my ass off every single day, working on *Amnesia of June Bugs* (published by 7.13 Books in 2022, just saying), studying Japanese, buying shrimp paste Banh Mih sandwiches at a nearby Vietnamese market for the first time since I'd lived in Little Vietnam, and getting a modest stipend to write, teach, and read amazing fiction (all privileges, but also completely earned).

11. Silent but firm **Buddhist** (Argentina and in grad school for my PhD): possibly connected to being in love and finding sustainable stability for the first time since junior high.

12. **Just here** with you in LA, Chicago, and A2 (as a **BAD FUCKING Buddhist** who should definitely sit more than he does but who is also at peace with his spiritual belief system and has nothing to prove to anyone, so eat it!).

There's a recurring theme here. I just can't quite put my finger on it right now . . .

次に/Next:
1. To snoop inside Jackson's satchel, go to page 119.
2. To see all the places Jackson has lived, go to page 38.
3. To read about the day Jackson almost lost LB in the hospital, go to page 246.
4. Or just turn the page.

69. How I Scotch Tape My Kami Back Together

一.

In order to exist as a complete human being, I've had to re-tape, re-staple, re-fold, and re-glue torn pieces of speckled kami back together my entire life, reassembling and reconnecting the severed scraps of the torn hapa body over and over again, suturing and collating fragmented scraps of wrinkled origami squares into a shifting taxonomy of geometric identities and paper morphologies. This life-long project to remain a whole person after each paper cut by the public imagination, this blind aspiration to remain intact as a fragmented creature devoted to his metamorphosis in the era of sharp objects and rasterized images, often feels like a form of insanity. But writing *Dream Pop Origami* helped me heal from the pain of disconnection, fragmentation, and dismemberment, becoming a four-way mirror to understand what I'm not, what I've always been, what I've become through the act of writing, dreaming, and folding, and what I'd like to become someday in this origami project. But this work is never done because real work never is. Even now, I'm afraid of tripping on my paper body since I'm a huge fucking klutz, the biggest ahondara you've ever meet, accidentally ripping off my scabs (scraps), the bruises in my bones, the paper cuts in my flesh, both singing songs of fracture and trauma, the qi in my body glowing like a soft overture of neon and dusk.

二.

Like every paper human in this world, I'm a deeply flawed work of hobbled selfhood: I've made progress in my spiritual evolution, but there are still sleeper cells of trauma, rage, sadness, and frustration inside me, a whole contagion of long-winded melancholy inside that I'm not even aware of until I cross an invisible boundary separating the land of the sublimation from the land of the paroxysm. I have my insecurities, delusions, and phobias like anyone else. I can be a TERRIBLE FUCKING Buddhist, a very flawed husband, and low-key feminist. I can be arrogant, moody AF, and argumentative when I feel cornered. I'm a documented night-snacker. I love romance, high school, and food manga. I can give women great advice on not judging their bodies by society's standards, but I can't follow any of that shit when I look in the full-length mirror and curse the rolls on my back. I can lose track of whole days when I'm on a mission on my PS4 and forget to answer my text messages. I love to dance, drink apple cider, fuck, watch sci-fi shows, play Nintendo, and organize my office when I smoke. I become shamefully happy when 20-something women flirt with me. My taste in cocktails is ridiculously girly (e.g., Margaritas, Daquiris, Cuba Libres, Piña Coladas, as well as Moscato and Rieslings) even though I despise stereotypical gender constructions, especially of taste, sensitivity, and sentimentality. I do enjoy a good scotch though, which is pretty damn bougie. I'm not apologizing, I'm just saying. Sometimes, I take more time getting dressed than LB does, I coordinate my outfits with my satchels, lunch bags, and jackets, which people tell me I should feel bad about, but I don't. Sometimes, I need a lot of space, but I can also be codependent. One of my worst defense mechanisms is that I think of inappropriate (and sometimes incredibly pornographic) things about the absolutely wrong people as we're talking about non-sexual things. I act like I'm not competitive because I'm so spiritually evolved, even though I totally am. You should watch me racing smug teenage punks on the treadmill or down the street. I can also be annoyingly nostalgic at times: for example, I miss my hair, my 20-year-old skin, my Mefloquine dreams in Burkina Faso, my daily merienda with mate and granola bars in Cap Fed, my high school sex drive, my former life as a smoker ~~and coffee drinker~~, my former life as a college student and incessant heartbreaker in Chicago. I wish sometimes I didn't give a shit about all the things I care deeply about now that have literally defined who I am, this contradiction being the perfect trapdoor to my own self-loathing and self-doubt. And yet despite the fact I can be maudlin AF, arrogant, and nostalgic, prone to contumacious smack talk and prosecutorial disagreements, despite my spectacular failures, missed opportunities, and nosedived aspirations in life (many of which I've mentioned in this memoir), the things that have saved me and given me refuge in this age of anthropogenic ecocide time and time again are love, traveling, and writing. If you think about it, those are all the same things. Since the day I kissed a girl named H. in a dark movie theater and wrote a manual on how to protect myself against bullies and traveled to México with my fam, since I started playing piano and found an alternate lexicon to express my emotions through art, since the day I became aware of my racial multimodality and cultural hyphenation, only writing, travel, and love have helped me escape myself, find myself, and become a whole entity again in the era of tiny earthquakes, permanent fragmentation, and scissored (im)migrant stories. Writing, travel, and love are the rope ladder that I clung to and climbed up to escape the sinkhole of my own heartache, the pit at the bottom of the world where I would still be now, stuck in Kōbō Abe's sand dunes that scorch and sparkle with the energy of fallen stars, decapitated origami cranes, and kamikaze comets electrifying the ground water.

三.

Even though *Dream Pop Origami* is an experimental, non-linear, permutational, postmodern memoir (quite the mouthful, innit?), it accidentally became a heuristic for me too. By writing about my life as truthfully as I could, I began to notice patterns I hadn't seen before and learn about myself in the process. Now, I want this memoir to be a lyric anthem for the intrinsic complexity of the (multiracial) self. I want this memoir to defend our right to ontological multiplicity, to defeat New Age sound bites about the laws of attraction and binary conceptualizations of desire, gender, class, and racial identity. I want to fight for the right to be both complicated and irreconcilable, vociferous and introspective, affectionate and stoic, optimistic and emocore, generous, loving, altruistic, and artistically obsessed, emotionally self-indulgent, imperfect, and overachieving, nerdy and gregarious, deeply flawed and hopelessly evolutionary. I want to fight for the right to have a metamorphic identity in this broken world of tectonic shifts and digital self-disfiguration. I want this memoir to destabilize the notion of the stable, static, unicellular self. I want to smash imagination into memory and reality into dreaming and emotion into thought and gender into culture and mind and heart and longing and body into performance. I want to turn desire into a radical state of permanent revolution against our own self-destruction. I want to construct a mosaic out of every chapter of this memoir, to hotglue every void, daydream, desire, fantasy, and trauma into a unified glasswork exhibition for the bursting choreography of the human space opera. I want to smash the boundaries between the people we think we are, the people we perform as, the people we want to be, the people we've forgotten, the different versions of ourselves that others see in us, and the parts of ourselves we are still excavating from the ontological rubble. I want to fight for the right of contradiction, metamorphosis, destabilization, and subjectivity, to see this memoir as an act of artistic insubordination against the reductive, static, convenient definitions of love and the circumstantial definitions of truth. I want to fight for the right against the tyranny of plot, against the occupation of narrative linearity, and against the nihilistic virus of unknowability instigated by illiberal actors, fatalists, narcissistic white nationalists, and part-time dictators.

四.

    After revising *Dream Pop Origami* for the past six years, I've made some legit autocognitive discoveries that you've probably figured out well before I did:

1. I find redemption in language, in the words I say out loud, in the words I grew up hearing, in the words I misspell, and in the word "hapa" that I discovered in New York back in 2006, which described my own mixed-race identity perfectly, all of which makes my shifting and protean identity feel less problematic.

2. I'm a hardcore daydreamer, so sue me!

3. It was easier pretending I was totally white than actually being hapa, which says a lot about the privilege of white passing and white supremacy in general but hey, who's counting?

4. I'm a nostalgic motherfucker. Also, there's nothing lonelier than being sick abroad.

5. My mom inadvertently gave my permission to see the world.

6. I have an amazing memory of my own pain.

7. Miso soup makes me feel closer to my obāchan and to my Japanese ancestry.

8. Music is not just my jam, but has actually framed each significant stage (or "saison" in the Rimbaudian sense of the word) of my life.

9. Love, appetite, and imagination are the fuel in my veins. They're literally why I'm here on this page, in this world, at this place, talking to you right now.

10. I have to build my own home—emotionally speaking—with my own hands for me to belong there, even if it's just made of gold-speckled origami paper.

11. I'm defined by my sense of longing, I get lost in the trap doors of my thoughts, and sometimes I take small vacations in my emotions.

12. I'm kinda mischievous, but also bad at spelling the words that describe me, which I'm sure is an unconscious rejection of categorical identity.

13. I realize now (even though I should have realized this like twenty years ago) that my parents were just as flawed as I was at their age and as I am now, neither worse nor better. The only difference is, I didn't have kids, so I didn't cause as much damage.

14. I'm pretty nerdy and I use hip-hop to cover it up.

15. I'm still evolving.

16. I was completely brainwashed by the masculinist Western Canon. J.D. Salinger though.

17. I still don't think war solves shit.

18. I'm a bad fucking Nisei and sometimes I'm cool with that (-10 points!). Hey, WTF?

19. Writing about my obāchan helped me understand her life, her tragic history, and her muted psychological grief. Writing about her also helped me understand transgenerational trauma. It helped me figure out what she meant to me through the void she left us after she died.

20. I'm incredibly lucky to travel as much as I do, mashallah. As it turns out, traveling is our kid.

21. I have a serious problem (some would argue *fetish*, but I would say minor league obsession at best) with lists, shopping, and facial products. Really, the evidence is too goddamn overwhelming.

22. The unspoken fear lingering in every page of this memoir is that you never made it this far. Let it not be true, dear reader. Let us be friends forever, ne?

23. I can riff like a motherfucker in my prose, which probably reflects the influences of Coltrane, Jay-Z, Common, Lydia Davis, Jack Kerouac, the Roots, Joan Didion, Junot Díaz, Erykah Badu, and Spoken Word poets, but I'm not bragging and I'm not apologizing, I'm just saying that's me. I'm just saying.

24. I know I have absolutely no future as a MC, but fuck it.

五.

Solitude, silence, and loneliness became my spiritual advisers as a latchkey kid. They taught me to be strong, mostly independent, self-reliant, focused, driven, and pathologically creative. At the same time, I'm still vulnerable to malice and criticism because I'm human goddammit and part of being human means being vulnerable to the world we live in. I fucking *hate* that word (vulnerable), I really do, but I'm trying to be brutally honest here since we ALL have issues. I often feel like an origami crane that a little kid made from discarded paper scraps. I often feel like I'm one relationship ~~and one teaching position~~ and one vocation away from a life of unmitigated sadness, self-loathing, and despair. This knowledge humbles me. It grounds me like a Japanese school monitor. What I've gained, what this memoir is giving me and what you (my beautiful reader) have given me, is a sense of purpose that I'll always be grateful for. Before you, I was just another writer lost inside his head and now I'm the proud author of an autobiographical maze. You have made me an author. You have made me whole again on this dialectical spectrum of writer, reader, editor, author, consumer, fan, critic, lover, and hater that we are all bouncing back and forth on. I thank you from the bottom of my 心 (heart) and I kiss your cheek for giving me a chance when no one else would. I also apologize for violating the rule of positive consent.

六.

I'm serious when I say that you have no idea how grateful I am to have you in my life. You could be Netflix and chilling right now. You could be binging on *Orange Is the New Black, Romance is a Bonus Book, Game of Thrones, House of Cards* (except the last season, that was fucking terrible), *American Crime, One Spring Night, Scandal, Insecure, Madam Secretary, Fresh Off the Boat, The West Wing, Attack on Titan, Because This Is My First Life, Terrace House, Psycho-Pass, Food Wars!, Itaewon Class,* or *Homeland.* Okay, maybe I just described my own binge queue, but so what? Anyway, the point is, you could be eating midnight nachos like I do when I'm depressed (or tipsy). You could be playing *Fallout 4* or *Candy Motherfucking Crush* or *The Last of Us Part II* until your thumbs are throbbing like mine were. You could be looking out the window (as I did the last time I revised this manuscript in DTLA in 2018, Ann Arbor in 2020, and West Hollywood in 2021). You could be at a dive bar right now looking for someone to hold hands with or have a one-night stand with or spend your last night on earth with or cuddle with to make you forget about your 9-to-5 or help you remember the person you used to be or the person you hoped you'd become. You could be like me in college and go out at night just to talk to someone at a café and maybe crush someone who meant something to you when your lips sparked in the spilled darkness of the punctured skyline after speaking in harmony for hours and hours. You could be at an overpriced Japanese restaurant right now looking for someone, ANYONE, who doesn't remind you of your own life. We're only together for three hundred pages, so in my own flawed, sentimental, on-the-nose maximalist sorta way, my affection for you right now is overwhelming. It's practically slobbering on the page. Go ahead and wipe your face if you want. I'll wait for you . . .

七.

Um, you didn't wipe your face. Listen, putting myself together after I've been fragmented into seventy-four scraps of origami paper, is an impossible mission because I can't reverse engineer emptiness and I won't recreate something that was never functioning or fix something when there's nothing wrong with me except my own fragmentation, transliterated clumsily into different genres: personal essay, autobiographical list, textual commentary, playlist, and reading paradigm. That's lit all I've got. But what

I can do here, what I'm trying to do, is understand the individual parts of my splintered self and superglue the scraps of torn kami back together, real gaudy-like, ripped shreds, missing color spectrums and corners and all, until I'm a (barely) cohesive reiteration of the human story again, even if I'm a wobbly and incongruous and flimsy and I don't know how to fly and I'm a patchwork monster attempting to become a series of metamorphoses in speckled kami, nevertheless, I belong here in this dramatically sharp-edge world, just as you do, just as all of us do who dare to refold ourselves into new creatures of fragmentation. We're not so different after all, you know?

八.

This patchwork memoir may seem sad and tenuously taped together and threadbare and top-heavy to throw out the window or hurl into the fireplace or smash into an envelope or stick into your partner's coat pocket, but it's functional. If you're reading this right now, then I still have hope. In the meantime, I'm taking breaths and listening to pop (Beyoncé's *Lemonade*) and dream pop (Beach House's *Bloom*) and hip-hop (Kendrick Lamar's *DAMN* on vinyl) and thinking about my daytrip to Santa Monica all day with LB (remind me to show you a pic someday). I'm revising this memoir right now as we speak. Here are the last seven timestamps for my manuscript revisions of this memoir:

1. 11 October 2016 at 10.20 am (via Amtrak, near Fullerton, CA)
2. 15 July 2017 at 12.46 am (DTLA, Los Angeles, CA)
3. 13 August 2018 at 11.13 pm (Thai Town/East Hollywood, Los Angeles, CA)
4. 13 August 2019 at 12.16 am (Old West Side, Ann Arbor, MI)
5. 19 September 2020 at 10.35 pm (Old West Side, Ann Arbor, MI)
6. 26 October 2021 at 9.29 pm (Hollywood, Los Angeles, CA)
7. 2 December 2021 at 4.46 pm (West Hollywood, CA)

Beyond that, I'm hoping I've published this memoir (sold to Unsolicited Press!) because that means you're reading it right now, which means I'm a published author (thank you thank you thank you, thank you goodnight), which means I might (or might not) be on tour, which means we may meet someday at a reading in the Last Bookstore or in out in the streets of Los Feliz or at Strand books or Skylight or Powell's or Literati or Unbridled or Elliott Bay Books or the Tattered Cover and maybe, just maybe, there's enough time for us to have tea together if I'm not exhausted and snippy and giving a reading at that exact moment, which means the universe might have collapsed into a fellowship of world-weary hope and rekindled joy after all, which means this shit life might not all be shit, and you and I might even exist together at last as people devoted to the redemption of language and storytelling, which is the marriage of the dream and the word.

九.

I want to say that I'm still breathing and writing almost every day and meditating (but not enough, never enough) and working hard to evolve as a flawed human being and artist and husband and global citizen and diehard klutz and shit-talking gamer and avid traveler and stalwart romantic and manga reader and urban liberal and unapologetic metrosexual who's basically straight but a little bit fluid sexually and sometimes non-binary and completely fluid romantically (at least theoretically) but also completely monogamous and deeply in love. I'm writing to tell you that I think of you with affection, even if we've never met. And in case you're curious, I won't stop holding LB's hand and half-wondering if the alphabet we pledge allegiance to becomes more beautiful the more endangered it becomes, the more unreal we become, as we all accelerate towards the end of the existential runway called old-age/global catastrophe/eco-apocalypse/pandemic shit show for the scientifically illiterate, as we glue and tape and staple the shredded confetti of our imperfectly designed ontologies into a wretched, maladroit, and sacred thing once more that we'll call humanity because really, nothing else makes sense except the elliptical pain and sublimity and ejection and impossibility. . .

次に/Next:

1. Remind me again what hapa means again. Sure, go to page 254, and get some fucking answers!
2. This is when Jackson started to feel old on page 63.
3. *Sung in John Coltrane cadence*: These are a few of my favorite WORDS, on page 173.
4. Of course, we all want Japanese okonomiyaki, but we're stuck here in America during this goddamn pandemic, eating 224 Pocky sticks a day. As they say in Osaka, "そかそれしゃあない。"
5. Or just turn the page or don't turn the page or turn it and then turn it back or . . .

70. Things I Learned from Reading My Baby Book

1. I was born at 5:30pm (which is often the time I leave the house when I stay up late the night before).

2. I was born on a Saturday, which happens to be my favorite day of the week (coincidence? I think not!).

3. I was born almost five weeks prematurely (because smoking and drinking while pregnant were totally cool in the '70s).

4. I weighed 5 pounds 9 ounces.

5. My complexion was listed as *red*, which sounds like a political slur or an allusion to my Maoist performance art project in college.

6. When I was born, my (racist, xenophobic, alcoholic, sexually-assaulting) grandfather said: *Fantastic!*

7. When I was born, my (spunky, generous, loving, hardworking) obāchan said: *Oh my God (a Boy)!*

8. When I was born, I screamed and cried the "second I was out" because I was evidently "eager to howl," which was the alternate title of this memoir by the way.

9. My first outing with the family was to Detroit for a picnic for *daddy's job via car.*

10. Possibly my favorite detail in the whole book: *[Jackson]'s first attempt at communicating with the world was around 2 months when he would smile and babble at the blk/wht lamp shade. Just lay or hold him anywhere that the shade was in sight and instant recognition + friendship!*

11. I also apparently loved staring at the ceiling and sitting on my dad's lap when he played piano, which makes sense now for so many reasons.

12. According to my mom, I was *known to babble on for ½ hour,* responding as if we were *carrying on a conversation.* For some reason, this last detail makes me both incredibly proud and also incredibly sad. It's like I was already trying to communicate with my parents before they disappeared. Like I knew they would.

次に/Next:
1. All the chismosos are meeting up on page 119 to rummage through my satchel like petty thieves. Stop them!
2. Metamorphosis from human being to magical realism, tonight on BBC-75.
3. To learn how Jackson's definition of "home" shifted over time, go to page 175.
4. To read a ~~derivative~~ memoir ~~that reads like every other memoir on the co-op table written by a white female author for a white female reader about being a white woman who goes to Italy or Bali or Vietnam or Argentina to find herself by exotifying local cuisine and sexualizing male bodies (of color) in the name of self-empowerment, simply google "memoir,"~~ please go to page 245 and kindly fuck off, but this time in the Loop because look, I'm not bitter, I'm not bitter ONE BIT at the way the Big-5 publishing industry has gendered creative nonfiction, memoir, and personal essays about infertility forever while telling men to evolve. Not one bit!
5. Or just turn the Gaga Googoo in your high-fashion meat dress.

71. My Maximalist Love Song for the Four Stars in 16 Movements

It's easy to croon nostalgic about Chicago once you've moved to another city and abandoned your dreams of hibernation in your avalanche of memories, daydreaming about funky Green Mill sets, Bahn Mi sandwiches on Argyle street with Jalapeños and shrimp paste, fresh Swedish cinnamon rolls and tempura udon in Andersonville, anorexic dinosaur replicas at the Field Museum, and the warm buzz of South Loop cafés after the first frost. It's easy to wax poetic about the Chi when you're just visiting for the first time or haven't been back in years, slowly leaving behind your buried frustrations, Sunday blues stages, scare jumps, and emotional disappointments in the snow-covered streets of Lincoln Park and the lingering chill of El tunnels in the early spring. It is infinitely harder to croon and remain faithful to your nostalgia after you've returned to the Loop and your chaotic reimagination has already blossomed into a full bouquet of agony, the humidity pickpocketing your qi with every labored breath, the grounded kindness of Chicagoans conflicting with the redlined segregation of your heartbroken city with its parallel worlds and Dickensian narratives, each one sharing the same Sinclairean jungle, the same green spaces of the south Loop, the same class envy in the Gold Coast, and the same buzz of knowledge and historical decay on the museum campus, always from different directions on the El. Chicago is a masterwork of contrapuntal narratives, everything turning to distorted fuzz as you leave, everything becoming a distant, Vaseline-smeared flashback to another time that really wasn't so long ago and really wasn't as awful or as beautiful as you remembered it.

Just as well since Chicago's redemption hides in a secret vault underneath the streets that only gangsters, historians, poets, and working-class heroes know how to excavate. In time, your memory erodes, unable to keep up with the nimble mutations of the city, your exiled revisionism, and the shifting stories you tell yourself about who you were when you last lived in Chicago and who you are now outside of it. Meanwhile, Chicago becomes another lesson in urban morphology: condos replace vacant lots, your favorite all-night haunt (the Third Coast Café) sheds its Escherian mirrors, rescinds its 24-hour service, and forsakes you as you knew it would, becoming a mediocre bistro for Old Town yuppies, the West Egg becomes another sushi joint with mysterious décor and blood red lanterns, Scenes Café becomes another Margarita joint, FAO Schwarz bids auf wiedersehen, the Red Line extends further into Chicago's parallel world, and Cabrini Green evaporates overnight, becoming a cautionary tale of ghetto liquidation and gentrified takeovers by stylish 2-garage condos with glass doors, stainless steel fridges, and broken-in concierges who remember when the neighborhood was a cautionary tale of urban poverty and before that, urban innovation.

Your teenage and college memories of Chicago have become slowly corrupted by reality, replaced and pilfered by modern condos, permanent construction sites, and uppity white commuters infected with historical amnesia, part-time racial blindness, and professional entitlement. The streets overflow with endless quantities of lost time, a classic moment of spatial defamiliarization for every misfit poet and quantum storyteller. Somehow in the middle of this acceleration of loss, there's me trying to reconstitute my hometown from the class conflict of DTLA, where I wrote this essay. Me, who is always five seconds away from obsolescence, me who is trying to hide behind the broken streetlights of Chicago, me, who cannot and will not let go of these memories because they have shaped me like primitive crafting tools, molding my form, my function, and the melodic universe inside my head. After all, it was in Chicago where I first:

1. HAD MY SEXUAL RENAISSANCE: after losing my virginity to J. in 11th grade at a forgettable party in Encinitas, I moved to Chicago my senior year, my ribcage fully ignited by the silent grief of heartbreak, the California divorce, and the strange desire of an adolescent romantic. In the following years, I dated and slept with girls who changed my understanding of my body, its syntax, and the linguistic exercise of Eros: M., a precocious girl from the Latin School who played Pink Floyd songs on her stoop and

came violently in my mouth the first time I went down on her after we smoked weed, X., a Greek gourmand who introduced me to spanakopita, souvlaki, ouzo, French Onion soup with a dash of port, the original Nintendo, Edna St. Vincent Millay, Karl Shapiro, and Kafka, S., who gave me head in her bedroom and took the El with me to the Art Institute after dropping acid, M., a desi classmate from Loyola who fucked a guy three hours before we did on our first date (the only time I've ever done that), R., a fierce Latina from the West Side who rammed her tongue down my throat in her car until I choked, S., a queer bartender I'd spent an indelible weekend with, who taught me to sing "Heigh-Ho! Nobody Home" in harmony on a perfect balmy afternoon as we walked around Evanston, smoking and talking about art and language and music and women and books, so many books, that eventually led to us going back to my place where we took a bath together and washed each other's bodies before she told me to touch myself so she could watch me come, which I did, then we had sex in my bed before falling asleep together, when I woke up the next day, she was gone, running into her only once after that on the El, when she walked up to me, hugged me, and then disappeared through the train doors like this memory. There were many girls, then women, I crushed on, made out with, thought about, and slept with because my hapa desire for wholeness was an awesome and insatiable thing, because I was independent for the first time in my life, because I was emotionally starving, ambitious, sometimes delirious, sometimes too emotional, sometimes too infatuated, and only love, sex, literature, and conversation mattered to me back then: a Latin School girl and a girl from Mango Street, an aspiring model, a British expat I called Little Debbie, a blond girl in knee-high boots who taught me how to do bong rips and then fuck in the middle of chaos, a mousey girl who offered me blowjobs in exchange for a relationship (nah!), a cerebral art history major who introduced me to tea drinking and undergraduate literary journals, a Seattle sociopath who didn't understand (or didn't believe in) foreplay, a mixed-race rebel who slept with me when she was unknowingly pregnant and still involved with a classmate (who tried to light my hair on fire during mass afterwards), the girlfriends of classmates who just wanted to talk on the phone for hours with someone who shared their love of music, books, and conversation while we secretly crushed on each other but never did anything except fantasize, college classmates from poetry and French class who invited me to their apartments in Rogers Park to drink cheap wine and eat college spaghetti, a Guatemateca I'd met who wore denim to every date and called me cariño in front of her tío, and a plus-size college graduate from Malibu who made out with me inside her condo, told me stories about celebrity run-ins in LA that made me miss California, and took me to gay bars in Boystown so she didn't have to go alone, even though I was underage and really just wanted her to sleep with me and hold my hand walking around Wicker Park and read poetry in the bathtub together. For six holy years, I was a human comma splice just like this paragraph, I was a bloom of the blossom, I was an urban disaster in training, only sex, novels, daydreaming, café conversations, long walks, and infatuation meant anything to me. Sometimes, it felt like I was all words, feelings, cigarettes, and pat gestures of romance. I was all nerdy romanticism, hapa prettiness, and unquenched bibliophilia. I was an argumentative atheist, an unoriginal iconoclast with dyed burgundy hair and preppy hand-me-downs and conflicting flannel shirts and fakeass Doc Martens. I was a smartass and an instigator of debates I always expected to win. I was an impulsive, insecure, pensive, passionate, deeply emotional, self-centered, affectionate, brash, preppy AF, energetic, vain, pain in the ass teenager (just like this autological sentence) who sought refuge again and again in the language of our existence, in our stories, and in the rapport of our bodies. I created one chapter of an alternative autobiography every time I stepped inside Chicago cafés scribbling in my journals, bumming cigarettes, going on dates in the afternoon, having 3 am conversations with strangers, and reading philosophy books that melted my brain. In Chicago, I learned about love and betrayal, desire and language, sex and plateau, desire and emptiness. Chicago gave me layers of existence, layers of self-expression, and layers of identity I didn't know I had or needed until I'd tasted my first cigarette and driven shotgun in a red sports car to Wicker Park and watched my first sunrise with a three-month girlfriend and made love on the Thanksgiving dining room table. This is why I will never stop loving

Chicago, why I refuse to, even when she breaks my heart, which is the prerequisite for falling in love.

2. SAW SCOTTIE PIPPEN PLAY AT THE OLD CHICAGO STADIUM: and he was more aerodynamic than a luge and more graceful and fearless than a murmuration of starlings.

3. BECAME OBSESSED WITH THE SMITHS: while I was living in Southern California, my friend Leta "lent" me one of her favorite tapes, which I, um, never gave back. *Louder than Bombs* became my teenage anthem. When I arrived in Chicago at the metamorphic age of seventeen, I'd finally returned home to the familiar shores of alternative music after an extended vacation listening to Brahms piano quartets, Rachmaninoff piano concerti, Mahler and Beethoven symphonies, Chopin ballades, sonatas, and nocturnes, Mozart sonatas, Dvořák symphonies, and Bach's cello suites at Interlochen where I was studying classical piano with the strict Dr. Yu, who used to slap my hands when I made mistakes and forced me to play scales during studio to "teach" me some fucked-up lesson about discipline (and humiliation). But Chicago brought me back to the beating heart of rock, alternative, grunge, and R & B, back to crashing cymbals, Sisters of Mercy synthesizers, Housemartin political slogans, '80s French pop songs, dream pop fantasia, Whitney choruses, and Gregorian chants set to break beats, which ultimately led to emo crushes and Johnny Mar riffs and Morrissey poetic lamentations, back to Manchester post-punk and fake Doc Martens (because I couldn't afford the real thing). In *Kill Uncle, The Queen is Dead, Your Arsenal,* and *Strangeways, Here We Come,* Morrissey and The Smiths became the soundtrack of my uprooted adolescence, my passionate obsession with words, and my fermenting scorn for injustice, hypocrisy, classism, and hierarchy. The Smiths became the soundtrack of my heartache, loneliness, ecstasy, and infatuation. I slipped grunge flannels into my preppy wardrobe, I dyed my hair burgundy, I scribbled in my journal every week, I read novels on the El religiously, and I freebased on the endless supply of melancholy in the alt subculture of Chicago because I was allowed to feel and think and write through my reality and also protest the self-blindness of class privilege and institutional racism.

4. VOLUNTEERED FOR AMERICORPS (& GOT MY FIRST DOSE OF THE URBAN EDUCATION CRISIS): teaching literacy in English and Spanish to Black and Latino kids at Cameron Elementary School for the University of Chicago's Center for Urban School Improvement, I saw how dysfunctional public education in America was. A series of interconnected problems involving stultified, overwhelmed, culturally disconnected white female teachers, ineffective and calcified administration, overworked, hostile, and/or indifferent parents, some of whom didn't speak English or hadn't graduated from high school or had their own stories of trauma from the public school system, mind-crushing bureaucracy, nonexistent school enforcement for disruptive behavior, a classist system of revenue collection based on property taxes, underfunded social services for students that needed social workers, counselors, and therapists, hidden drug addiction and sexual violence inside single and two-parent households, lack of state and federal economic investment in low-income neighborhoods, absurd teacher union policies like getting rid of recess and ending classes at 2:30 pm, hidden family malnutrition, and early teenage pregnancy. I saw it all and what I saw broke me. I tried living on the $700 a month Americorps stipend, which was so little money for Chicago, I qualified for food stamps and then saw firsthand what poor people went through just to exist, what we put poor people through to justify their survival, and it bruised my soul. I formed friendships with students who moved me, humbled me, and taught me about the indomitable spirit of the underdog and the subaltern. Being an Americorps volunteer in the West Side taught me more about systemic racism than every book I've ever read.

5. EMERGED FROM THE CHICAGO CHRYSALIS: my dad and I drove from Chicago to Oberlin College. I moved from Chicago to South Bend with the help of my friend Mona to start my MFA at Notre Dame. After we fell in love, LB and I moved from Chicago to Buenos Aires with the money we'd saved up to improve our quality of life (and also to avoid the 2008 Recession). A year later, we traveled from Chicago to Spain, France, the Netherlands, Switzerland, and Morocco together before we spent the summer in Lakeview. At the end of August, I boarded the Amtrak

Southwest Chief at Chicago Union Station and traveled across the country to LA to start my PhD at USC. Chicago was first my chrysalis and then my hub to other destinations, both my site of transformation and later my waiting room for the next metamorphosis. Unlike Kanye, though, I will never take the Chi for granted or sell out to white nationalism.

6. STARTED SMOKING: it all started when I listened to *Louder than Bombs* in SoCal, moved to Chicago, attended a Jesuit prep school in Wilmette, and became the token atheist, the mixed-race pretty boy, the argumentative city boy, and the lower middle class hapa Caulfield. I began smoking weed, commuted from Uptown all the way to Wilmette every day by taking two trains and a bus. I made out with rich white girls at Catholic prep school parties who had names I'd never heard before, fancy cars I'd never been inside, and European vacation stories I couldn't relate to. Even my two best friends from Loyola Academy were loaded (but not entitled, thank god). Smoking was an act of class horizontality for me, but it was also a form of adolescent diplomacy that crossed racial, geographic, and class boundaries as well. The first time I bought smokes, I felt like I became an adult. It was half past eight and I was studying for a Latin test, listening to Morrissey, the apartment all to myself. I'd been bumming smokes from friends at parties at beautiful North Shore houses for months, and then one night with a couple bucks to spare, I realized I could be my own provider since no one checked ID in Chicago, so I walked inside a musty Chinese restaurant in Little Vietnam and bought a pack of Camels from a cigarette machine even though I was seventeen. I walked outside afterwards and lit my first purchased smoke like it was nothing, the darkness outside forming a hoodie around my cherubic face. Smoking became my gateway drug to an imaginary adulthood. I started smoking at the same time I learned to navigate the El. Soon, I smoked with my best friend Sébastien, I shared a half-full box of Marlboro Lights with the ox-eyed Regina Dominican class president at a Loyola Academy football game after she'd offered me a sip from her tiny flask. I smoked weed and Camels with my best friend Brendan in a forest in Winnetka with the fading sunlight trickling through the treetops in flash benediction as the evening landed on top of us. I smoked during long walks on the Northwestern campus when I was high or tripping

on acid, the color symbolism of the kelly-green grass, earth tone leaves, and the fall sweaters of students all wheezing into the air like punctured paint cans. Smoking became my romantic gesture of punk rock freedom and self-destruction, a marker for my new role as the misplaced writer and the alienated intellectual from the rough part of town. Smoking was five minutes of silence, an unjustified reward that felt Mephistophelian but also Joycean (pic-pac-poc). Smoking made me feel like a bad hapa subject but also a school insider where every student at my school had a personal relationship to tobacco. Smoking turned me into a figment of my novelistic imagination but also a total stranger as I looked at myself in the mirror of prep school stylization only six months after I'd skipped class and gone to LA with friends from California. Smoking was a tiny performative utterance of my independence that made me urbane, rebellious, Eurotrashy but also Asian, fictional, timeless, and Salingersque. Smoking helped me become a city boy, a literary protagonist, an honorary European, and a latter-day sensualist.

7. LEARNED THE GIFT OF MOBILITY & SELF-RELIANCE: I learned my civic lessons about freedom, mobility, self-reliance, and courage by taking mass transit. I took it every day to high school and then to college except on the days that I skipped, which were always my favorite days in Chicago, even better than the weekends when sloppy couples and grinning families were on full display, which made me feel suddenly alone. Sometimes, I took the El back home at four in the morning after studying all night at the Third Coast Café, whose walls were once drenched in various mirrors of different sizes and lengths, turning the café into a complicated equation of infinity. For the first time since childhood when I used to ride my bike everywhere, I didn't rely on other people to get around. Not my parents, girlfriends, classmates, or friends' parents. Not my morphing crew of friends, debate team coaches, or friends of friends of friends. I traveled on the train from the pristine lawns of the North Shore to the rocky beaches of Evanston, from eclectic Lakeview to get fresh ink, vegan Reubens, and cubs tickets, to the other side of hipster paradise to drink mochas, read Russian novels, and smoke English cigarettes in Wicker Park, from the vibrant color tours of the Northwestern campus to the

parallel universe of Hyde Park bookstores, vegan soul food restaurants, and backyard gardens in the South Side, from the boarded up apartments in Little Vietnam to the white flight suburbs and exurbs of Schaumburg, Kennilworth, and Lake Forest, and then to the flyover city of Rosemont to buy anime videos, Japanese groceries, and ocha at Mitsuwa. I could do these things all by myself in Chicago, whenever I wanted to, whenever I needed the warm, inviting spaces of café chatter or the solace of long, snow-crunching walks through Streeterville or chilly Autumn strolls down Michigan Avenue over the bridge to Millennium Park or the therapy of German chocolates filled with marzipan and pistachios in Lincoln Square. The El, in particular, was my busted-up chariot crashing through divine gusts of wind, the bolts groaning in the train cars, the windows frosting in the subarctic temperatures, but always delivering me safely to Ithaca, and by that, I mean to Berwyn, Davis, Argyle, Belmont, Chicago, Fullerton, Adams, Western, and Damen. The El was the most reliable companion I had in Chicago after my journal.

8. CHEATED ON SOBRIETY: I dropped acid and walked around Evanston in a daze, the Northwestern campus becoming my hajj, my dream quest to a higher level of consciousness. I stayed up all night walking around Lake Michigan with X. before eating eggs and sausage at a greasy spoon in Andersonville. I listened to the Cocteau Twins' *Treasure* on repeat and tried to levitate by jumping into the air. I smoked weed and then wrote gimmicky poetry that deserved to be burned. I wrote manifestos to my childhood, I wrote theorems about organized religion as a form of mind control in my journal for religion class. I met girls who pulled bowls out of their purses and asked me to fuck them in their new Rogers Park apartment, we had sex inside their Jeeps in dark alleys at two in the morning and sometimes in broad daylight with our pupils wide as satellite dishes. I raided my dad's Christmas gift baskets when I got the munchies. I went on long walks through Uptown, Edgewater, Rogers Park, and Lakeview. I called Jenny in Michigan and Leta in California just to hear their voices and remember what it felt like to be known. I watched late-night cable with my brother and laughed at cheesy music videos and local commercials. At North Shore parties, I drank gin cocktails with my friends and screwdrivers and shots of

straight vodka that tasted like paint thinner, the enamel practically disappearing on my teeth, I downed shots of Jameson that ripped through my empty stomach like a nuclear isotope. My brother and I once even tried smoking nutmeg and banana peels after following the "recipes" in *The Anarchist Cookbook*, which were both horrendous, like trying to inhale an electrocuted orange. Chicago became my laboratory of exploration both within myself and also within the multicultural fractal of the city.

9. WROTE MY FIRST—AND TOTALLY SHITTY—POEM: my poem made a political statement about the savagery of war by juxtaposing war crimes to a Caesar salad. It was an unforgivable double entendre (I know, I know), but the important thing was that I found refuge in writing, I found a reliable listener and mentor in narrative and in language, I found self-empowerment and self-defense in the dojo of the blank page, I found the arrowhead of my tongue and the realpolitik of my words, which I launched at my enemies, my buried fears, and my undocumented obsessions. I found dual citizenship in prose and poetry. I found repatriation in the syntax of failure, excavation, and reincarnation.

10. SAW MY FIRST MUSICAL (& BAWLED MY EYES OUT): I went to *Les Mis.* with my dad, dressed like Ricardo Tubbs. I'd borrowed one of his Miami Vice Jackets and slicked back my hair for the hell of it. From the first note of "Work Song" until the last note of "Do You Hear the People Sing?" from the instrumental overture until the final curtain call, I sang along and cried almost continuously until my dad was forced to ask me if I was okay. I wasn't. My first summer in Chicago had been one of the most painful moments of my life and he didn't know because he didn't ask and didn't care. Three months earlier, I'd left California to move in with him and he'd abandoned me the very first week, leaving me alone in his half-furnished apartment in Uptown until late at night with a near-empty fridge where I was stuck in the sweltering apartment all by myself, a little bit freaked out about living in the city for the first time next to a cemetery, and forced to wait for dinner every night like a prisoner. Pops would saunter home sometimes at eight at night, sometimes at one in the morning, completely unconcerned about me, never wondering how I was holding up, and never interested in talking to me, his face punch-drunk with booze and

Camel unfiltered cigarettes from another night on the town with coworkers. This was his formula: he'd say hi, plop a Styrofoam container of food on the kitchen counter, brush his teeth as I inhaled a lukewarm hamburger and tested my gag reflex cramming starchy bouquets of wedge fries down my throat, and then he'd close his bedroom door without a word as I was wiping my mouth. For months, I couldn't shake the feeling that I'd made the biggest mistake of my life because he didn't want me. If my dad's intention had been to try to deny my existence or treat me like I was nothing but a hassle and a chore and an obligation and a colossal mistake and an unfortunate leftover from a bygone era, then he succeeded. But if his intention was to erase me, then he failed. The signs were all there anyway: he didn't show up to see me debate during Nationals after I'd qualified in the Southern California district (a tournament that just happened to be in nearby Glenbrook that year), he never talked to me when he came home at night reeking of cigarettes, beer, and fried food, he never walked around the neighborhood with me or took me out to dinner or showed me how to get around the Loop or spent any real time with me, he barely acknowledged my existence on the rare nights he was home, and even then, he looked annoyed like I was a bad dream that wouldn't disappear. It's hard to put into words what it felt like to know (to have always known) that your dad saw you as dead weight, to know that your existence was an obvious burden to the one person who'd already left so much negative space inside you, the person you'd ironically run to when California had crumbled into the sea like every geologist said it would. After I'd moved to Chicago, my dad had almost sent me to Florida to live with my mom, which confirmed everything I'd felt that summer. Two weeks before the musical, I'd called up Sarah, a friend from summer camp. She told me to take the #22 Clark bus to Belmont and Clark. She said the fare was $1.25. She said to meet her in front of the Dunkin Donuts, so I hopped on the #22 bus, scared and relieved to leave the apartment like an abused Dachshund with a broken leash that I dragged on the ground behind me. We walked to Scenes Café, ignored its self-irony, and talked forever. For a few hours, I felt like a normal teenager again. When she dropped me off at the bus stop and kissed me, I had to stop myself from crying. Sarah made me feel human again and I wanted to take her home with me. Two weeks later at the Auditorium Theater dressed like a DEA agent from Miami, I had so much uncountable sadness, resentment, and anger to let go of, so I sang along to every song and bawled my fucking eyes out because it was the only place I was allowed to have emotions. *Les Mis* was the only opportunity that summer to let go of my confusion and shame and betrayal and anger and loneliness, an unconscious way to force my dad to accept my feelings even if he didn't understand them, the way I forced him to acknowledge my pain and my loneliness and my subjectivity, even if he didn't want to. It was a musical I knew by heart that felt like home to me in this city full of strangers, dirty streets, and absent divorcés. Some songs can't be unheard, though he tried.

11. WENT TO MY FIRST MAJOR LEAGUE BASEBALL GAME: after I'd complained to my dad that he never spent any time with me (a incessant motif in this memoir), he took me to a Cubs game and just like in Hollywood movies, the home team came from behind in the final inning to win. Cubs fans gave each other high-fives, screaming in celebration, wobbly from beer served in Solo plastic cups, and then we high-fived too, possibly for the first time. Our performative joy felt viral. This was probably the manliest thing my dad and I ever did together as grown men. For a few brief seconds, it felt like we were friends, a feeling I relished because of its fragile untruth.

12. READ MY FIRST POEM ON OPEN MIC NIGHT: it was a shitty, pretentious poem (I still apologize for nothing!). I read it to a group of cynical teenagers at the No Exit Café, all of them trying hard to act like Beatnik geniuses and Bukowski clones. Geniuses they weren't, nor Sartre fans or beat readers for that matter. They were a tough crowd though and I felt their disapproval (and my own power) in every word that I fired from my mouth. Sometimes, you have to walk through fire to understand how much of your writing needs to be burned. Remember: you can baptize yourself with your ashes.

13. FELL IN LOVE WITH KANDINSKY & CHAGALL EVERY SATURDAY: once I was comfortable taking the El around the city, I spent every Saturday afternoon in high school going to the Art Institute of Chicago and spending the day looking at *Painting with a Green Center, The*

Praying Jew, and my favorite mosaic of all time, the metatextual *American Windows*. Modern art made me feel complex, lost, centered, awake, inspired, and deeply understood. Sometimes, I wondered if it was possible to date a painting, which was the inspiration behind my short story, "When Silence is an Old Warehouse and Love is a Pocketful of Rocks." Not that you asked.

14. EXPERIENCED DISCRIMINATION: though absolutely nothing compared to the shit my Black, Native, and Brown friends have to deal with every day of their lives, I was racially dehumanized. Back in the day when the Rainbow Roller Rink was still a thing, I'd just begun exploring Uptown on my own and was walking down Clark Street late one summer night. I was halfway across Lawrence when a car raced down Clark Street and tried turning left at the light, practically running me over. When I looked at the car in disbelief, the Black driver shouted: *You stupid-ass white boy! You stupid fucking white boy! Get the FUCK out of the street!* I was speechless. My Black, Asian, Latino, Arab, and White friends had never talked to me like I was human garbage before, even during the most heated arguments, so the shock and the humiliation I felt were real. The irony was, I'd had the right of way. I'd started walking when the light turned green, and I was halfway across the street before she'd raced to the intersection to make the light, but she'd still managed to make me feel bad about something I couldn't control, making me aware of my (partial) whiteness, its (potentially) oppressive signification to Black people, its default power to protect me from (police, racial, and class) trauma if I'd called for help, but also its simultaneous illegibility to white people and people of color, who couldn't see me as I was (a mixed-race, Nisei, hapa teenager). To her, I looked like just another clueless white guy demanding space he didn't need. She made me feel like I didn't belong in my own neighborhood, a feeling I still get sometimes when I walk around Chicago by myself. After I'd crossed the street that night, shaking my head in disbelief, three Black teenagers who'd been watching the drama unfold, crossed the street and followed me down the sidewalk. I tried not to look back, but I was a little freaked out and a little confused, the night spiraling out of my control. At one point, someone muttered under his breath: *Go ahead, call us n***** and we'll bust*

yo' ass. I'd never felt so misunderstood, so lost, so pissed off, or so powerless before.

15. DANCED ON MICHIGAN AVENUE IN THE MIDDLE OF TRAFFIC: during my second summer in Chicago, Sébastien and I were walking down Michigan Avenue when traffic came to a dead halt in front of the Art Institute. By the time we'd pushed our way through the traffic jam, we spotted a large crowd of people dancing to African Drums and shaking it to a Brazilian band playing in the middle of the street while cars stopped in a trance and passengers looked on, completely stunned. Sébastien and I jumped right into the throng of dancing people and got down because youth. We danced in the street with Polish grandaddies and old Puerto Rican women, Black and White people, tourists and drunk frat kids, an Asian girl and her sister. It was an insane and crazy moment of class synchronicity in Chicago. Afterwards, we walked onto the sidewalk again to catch our breath when a middle-aged Black guy turned to me and said, *Isn't it amazing how music can bring White and Black folks together like this?* I nodded in agreement. Suddenly, I felt grateful to be in this city, grateful to see the collective humanity of Chicago harnessed through music and shared common space, expressed through flash mob and infectious rhythm, sweat and trance, shock and laughter. This was the thing I'd needed after the Rainbow incident. I witnessed the sheer force of community art and collective jubilation in Chicago for the first time and it changed me. I learned that art could disarm the landmines of class and racial conflict for one particular moment.

16. WENT ON MY FIRST DATE WITH LB: I had an ugly lip piercing (should have gotten it in the middle, not the side) and I was wearing a ready-to-wear gray pinstriped suit from Banana Republic that was boxy and big in the shoulders because I didn't know what bespoke meant. Even worse, I was late (a terrible habit of mine). I wore the suit for the worst interview I've ever had with the JET program where I was told (tacitly, of course) that I was too old for the job, that my lip ring was a distraction, and that my stint in the Peace Corps made me a flight risk for a job teaching English in Japan because you know, West Africa and Japan are practically the same thing. I was late to my first date with LB because I was buying a

new pair of Kenneth Coles for her, not for my bullshit interview with the JET program. One thing Pops taught me, which I actually appreciate even now, is that you can learn a lot about a man by his shoes. Despite my sexual renaissance in Chicago in high school, LB was the one and only person I ever fell deeply in love with in Chicago despite the myriad crushes, daydreams, hookups, and make-out sessions that had transformed me into the person I became. My date with LB in the dead of winter was the one and only time I bought shoes for a first date. It was the first time I knew exactly who I was, what I wanted, and where I was going, all at the same time. The emotional synchronicity would have been sickening if it hadn't been so joy-making.

次に/Next:

1. To watch Jackson taping torn pieces of his origami together, go to page 260.
2. To learn about Jackson's favorite childhood video games, go to page 85.
3. To see why Ashton Kutchner was the wrong host for *Punked,* go to page 129.
4. There's nothing more terrifying than giving an oral report in French class. Let's eavesdrop on another compromising moment for Jackson on page 159.
5. Or just turn the page.

72. My Pro/Con List About Living in Buenos Aires

CON LIST (Ya!)

1. Ubiquitous dog shit, dog piss, construction, and garbage on almost every single block in Palermo Viejo

2. Living on empanadas, pizza, arroz chaufa, spaghetti, and salads (when we had enough money) as vegetarians

3. The water in our apartment that gave us eczema

4. The air quality when colectivos pass by

PRO LIST (Sí)

1. Little kids in Cap Fed all dressed up in little person suits and dresses, speaking to you in adorable sheismo

2. Argentines' sense of humor, which is completely infectious

3. Viejitos when they tell you about their life in Italy, or how they knew Borges, or what life was like in Buenos Aires in the 60s, when their skin was smooth and their mannerisms were romantic and exaggerated

4. Parque de Palermo Viejo (where LB and I used to drink mate together) and Esquina de la Flores (a refuge for vegetarians living on honey granola bars)

5. Insane drivers that accelerate towards pedestrians and red lights

6. Our neighbor downstairs who spent all weekend yelling into her phone

7. The Coto loading dock across the street from our bedroom

8. The guilt of having a cleaning lady we never wanted who came with the rental

9. Flash inflation

10. The prospect of contracting Dengue Fever

11. The Maradona cult (RIP, chico)

5. The love Argentines have for their family, gorditos, and friends

6. The redemption of city lights at night (especially in Microcentro)

7. The detailing, the embellishment, and the color scheme of porteño doors

8. Riding a crowded Subte that's scorching, especially when passengers are pushing me against a beautiful mina against my will, who smiles at me (what can you do, man?)

9. Argentine passion and bluntness

10. Porteñas in sun, black-wrap, and leopard dresses in Recoleta, Maxi and pinafore dresses in Palermo Hollywood, miniskirts and oxfords in Microcentro, cardigans and tank-tops in Palermo SoHo

11. Hearing the word *chau* each and every day

12. Being so far away from my fam

12. Kissing absolute strangers on the cheeks before I can even decide if I want to

13. The coin shortage in Cap Fed with all of its accompanying conspiracy theories (e.g., it's Chinese immigrants, it's the Mafia, it's a cartel—no bitches, it's the National Mint)

13. The satisfaction I get when my Spanish works on autopilot

14. Subte rides where viejitas pass out because it's so fucking hot and the AC doesn't work

14. Learning to be happy so far away from home

15. Expat tangueras who think they "know" Argentina because they spent three weeks in a milonga dancing with dirty old men and opportunistic male chauvinists who assume tourists are easy to sleep with

15. The religious ritual of the daily merienda

16. The tiny fear I have of getting jacked, robbed, or kidnapped every time I walk to the ATM machine or leave our apartment at night (because it happened to almost everyone we knew)

16. Having a life that is so vastly different than that of my American friends

17. People who say, *así no se dice acá* every time they hear something that's not Argentine, as

17. Argentine wine, in particular, *Trumpeter*

if our only obligation is to
replicate Argentineness

18. National cynicism,
resignation, and apathy as a
pretext for not doing shit so one
can continue to be cynical,
resigned, and apathetic

19. Hanging out with Argentinos
who obviously hate my country,
but have never visited it and don't
know shit about it

20. One-hour lines at the
supermarket and the bank, after
which, a repetition of #16

18. Dinners with expat friends
from England, Australia, Sweden,
France, US, and Singapore

19. Teenage girls flirting with me
in Nuñez

20. Talking fiction with Jon, my
Aussie friend at Plaza Holanda

21. Seeing the whole city
illuminated from Annie and
Jimmy's rooftop

22. Jokes my English students at
Accenture made about nude ping-
pong, Viagra addiction, sexually
insatiable wives, and trans
fantasies

23. Fresh OJ stands in
Microcentro

24. Making love with LB in the
afternoon, just as the city is
sighing

25. Walking through cobblestone streets in San Telmo as a fiction writer

26. Remembering the important things in life (e.g., love, laughter, fresh food, health, joy, patience, kindness, language, music, red wine, nourishment, laughter, and evolution)

27. Spring's vegetarian buffet, brownies and licuados at Dave's Café, and all-you-can east vegan buffets at Los Sabios

28. The Sunday venders selling hand-made necklaces, Crayola soap bars, mate gourds, chrome wind chimes, knock-off baseball caps, homemade incense, and lots of intricately constructed wire things I could never understand

29. Futból passion

30. Tons of great used bookstores that put America to shame

31. Listening to Bebel Gilberto as I crossed El 9 de Julio and taking long showers on the weekend

32. (Green) High Tea and Vanilla coconut cake dates with LB at Último Beso

---

Cap Fed wins, 32-20!

次に/Next:

1. To see Jackson and his brother smoking weed, ~~driving up the 101 in a shiny Turquoise Lowrider Impala with chrome, wire-rimmed spinners, listening to *The Chronic,* and drinking 40's with environmentally friendly metal straws,~~ go to page 50.
2. "I heart lamps," said the newborn Jackson on page 271. Wait, WTF?
3. Watch Jackson kiss LB on Charles Bridge on page 99.
4. Create a sentence from the following letters: n, u, s, h, e, t, o, j, e, t, r, u, p, a, t, r, g.

73. My Promotion to the Elephants

In 1st grade, my teacher demoted me to the elephants, the slowest reading group. Some of the kids in this group had legit learning disabilities. For the next five years, I had to live with the knowledge that my teachers thought I was almost illiterate. I knew they were full of shit, but I couldn't do anything about it except remember. When I was placed back in the highest reading group in 6th grade after an external literacy coordinator gave me a diagnostic exam and encouraged me to correct my own mistakes (god bless her), the damage was already done. I knew what teachers thought (or had failed to notice) about me, so I stopped caring about literature or writing until I was accepted into the honors program in 10th grade. Twenty-two years later, I revisited my elementary school and walked inside my old 6th grade classroom where I saw my old teacher. Wearing an avuncular cardigan and a flannel oxford, Mr. D. looked exactly as I'd remembered him, except for streaks of silver in his receding hairline and sunken red cheeks. I asked him if he remembered me. He shook his head apologetically. I knew it was probably better that way. After all, it had taken me years to forget my own stigma. I'd been brandished with the stamp of intellectual inferiority. Now, standing inside his classroom with the tiny desks and construction paper art covering the walls, a defiant and bruised part of me wanted to be remembered, I wanted impossible things from him, I wanted him to remember my stigma, mislabeling, and erasure, I wanted to tell him how wrong the system had been, how wrong all of them had been, how I was just a microcosm of every smart, creative, inquisitive, countercultural, mixed-race, non-white student to go through the public school system in America. I wanted to drop on his lap a long, damning speech about how schools shouldn't mistake creativity, independence, heterodoxy, and skepticism for recalcitrance, defiance, ignorance, and inability. I wanted to tell him that schools should encourage their students to think for themselves and question everything, even the questions themselves, and embrace their unique ways of learning, interpreting, feeling, understanding, and engaging with reality. I also wanted to thank him for calling me an elephant (even though it was my first-grade teacher, not him), because elephants are such beautiful, altruistic, and evolved creatures. They have the Buddha nature, they love being near water, they're Asian or African and they have adorable, floppy ears and gargantuan brains, they're vegetarians and they communicate through touch, just as I do. And they're empathetic, self-aware, and endangered animals trying to survive in this violent and harsh and greedy and masculinist world that humans have made in their most domineering, relentless, and destructive image. Above all, I wanted to thank him as the signifier of my elementary school for making me an accidental symbol of good luck and a gorgeous beast of immense strength and devotion in this heart-breaking and heart-broken cage-fight of a world. We were sweet, sensitive, and clumsy creatures living in an ecosystem that didn't know how to sustain us, but if you hurt us or devalued us or treated us like objects, we wouldn't hesitate to stomp on the ring master and crash into the bleachers.

次に/Next:

1. Because life isn't depressing enough, maybe it's time to wander to page 141 and get HIGH ON DEPRESSION! Emokids, unite!
2. Curious to see which religious phases Jackson went through (what do you mean, NO? How *dare* you!), go to page 257.
3. To see Jackson walking through Istanbul in a daze, go to page 133.
4. Or just turn the page.

74. How (Not!) to Spot a Hapa

At some point in your reading of this permutational memoir, you'll end up here at chapter #74. For most readers, this chapter isn't the end of your reading, it's just a flyover page in a much longer journey and having grown up in Chicago (and before that, Michigan) before my move out West, I'm particularly sensitive to being a flyover anything, especially from those coastal elites who are always rejecting my manuscripts due to matters of taste, racial illiteracy, cultural ignorance, and perfectionism (*there's much to admire in this manuscript but it wasn't a perfect fit*) and infatuation (*I didn't completely fall in love with your mixed-race protagonist because whiteness is all I know*) before giving million-dollar advances to white women novelists who write about greedy and dysfunctional white East Coast families and white women traveling to Bali and Tuscany and Martha's Vineyard to find themselves, but that's just a clumsy generalization based on my own personal frustration and the goddamn gospel truth.

For a few of you (the lazy, the unscrupulous, the unengaged, some of my jealous classmates and frenemies who always hated me for being mixed-race cute and having soft hands and dressing like a French schoolboy or a Cranberries fanboy or a G-star urban stylist or a Japanese MC or an English hipster, as well as those I've hurt at some point saying stupid, insensitive, and obnoxious shit to growing up—gomen, ne—not to mention those trying to impress their partners, spouses, friends, and snotty classmates, especially the really pretentious ones who act like they've read everything, even though most of their knowledge comes from late-night Google searches and bookmarked LitHub interviews), you'll stop reading here just because numerically speaking, it's the last chapter. So, to channel Queen Bey, bye reader bye! I don't hold it against you at all and I thank you for ~~buying~~ reading this book.

But for most of you, the "ending" of *Dream Pop Origami* is really wherever and whenever you decide to call it quits, which, if you think about it, is a huge responsibility. I mean, what if you pick a really shitty chapter to "end" this memoir, then you'll have a terrible taste in your mouth and you'll blame me for it. You'll be talking about this memoir with a friend at a tiny bar that charges twenty bucks for a glass of clumsy California Chardonnay in Silver Lake (or the Village or Wicker Park or Queen Anne or Alberta Street or Dupont Circle or the French Quarters or the Mission District or Harvard Square) and then you'll confess that you "didn't love the ending," even though the "ending" was your decision completely, no one else's, and then, just as you say that, you'll make a mental note to read a few more chapters of this memoir so you like the ending more (and who can blame you?). But what if you pick a really awesome chapter to "end" *Dream Pop Origami* with and then when you try to talk about it with one of your snotty, pretentious classmates who acts like they've read everything even when they haven't (including THIS MEMOIR, which they've NEVER HEARD OF!) or like, with your close friend at that tiny Silver Lake/Los Feliz/WeHo/DTLA bar with the annoying jukebox of bad '70s hits and the pealing stools and the C-list celebrities all dressed to lay and the musty books used as props in the fucking background because Angelenos don't read shit besides IMDB and IG comments, you eventually realize you've "ended" this memoir at totally different places, so the two of you can't even AGREE on how this memoir ends or even in which direction the storytelling went. No one can! Imagine how fucking frustrating THAT shit would be. Usually, reading is a low-stakes consideration, but as you know, in THIS memoir, reading is high stakes because you decide HOW this memoir begins, you decide WHERE it goes, and you decide WHEN this memoir makes it closing remarks, at least until you pick it up again or treat it like another book of Borgesian infinity that just goes on forever until you go batshit crazy or hurl the book out the window, which is actually one of the instructions at the end but like, no pressure.

So, if you think about it, dear reader, you and I are a team, which is kinda dope. Yes, I wrote this book, but you're choosing HOW this piece of creative nonfictions unfolds and also how long this memoir is, which means in a way, YOU'RE writing this memoir too to the extent that deciding, editing, choosing, and altering a text constitutes a version of writing, which it ABSOLUTELY DOES. What that means is that you (dear reader) and I (Jackson I wish I had a Japanese surname Bliss) are in this together as partners in crime, so to speak, for as long as you read this book. And thank you, by the way, for reading *Dream Pop Origami*. ~~I know there are a million other experimental, permutational memoirs out there, so~~ it means a great deal to me that you picked DPO and not another memoir, say, about white women who go to Provence or Amsterdam or Bali or Naples to find themselves through yoga, sex, culture shock, and gluttony before writing a memoir that gets a three-million advance that they don't need, don't deserve, and don't even fucking spend well (and by the way, I'M NOT JEALOUS AT ALL, NOT EVEN A TINY BIT).

But for those of you longing for something more definitive in a memoir (and I think we could all use something more concrete in the era of the perpetual Trumpian crisis where everything is awful, unstable, and nothing seems real anymore), I'm "ending" *Dream Pop Origami* with a short checklist for you. Please feel free to read another chapter if you're not feeling it. This memoir gives you that right.

So, here we go. Just for you (and the other three thousand people who bought/stole/memorized a Wikipedia entry for this memoir):

HOW TO SPOT A HAPA

1. ~~Go to the nearest indie bookstore and look in the Asian language book aisle.~~

2. ~~Attend the next Mixed Remixed festival in LA & be sure to demand (don't ask, demand) that Jackson Bliss be the keynote speaker.~~

3. ~~Read *Part Asian, 100% Hapa*, check out the Hapa Japan Project online, or stroll through San Francisco with a notepad and a rice cooker/time machine.~~

4. ~~Travel to the big island and shout, "Are you hapa?" to every Pacific Islander surf dude. It'll be a big hit for sure, trust me.~~

5. ~~Open your fucking eyes, bakayeroi!.~~

6. ~~Climb up a tree and watch the Nisei Festival with a pair of binoculars.~~

7. ~~Just read this memoir, like duuuuuuuuh.~~

8. Hang out in noodle shops all night long.

9. Take the Bad Nisei Quiz (p. 42, as luck would have it).

10. Fly to Japan and look up every mixed-race model.

11. Go to a poke bar in Honolulu and take notes.

12. After you've incorrectly guessed someone's racial, class, and cultural background inside your head, take a good look at their face and then ask them out loud about the story of their life in any way except, "What ARE you?" and "Where are you from?" They'll be happy to tell you. Hapa, hafu, and mixed-race people are hella vain, as it turns out, and they really love their grandmas.

次に/Next:

1. The day Jackson became a Sufjan Steven's album (but like, not *The Ascension*, sorry Sufjan), on page 273.

2. To watch Jackson finish his existential Lego set (um, YEAH, dude), go to page 260.

3. "Miso and the Wonders of the Spirit World Tonight on Channel 126!"

4. Or just flip to the beginning of this memoir, cuz this is where the magic carpet ride ends, Aladdin.

HOW (NOT!) TO READ *DREAM POP ORIGAMI*

-**Calvinist Method**: Read this book from beginning to end like you have no choice, ignoring options for exercising your own free will after every chapter.

-**Choose-Your-Own-Biography Method**: Pick a number between 1-74 and/or read first chapter and/or then choose exclusively from the option mention. Celebrate the permutational autobiography for what it is and/or for what it can/should be and resist the tyranny of plot (which is an artistic marker of capitalism and a cultural marker of the aristocracy), comrade!

-**Rando Method**: Flip to a random chapter and start reading. Memorize the highlights. Later, walk up to a complete strange and start talking to them for no goddamn reason like you're finishing an earlier convo: —So, going back to our earlier conversation, I think this memoir is fucking crazy! You hear me? Fucking insane! Wait for bewildered look. Then moonwalk away.

-**Origami Method of Dirty Love:** Gently (some might say *lovingly*) rip a page from this memoir and fold into an origami crane (or other creatures in your Pokémon dungeon). Continue folding each page until paper metamorphosis is complete. Toss origami through window until the sky is filled with words spiraling to the ground like deciduous leaves. Ask strangers on the sidewalk to collect your word origami, in a bucket. Give them your phone number and ask them to call you after they've unraveled your each paper metamorphosis, and then read them to you. Finally, make out with said stranger because YOLO and the aphrodisiac of hot language burning on your tongue.

-**Iconoclastic Method**: Start reading from END of book, just because you can. This way, you can be the baddest motherfucker in the café or the classroom or the train or the hot air balloon.

-**Paint Gun Method**: Steal paint gun from Minutemen wannabe neighbor/ex-militia uncle convinced that Biden is going to steal their guns and/or that there's a celebrity pedophilia ring, and then shoot at your copy of *DPO*. Finally, read paint-splatted chapters exclusively.

-**Violent Brainwash Method**: Throw book on floor and read open chapter or read first torn page after apologizing profusely to your partner who was doing yoga on said floor. Consider buying partner tulips and duct-taping spine. Yours, I mean! Do you do everything an author tells you to do? Please say no.

-**Mom (Probably) Knows Best Method**: Call Mom up and tell her to pick a number between 1-74, then read appropriate chapter. If she tells you to call her more often, do it! You can always buy another copy of this (amazing, breathtaking, once-in-a-lifetime, sui generis) memoir, but you can't buy another copy of your mom.

-**Game Play Method**: Steal dice from unused Parcheesi set in parents' dust-covered game cabinet or from D & D-playing friend who still regularly wears Merlin cosplay to parties, even after you beg him not to. Then, roll dice, add up numbers (in your head!), and begin reading appropriate chapter. Repeat!

-**Hungry Shih Tzu Method**: Show book to your chubby Shih-Tzu (or any four-legged friend), spilling (dog) biscuit crumbs between pages. Read all licked pages.

-**Punk Rock Method**: Ignore everyone and everything and just read whatever the fuck you want, when you want to. Lip snarl is totally optional (but strongly encouraged to provide refuge for errant flies).

-**Flipper is My Homie Method**: Being flipping pages at medium speed from the front and back covers simultaneously and then tell your friend, *Okay, tell me when to stop.* Read appropriate chapters.

-Fibonacci Spiral Method (also doubles as the Fuck, I-Have-to-Write-a-Book-Report-Tomorrow Method): Dog ear the twelve pages that correspond to the first 12 values of the Fibonacci Sequence:

> Page 1 (wait, where *is* page 1?)
>
> Page 1 again (wait, what?)
>
> Page 2
>
> Page 3
>
> Page 5
>
> Page 8
>
> Page 13
>
> Page 21
>
> Page 34
>
> Page 55
>
> Page 89
>
> Page 144

-College Method (also known as the Fake-it-Until-You-Make-it Comp Student Method): Read the first twenty pages, the Maximalist Love Song of the Four Stars chapter, and then the "last" chapter, which as was already discussed, is controversial. Be sure to write that in your book report. Then, Google that shit to see what you missed (the answer: everything). Finally, write that two-page essay, even though it sounds WAY more informed than you are. At least you gave it the Ole College Try, which should suffice for a while, or at least until you talk to someone with actual standards or a real work ethic or until you can call up your nerdy friend who actually "read" this whole memoir and can smell your bullshit a mile away but no judgments or anything.

-Poplisticle Method: Read only autobiographical lists (-), then pretend you're an expert on my life like every other Wikipedia genius like the basic bitch that you are.

-Creative Nonfiction Snobby Bitch Method: Read only lyric and personal essays (•) while ignoring listicles (-) like the brand-new bitch that you are.

-Oddball Method: Only read odd (or even) numbered chapters because you're fucking crazy and shit.

-Eclectic Motherfucker Method: Combine the above methods as your little heart desires. You don't have to explain yourself to no one! Also: yolo to avoid fomo, mofo!

-Random Twitter Method: Tweet someone (not me at @jacksonbliss) and ask them to randomly send you three numbers between 1-74. Read those chapters first, and then take it from there. No need to tell me about it at @jacksonbliss.

-Spiteful Non-Randomized Twitter Method: Tweet someone besides me PLEASE. Not me, but of *course* it's gonna be me because you're feeling frisky right and mischievous (←incorrectly spelled yet AGAIN) and ask them (me at @jacksonbliss) to randomly send you three numbers between 1-74. Read those chapters first and then see where you spiteful unrandomness takes you in life. Here's a hint: nowhere except back here.

-Numerology Method: Add up the numbers in the year you're reading this memoir (or I dunno, the year you were born) and then read appropriate chapter. For example, 2014, the year I started revising this memoir, equals 7 (2+0+1+4). Start with the chapter 7 in *Dream Pop Origami* entitled Flowchart Reincarnation. This is like a narrative essay in numerical form. Now do the same thing with your own numerology. When you get to the appropriate chapter, pretend it was destiny that brought us together because it was, until it wasn't.

-Random Dictator Method: I order you to read the following chapters now! Chapters 41, 9, 64, 38, 17, 22, 73, and 55.

-**Skim, Skimerie, Skim Skimerie, Skim Skim Skaree Method:** Skim the index for words that call to you (because who needs to read essays or even entire sentences when we can just skim shit and act like we read the whole thing?). Later on, when someone else says something really smart about this memoir you don't "remember," skim some more to convince yourself you're not like those other slackers who bullshit their way through lit class. Then, promptly watch something on Netflix and escape from your own defensiveness, which is probably a big world.

-**Who's the Big Winner? Method:** Look up the lotto numbers for today. Read appropriate chapters.

-**Whole Paycheck Method:** Keep your next Whole Foods receipt, rounding up the change. Go to page number corresponding to receipt amount. Try not to act shocked and horrified and angry at said amount.

-**Trader Joe's Method:** Okay, let's try this again. Keep your next TJ receipt, rounding up the change to a whole number. Go to page number corresponding to receipt amount. At least we know you can afford that page, but can you afford the truth?

-**Frankenhapa Method:** He's alive! Just as a patchwork hapa monster. Only read chapter 69 and then put Jackson together piece by piece like those two nerds in *Weird Science,* but like, without the gorgeous actress with the killer accent and magic powers. Think of the science experiment as a metaphor of the mixed-race nerd.

-**Annoying Wanderlust Method (for the Rich & Entitled):** Simply skip from one page to another, coming and going as you please. When neither money nor time is an option, you (and only you) can afford to just "vibe" with each new destination and stay as long as it "feels" right to you. But let's be honest, Daddy's Amex doesn't hurt, you vapid dickwad!

-**Speak Amairkin, Motherfucker! Method (Doubles as They Hate Us Because We're Free Method)**: The rest of the world sucks. Read only chapters that take place in the good 'ole US of Hey—wrong autobiography, dude! Read EVERYTHING you can get your hands on, my white trash reader friends, because this is an immigrant nation founded on colonization, institutional racism, and slavery, and this memoir was written by the son of a Japanese immigrant. Don't like it? Go back to your suburb, Karen & Ken.

-**I Knew this Dude Before He Was (NOT!) Famous:** Because I've met you at some point in my life (i.e., maybe you're an old childhood friend, maybe we had sex in your car while on drugs, maybe you're a former student of mine that wished I didn't talk so much, maybe I crushed on you in high school and never told you and you have undiagnosed telepathic abilities that you didn't even know about until you read this memoir, maybe I recited fake Shakespeare poetry to you at a junior high party on the rooftop because I was trying to impress you so you'd kiss me, and maybe you're just a raging narcissist who wondered whether I might have written about you because, why *wouldn't* someone write about you in their OWN MEMOIR, since you're obviously interesting enough to be writtenaboutable), read only chapters that could possibly be about you, which will be none . . . but still, keep hoping!

-**House of Pain Method:** Jump up, stumble, adjust your pants, and get down! And while you're doing that, throw this book in the air and whatever chapter "opens" up, jump on that shit (I mean, jump *into* it and, whatever, you get the point).

-**Mothra v. Godzilla Method:** Imagine you're in the middle of an epic metaphorical fight in a fake model city where aliens are white people and the great savior of this world is the Asian race. Claw random pages of this memoir as Godzilla would have done and then read the page fragments that you scratched with your chewed-off fingernails. Next, do the same thing with a mouthful of water as Mothra would have done if instead of giant laser beams, he spat filtered water coming from your Brita filter instead. Then, read only the wet words. Now, decide which "reading" was better:

the scratched version or the wet one? Whatever you do, please do NOT Tweet me @jacksonbliss and tell me who won this stupidass fight, okay?

-**Batshit Crazy Method:** Once your brain hurts from reading this memoir, hurl the book out the window. After you retrieve it, call up one of your friends (preferably the really pretentious one who pretends they've read everything even when they haven't and who insists on paying twenty dollars for clumsy California Chardonnay) and tell them to start reading wherever your book was open to after you picked it up. When they say they've already read it, say, "uh-huh" and then tell them that *Dream Pop Origami* is Borges's "Book of Sand," so it can't be "read" since there is literally no official beginning and no official end. This means your pretentious friend can "continue" reading this memoir anywhere and it'll be a new beginning of a new text that all started with your own insanity. Once you're "done," send your pretentious friend a bill for all the time they've wasted in your life, which you'll never get back except through cold hard cash, which they (but it's probably a he) will pretend not to have when it's payback time.

MY ENDLESS LOVE, GRATITUDE, APPRECIATION, & RESPECT TO:

LB, otherwise known as Little Bug, otherwise known as Baby Moonshine, who is the love of my life. You are my greatest joy. You are my greatest passion. You are my greatest pain. You are my brilliant Peruvian mermaid with the melting chocolate eyes, honey drizzle cheeks, and ribbon hair. Te amo, te amo, te amo. Without your endless love, I wouldn't be here right now. Facts! I can't thank you enough for the way you supported me and loved me, even when I spoke in obsessive circles and my heart was obliterated from years of constant rejection by the publishing industry that still doesn't give a shit about mixed-race identity or fertility narratives told by men or personal essays about growing up illegibly Asian in the Midwest, but you encouraged me, you told me never to give up, even when it felt like my writing career was dead and all my writing friends were on tour and I felt like a complete failure. My love for you I carry deep inside me, into the cells of my being, now and always. Your love guides me in this massive, dark universe like a cosmic firefly.

おばあさん (obāchan)、お母さん (Mom)、and チャッド (Wick), I love you all so much. Thank you all for your community, trailblazing, vulnerability, and humanity. We've traveled through so many parabolas in our separate but intersecting lives. Through it all, the things that broke us also saved us: our stubborn love, our stories, our navigation of American culture, our iconoclastic and wandering souls, our sense of humor and diehard idealism, our insistent and flickering joy in the face of nothingness, and our flawed love for new beginnings, most of them in the West Coast. The best coast. I couldn't have made it here without you three, who are all here in flesh and spirit. I love you all so much. Double shout-out to Wick who was my first partner in crime and the best friend a teenage boy could have. Thank you, brother, for your companionship in this dysfunctional and lonely world.

The hapa community, *Discover Nikkei*, Kip Fulbeck for his life-changing book, Duncan Williams, my hapa thesis adviser at USC and founder of the Hapa Japan project, Heidi Durrow at the Mixed Remixed festival in LA, Aya Mac, my mixed-race photography star, Yo my big Japanese kuma of a friend and brother, Joy Huang-Iris, my talented soul person, fellow hapa fiction writer, and friend, and Emily and Ernie, the tonics for my soul in these troubled times.

I want these people to know how much I love them. I want them to know that I think of them all the time: Jim W., Mona, Joy, Rebus, Anita Monita, Luis, Fia, Leo, Joe, Tara, Rachel, Sarah J., & the people of **Chicago**. Romeo, Keith, Grace, & the people of **SF**. Ivory, Sejal, Frenchie, & the people of **Boston**. Molly, Chiwan, & the people of **Pittsburgh**. Sébastien, & the people of **London**. Brendan, & the people of **Amsterdam**. Kelley & John, Inuka, Amy M., D., Aimee, Laura, Richard C., Lovie, Megan, Yo, Regina, Aimee B., & the people of **LA**. Eikichi & Megumi, & the people of 東京. Alana, Leigh, Kevin, Nancy, Jacose, Nathalie, & the people of **PDX**. Barbarella, Alexa, Mike C, Jackie & Seamus, Angie, Micki, & the people of **Traverse City**. The Traoré fam in Bobo-Dioulasso, & the people of **Burkina Faso**. Maribaum, Shahbaba, Sara, Sevda (wherever you are), & the people of **Azerbaijan**. Chie, Aunt Shizuko, & the people of 大坂. Helmut, & the people of **New Haven**. Coleen, Dave G., Valerie, & Steve T., & the people of **South Bend**. Renée, & the people in la **Suisse**. Jennifer D., Lily H., & the people of **San Diego**. Laura F., Grace (JL), Pei-ling, Lisa K, Nika, Megan, & the people of **NYC**. Niki, Carla D, Abdul, Steven, Frances, & the people of **Baltimore**. Randa, Marc O., Nick G, & the people of **D.C.** Alex, Merve, & the people of **Istanbul**. I love and miss you all like crazy & hope we get to kick it together someday in the future after we've retaken our lives.

The many sharp, generous, and talented editors who first published sections of this memoir in various forms and versions, including Miya Lee at the *New York Times,* Raluca Albu at *Guernica,* Simon Waxman at the *Boston Review,* Sari Botton at *Longreads,* Jennifer Derilo at *Kartika Review* and the *2012-2013 Anthology of American Pacific Island American Literature,*

Tara Betts, Cathy J. Schlund-Vials, & Sean Frederick Forbes, the Anthology project editors of *The Beiging of America*, Grace Jahng Lee at *Guernica,* and last but not least, Lisa Hickey at *The Good Men Project* for publishing so many of my essays on contemporary masculinities & feminism.

A huge hug, fist-bump, and shout out to Esme, Kristen, Katie, Summer, and the other editors and graphic designers at Unsolicited Press who took a risk with this experimental memoir and gave me a voice when no one else would, I thank you from the bottom of my heart and will love you forever. Please come visit me some day in LA and I'll make buy you all a perfect Vanilla Oat latte.

And lastly, a massive hug to you, my beautiful reader, for reading this book and sewing me back together. I love you like I do.

WANT TO EXPERIENCE *DREAM POP ORIGAMI* IN AN INTERACTIVE DIGITAL WAY?

HEAD TO DREAMPOPORIGAMI.COM

About Jackson Bliss

Jackson Bliss is the winner of the 2020 Noemi Press Award in Prose and the mixed-race/hapa author of _Counterfactual Love Stories & Other Experiments_ (Noemi Press, 2021), _Amnesia of June Bugs_ (7.13 Books, 2022), and the speculative fiction hypertext, _Dukkha, My Love_ (2017). His writing has appeared in _The New York Times, Tin House, Ploughshares, Guernica, Antioch Review, TriQuarterly, ZYZZYVA, Columbia Journal, Kenyon Review, Longreads, Witness, Santa Monica Review, African American Review, Fiction, Boston Review, Joyland, Arts & Letters, Quarterly West, Stand (UK)_, and _Multi-ethnic Literature of the United States_, among others. He is the Distinguished Visiting Writer at Bowling Green State University and lives in LA with his wife and their two fashionably dressed dogs. Follow him on Twitter and IG: @jacksonbliss.

About Unsolicited Press

Unsolicited Press based out of Portland, Oregon and focuses on the works of the unsung and underrepresented. As a womxn-owned, all-volunteer small publisher that doesn't worry about profits as much as championing exceptional literature, we have the privilege of partnering with authors skirting the fringes of the lit world. We've worked with emerging and award-winning authors such as Shann Ray, Amy Shimshon-Santo, Brook Bhagat, Kris Amos, and John W. Bateman.

Learn more at unsolicitedpress.com. Find us on twitter and instagram.